EMORY BUCKNER

Overleaf

Emory R. Buckner, taken when he was United States Attorney (1925–27), and three of his assistants: William E. Stevenson, Herman T. Stichman and John M. Harlan.

EMORY BUCKNER

BY *MARTIN MAYER*

WITH AN INTRODUCTION BY *Justice John M. Harlan*

PUBLISHED UNDER THE AUSPICES OF

THE WILLIAM NELSON CROMWELL FOUNDATION

BY HARPER & ROW, PUBLISHERS

NEW YORK, EVANSTON, AND LONDON

LIBRARY OF CONGRESS CATALOG CARD NUMBER: 68-15965

C-S

To the memory of

ELIHU ROOT, JR. (1881-1967)

and

GRENVILLE CLARK (1882-1967)

CONTENTS

ACKNOWLEDGMENTS

The story of the origins of this book is told in its opening pages, and I am of course grateful for the help of all those mentioned there. I owe a special debt of thanks, however, to Leo Gottlieb, Esq., who organized the job with remarkable efficiency, patience, insight and generosity—and to Mr. Gottlieb's secretary Betty Landis, who saw that the organizing worked.

I am grateful also to the firm of Dewey, Ballantine, Bushby, Palmer & Wood—successors to Root, Clark, Buckner & Howland—which placed at my disposal the resources of its library and gave permission for the many excerpts reprinted here from its inside publication *The Bull*. U.S. Attorney Robert Morgenthau kindly gave me access to the library of the Southern District of New York and to *Scraps*, the weekly journal by which Buckner sought to import to public office the *esprit* of his private practice.

Thanks are due also to the Harvard Law School Library for the correspondence between Buckner and Roscoe Pound (and to Vice Dean Livingston Hall for making the arrangements); to Norris Darrell, Esq., for his consent to my use of some of the Buckner–Learned Hand correspondence; to Frederic S. LaCroix of the University of Nebraska Libraries, who unearthed material about the Class of '04 (and to Herbert Brownell, who got the University interested, finally, in a biography of one of its most distinguished alumni); to the Association of the Bar of the City of New York for several rare items fortunately preserved in its library; and, as always, to the New York Society Library.

Assistance that could have been given by no one else was provided by Emory Buckner's daughter Ruth Gouverneur; his nephew James N. Buckner; and his secretary Mathilde Sandstede.

—MARTIN MAYER

INTRODUCTION by JUSTICE JOHN M. HARLAN

The New York Bar has given to the country many distinguished lawyers, but few of them, I venture to say, have left so deep an imprint on the next generation of the profession as has Emory R. Buckner. The true source of that imprint is not to be found, however, so much in his abilities as a lawyer, in his skills as an advocate, in his architecture of one of New York's great law firms, in the renown of the cases that he handled, or in his achievements in public office—notable as each of these facets of his career was—as in the remarkable gift he possessed for training and inspiring young lawyers and launching them on their careers. His influence was not of the pedantic sort, but was born of the human and professional stuff that sticks with those who were exposed to it. To vouchsafe that there have been countless instances when lawyers bearing the responsibility for ticklish decisions have first asked themselves, "What would Buck have done?" is not to indulge in hyperbole. This book has its origins in the belief of some of those who held Emory Buckner in high esteem and affection that an account of his life is a legacy which should be left to oncoming generations of lawyers. As one of those, I am grateful to the others, to the author, and to the Cromwell Foundation which has ensured the accomplishment of the project, for allowing me to introduce this book to its readers.

The essence of Buckner's method for indoctrinating young lawyers, which because of his own professional calling lay primarily in the field of trial and appellate practice, was to place real responsibility upon them at the earliest stage and to hold them strictly accountable for their performance. A "first-year man" who was given a memorandum of law to write was made to feel that his legal conclusions upon the point involved would be accepted at face value. The novice examining for the first time a witness in open court under Buckner's eye was largely left to his own devices. And the more mature man who was put in charge of a case as Buckner's first assistant, called by him the *tenant in capite,* was looked to by Buckner as the ring-master of the entire operation. If soft spots developed in the performance of his associates at any point, Buckner preferred to ride them out with his client or the court rather than to unmask such deficiencies "in public," and to leave retribution, always straight-forward but nonetheless considerate and kindly, to another day. More important from the standpoint of his fledglings, Buckner was always at pains, usually at the inception of his retainer, to warn the client that Mr. so-and-so would play an important role in the management of the case. Time and again I have seen him do this even at the risk of forfeiting his retainer to another lawyer not so prone to delegate major responsibilities to juniors.

The cornerstone of the Bucknerian litigation method was objective and relentless preparation. Buckner was never content simply to do the best he could with the case as put to him by his client, but insisted upon making his own investigation of every fact and circumstance before reaching his estimate of the situation. He conceived the duty to his clients to lie quite as much in disentangling them from unwise or improvident litigation as in pressing an unquestionably good claim or defense to a successful conclusion in court. It was not a rare occurrence for a client to find himself astonished by the different aspect which his case assumed under the spotlight of a Buckner-type investigation.

I would describe the type of investigation that was Buckner's forte as something akin to what in scientific terms is called pure or experimental research, that is, Buckner turned his young lawyers loose to ferret out the facts and to discover the controlling legal principles untrammeled by any preconceived framework of the case. He was unsparing in his use of manpower, often recruiting from the outside on an *ad hoc* basis when the size of the organization deemed necessary for a particular case would unduly tax the resources of his own office staff. He looked for imagination as well as industry in those who worked for him, and was always receptive even to the most fanciful ideas of the youngest man on the totem pole. He was accustomed to tell his staff that he expected each man to do his segment of the job as if he were solely responsible for it, and that after he was satisfied that he had done his work "one hundred percent" he should then put in an "extra ten-percent" effort; only then should he submit his work product for the consideration of his superior.

The Bucknerian process was necessarily expensive for those who could afford to pay, but, though never willing to trim the thoroughness of the process, Buckner always saw to it that it was never so to those who could not stand the cost. Sometimes the rigor and dispassionateness of the Buckner method was irksome to clients who had an *idée fixe* about their cases, a feeling that was usually dissipated however by the rewarding results, whether by way of a negotiated settlement or a court judgment after trial, that more often than not followed in its wake.

In his choice of assistants Buckner looked for brains rather than experience. He seemed to feel that bright ideas and imaginative courses of factual and legal investigation were more likely to spring from those as yet professionally untutored than from the often more conventional approach of the experienced. Buckner's reliance on young-lawyer manpower finds no better manifestation than in the selection of his staff when he became United States Attorney for the Southern District of New York in 1925. He replaced or augmented the staff of his predecessor largely with youthful talent drawn fresh from the high-standing men of the graduating classes of the leading law schools and from the lower echelons of law offices. In the later years of his private practice when physical infirmities forced him to curtail his direct professional activities, his faith in his young protégés was further made apparent by the great and usually successful lengths to which he went to persuade his clients in important cases to allow his top associates to "carry on" in his stead without bringing to their side the leadership of some older lawyer of firmly established reputation.

Beyond this, Buckner's interest in the young lawyer reached far beyond those who were fortunate enough to have the opportunity to work for him. He had an uncanny way of holding the looking glass before those who came to him for advice about the next step in their careers. Private practice, the public service, business organizations, and law school faculties still contain many who will acknowledge a debt of gratitude to Emory Buckner for giving them a helpful steer at a pivotal point in their professional lives.

Preparation of a lawsuit, however thorough, avails little apart from the use that is made of it, and hence it is appropriate that something should be said about Emory Buckner's qualities as a barrister. Epitomizing, I would carve those qualities into four parts: an unerring instinct for getting at the jugular of a case and holding his adversary, the court, and the jury to it; a capacity to simplify and synthesize even the most complicated set of facts into a harmonious, understandable, and satisfying picture; the use of cross-examination to make of his adversary's witnesses affirmative elements for his side of the case— by putting them "under ether" as Buckner used to say—and not merely as an instrument for destroying credibility; and a genuine and disarming sense of fairness to his opponents which never failed to add strength to his own client's cause.

An examination of the records in any of his important cases will abundantly illustrate these characteristics, as Mr. Mayer's book well shows, but for this thumbnail sketch it will suffice to say that Buckner was a pre-eminent master in the handling of facts. He had a faculty for bringing the factual bits and pieces into an over-all focus which irresistibly commanded respect from the trier of the facts, be it court or jury, and usually fitted into established legal principles or led to the formulation of new ones favorable to his client's position. He was not much given to reliance on legal technicalities, and usually sought to postpone judicial assessment of his case until after the factual situation had been fully developed. He was distrustful of "motion practice" and for the most part eschewed interstitial legal tactics, believing that preliminary skirmishes often tended to embarrass the ultimate outcome of a case because the judicial rulings they invited would occur in a context short of a portrayal of the full setting of the issues. In his development of the facts Buckner was always on the affirmative, whether acting for the plaintiff or the defendant, never relying merely on the weaknesses of his opponent's case and rarely even objecting to any evidence that his adversary wished to introduce. His aim was always to demonstrate the factual and legal righteousness of his client's cause standing on its own bottom. He was accustomed, particularly in complex litigations, to bring his side of the case into the open at the outset of a trial by making a compendious opening statement. As his evidence went in he sought whenever possible to orient contemporaneously each important item with relation to the picture he had painted at the beginning of the trial. And in summation he had a remarkable faculty for focusing attention upon the master issues by the use of picturesque phrases and homilies, avoiding for the most part histrionics.

A word should be added on one of the intangibles in Emory Buckner's makeup as a trial lawyer. He possessed to a remarkable degree what he used to describe as "courtroom antennae," that is, a capacity to sense and adapt himself to the subtle changes of atmosphere that often occur in a protracted trial, and to summon to his aid the "flash of genius" usually necessary to dissipate or neutralize the impact of an untoward trial event.

Buckner entered the courtroom prepared to do battle, with the precision of a military commander who has skillfully deployed his troops. He considered the mechanics of presentation almost as important as the contents of his case, believing that the orderly and rapid-fire development of the facts and legal points tended to undermine the opposition and to instill confidence in the court and jury for his side of the case. Every witness was on deck when his appearance was called for; every exhibit was snapped into play in accordance with the trial plans; and preprepared memoranda of law were always at hand to assist the court with respect to points on which it had been anticipated rulings might have to be made. Nothing annoyed Buckner more than to have an assistant fumble in the courtroom the mechanical handling of the part of the case which he had been assigned to prepare. Yet when trial vicissitudes seemed to indicate the desirability of changes in the grand design, Buckner, through overnight or recess conferences with his staff and sometimes even by pure improvisation in the courtroom, always seemed able to contrive a reoriented presentation that proceeded as smoothly as if it had been originally planned that way.

Lamentably, Emory Buckner before he had reached his mid-fifties and at the very peak of his reputation was taken from the active trial bar by a succession of illnesses. His last major jury trial took place in 1932, a case in which he represented one of the principal executives of the Bank of the United States, involving a New York state criminal prosecution arising out of the Bank's failure during the great economic depression of that period. Notwithstanding his infirmities Buckner continued during the last ten years of his life, which ended on March 11, 1941, to draw important litigation to his firm, although, to be sure, not in the quantity that he had attracted before. While he continued to supervise the office litigation with his accustomed care and imagination, the actual courtroom work passed more and more into the hands of his younger partners and principal associates. For most lesser men this would have been a disheartening, if not devastating, chapter in their careers, but not so with Emory Buckner, who seemed to regard the passing of the torch to his "boys" as the true fulfillment of his own professional philosophy.

Turning, in conclusion, from the subject to the author, the highest compliment I can pay this book is that it has withstood the critical "vetting" of not a few of the "Buckner boys" who are still around to see the fulfillment of a project that has been very dear to their hearts. From their standpoint, they are in Mr. Mayer's debt for having succeeded in portraying the image of this remarkable man in a manner which without his painstaking and understanding research, his literary talent, and the fortunate circumstance that the Buckner-Frankfurter correspondence has been preserved, might not have been possible. More important, unless I misjudge the real values that make for sustaining the standards of our profession, this book will prove to be a continuing source of inspiration for future generations of lawyers.

EMORY BUCKNER

CHAPTER ONE *Out of the West*

1877-1907

"The first day Buck was in New York," Felix Frankfurter recalled, thinking back almost sixty years to 1907, when he and Emory Buckner were starting out in the law, "I asked him to dine at the old Holland House near Grand Central. We had a very good dinner because we both liked good food—I introduced Buck to wines. He was a sheer joy as a human being—you couldn't have anything but an exhilarating time with him. He would have made a great governor—he would have made a wonderful President, would have done what Jack Kennedy could never do, lay out these problems so people would understand them.

"I remember, some years later, a New York lawyer came to me and said, 'I've got a very complicated shipping case, admiralty case. And as you know, in shipping cases all the witnesses are liars. Who should I get as my trial lawyer?'

"I said, 'Get Emory Buckner—he's the best trial lawyer in New York. That makes him the best admiralty lawyer, even if he's never had an admiralty case.' "

Buckner had been dead more than twenty-three years when Frankfurter spoke of him. The old man, crippled by his stroke, himself to die in a few months, added sadly, "I miss him deeply. Often I say to myself, 'Wouldn't Buck enjoy this?' or 'Wouldn't Buck be outraged?' " Then the visitor's hour was up, and Frankfurter, who re-

1

tained considerable vigor into his final illness, threw him out.

During the 1930s, while Buckner was visibly declining in health, Frankfurter (then a professor of law at Harvard) and his wife Marian assembled much of the correspondence the two friends had exchanged in periodic bursts starting in 1911, when the future Justice first went to live in Washington. Among those who visited Frankfurter often in the months after his retirement from the Supreme Court was his recent colleague John M. Harlan, who many years before had been Buckner's chief assistant in private practice. One afternoon in early 1964, Frankfurter produced a large folder of papers and gave it to Harlan with the words, "You'll probably write a biography of E.R.B. some day." Supreme Court Justices, unfortunately, do not have time to write biographies. With Chief Judge J. Edward Lumbard of the Court of Appeals for the Second Circuit and Leo Gottlieb of the New York Bar, men with the deepest feelings of gratitude for the generosity and professional guidance of Emory Buckner, Justice Harlan formed an unofficial committee to make arrangements for such a biography.[1]

Emory Roy Buckner was a lawyer in New York for more than thirty-three years, and for a quarter of a century a leader of the New York Bar—one must certainly award that title to a man not yet forty who was chosen in 1917 to chair the Fusion Committee on the Judiciary. In 1913 he was one of the founders of the firm of Root, Clark, Buckner & Howland, which from 1919 on was one of the most successful such establishments in the country (and indeed still is, under the name of Dewey, Ballantine, Bushby, Palmer & Wood). His two periods of greatest public prominence were 1912-13, when he was counsel to the Aldermanic Committee to Investigate the Police Department, and 1925-27, when he was U.S. Attorney for the Southern District of New York, padlocked any number of speakeasies, sent Earl Carroll to jail, and, against the wishes of the Coolidge administration which had appointed him, prosecuted the Attorney General

---

[1] The other members of the unofficial committee were Leslie H. Arps, Herbert Brownell, Grenville Clark, William Dean Embree, Henry N. Ess, III, James A. Farmer, Raphael P. Koenig, Cloyd Laporte, George S. Leisure, Sr., Benjamin A. Matthews, Carl E. Newton, David W. Peck, C. Frank Reavis, Jr., Elihu Root, Jr., Alexander B. Royce, Arthur H. Schwartz, Edward S. Silver, Herman T. Stichman, Lowell Wadmond, Bethuel M. Webster, and C. Dickerman Williams.

of the Harding administration for "conspiracy to defraud the government of his best services"—i.e., bribe-taking. Frankfurter believed Buckner could have been Governor of New York in 1928, when Franklin D. Roosevelt, running against a much weaker candidate, barely survived the Republican tide which carried the state for Hoover. The newspapers of the time (though perhaps not the Republican leaders) certainly considered him a desirable choice for the nomination.

The cases Buckner tried as public prosecutor, defense counsel or private lawyer in commercial matters offer fascinating insights into the social history of his period, revelations of the sort that often elude the conventional historian. Several of these cases were thoroughly reported in the newspapers and magazines, and many were appealed, which means that the trial record was printed for the edification of the upper courts and is still available. A biography, of course, must deal primarily with what a man did; and these documentary sources, plus a *New Yorker* profile, a biographical article in *Success,* transcripts of talks given at bar association meetings, Buckner's own biographical and other writings in the internal house organs of his law firm and the U.S. Attorney's office, provide much of the information for this book.

Even more important, however, have been the grateful recollections of scores of the young men (among them the author's father) who were introduced to the practice of law in New York by Emory Buckner, and who went on to grace both the federal and state benches, to various other public offices, to the presidencies of Manhattan's two bar associations, to the senior partnerships of many of the city's law firms, to the presidency of major corporations. All had admired—and enjoyed—the man; all felt that his example, and the guides of conduct he had given for the public profession of the law, had made a significant contribution to their own self-respect in their life's work.

Buckner's correspondence with Roscoe Pound and Learned Hand (generously released by the Harvard Law School and the Hand estate) has also been invaluable in picking out incidents from his life that would otherwise have remained unknown. But this biography would have been far less informative, lively and revelatory of personality without the Frankfurter-Buckner correspondence, and the friendship which began between them at the Harvard Law School in 1904. It was a friendship very strongly felt, of the kind not uncommon among young men. "Though I saw you yesterday," Buckner began a letter about a Frankfurter brief in 1911, "shall see you today and of course tomorrow."[2] In 1914, when Frankfurter was appointed to the Harvard Law School faculty, Buckner would identify him for Roscoe Pound as "the closest friend I have and the real thing."[3] But the roots of the friendship were deeper than the usual young man's need for alliance against a threatening future, and its intimacy persisted. "FF," Buckner wrote Learned Hand in 1933, "has been away from New York ever since Stimson went to Wash. as Sec'y of War. . . . We don't see each other for long intervals or write—but we always begin where we left off—no apologies or self-consciousness."[4] It was a friendship that could have ended only as it did, with Buckner's death in 1941, and Frankfurter's telegram to his widow: "You know that I have a right to say how much I share your grief and that of the girls. . . ."[5]

It was at the start an implausible friendship, one that could have begun only in the artificial and isolated community of a residential university, and could have flourished, perhaps, only in that time of fiercely innocent belief in Americanism, in the democracy of intellect and of hope, which took its inspiration from Theodore Roosevelt. The two young men shared poverty and a brilliance immediately obvious to those around them because it came out in streams of verbal byplay; and both were unusually short, Frankfurter slim and apparently anemic, Buckner already tending to the pudginess that would contribute to his rapid physical decline past the age of fifty.

In situation and in background the two men were as different as could be. Frankfurter, though a year ahead at law school, was five years younger, a bachelor, not infrequently on the prowl. (Buckner wrote Frankfurter in 1940 that Judge Thacher of the New York Court of Appeals had asked him one day "walking up the street, 'What did Felix do in those early days? Run around with pretty girls?' I told him you were never interested in any girl that I knew of—but I did not tell him it was the sex as a whole."[6]) By contrast,

---

[2] Buckner to Frankfurter, 6/22/11.
[3] Buckner to Pound, 10/29/14.
[4] Buckner to Hand, 6/16/33.
[5] Frankfurter to Mrs. Buckner, 3/11/41.
[6] Buckner to Frankfurter, 3/8/40.

Buckner had been married three years before he went to law school, and in his third year at Harvard he became a father.

Frankfurter had worked a year in the then equivalent of the New York City Welfare Department between City College and law school, and had saved enough money to pay all his bills for three years in Cambridge. Buckner had worked five years between high school and college, but whatever he had saved then was long gone (saving money was never one of his talents, anyway); he had borrowed to come East, and he had to pay all his bills as they came up.

In his reminiscences, Frankfurter, who led his class all three years, tells of a rich young man who came to him for tutoring help, and of his decision to give the help on the understanding that it was a comradely favor not to be recompensed. From the point of view of a Buckner, who was third in his class and often solicited in a similar manner, Frankfurter was scabbing; tutoring was among Buckner's more important sources of income, especially in the third year. Buckner acquired a life-long dislike of Professor Edward "Bull" Warren ("the C-man's delight and the A-man's puzzle," he wrote scornfully to Frankfurter thirty-three years later[7]) because of Warren's rough treatment of Ogden L. Mills, later to be Hoover's Secretary of the Treasury, then just one of the high-living Gold Coast boys Buckner was tutoring.

But the great difference, of course, was in their origins and upbringing. Frankfurter was a Viennese immigrant, brought to the promised land shortly before his twelfth birthday, growing up in the steaming, unbelievably crowded, desperately ambitious Jewish slums of New York. Buckner was a product of the Great Plains and a descendant of the continent's earliest Anglo-Saxon stock, tracing back eight or nine generations.

2

There have been Buckners in America since the seventeenth century, among them John Buckner, who in 1682 was fined by the Royal Governor of the Colony of Virginia and his Council for printing a pamphlet "without his Excellency's license."[8] A cadet branch of the family went off to North Carolina, where Jackson Buckner, according to family legend, ran away from a disliked stepmother

---

[7] Buckner to Frankfurter, 2/14/?, probably '40.
[8] Douglas, *An Almanac of Liberty*, Dolphin ed., p. 250.

at the age of twelve and spent his adolescence on the farm of his father's brother John. In 1841, shortly before his twenty-first birthday, he married Jemima Pike, then eighteen, and settled briefly on a farm about forty miles west of Raleigh. In March, 1844, with their slaves and an infant son, the Buckners went off to Missouri in a covered wagon.

"Unreconstructed to his dying day," as his grandson Emory would later testify,[9] Jackson Buckner moved out of Missouri during the troubled times of the Civil War, and eventually settled in Pottowattamie County, Iowa. There Jackson and Jemima Buckner raised twelve children who lived long enough to marry and have children of their own; from 1915 to 1940 an organized Buckner Family would meet for a picnic and photo session in Council Bluffs, Iowa, on the anniversary of their ancestors' wedding. Jackson Buckner was a farmer all his life, but also a lay preacher who would rouse his neighbors to follow the Bible at camp meetings in the farm country.

The seventh of Jackson Buckner's children was James Dysant Monroe Buckner, who was determined to become a real preacher; and for this purpose, even on the frontier, it would be necessary to finish high school. Love struck first: at the age of nineteen, he eloped with a neighboring girl at Wheeler Groves, Sarah Addie Ellis ("Aunt Addie" later to her grandchildren as well as to her multiple nephews and nieces). The young couple lived at Jackson Buckner's farm, "J.D.M." riding off to school in the morning. His grandson James N. Buckner remembered talk in the family that J.D.M. was joshed by his brothers and sisters, who claimed that his reason for insisting on school was laziness around the farm.

The first child born to J.D.M. and Addie Buckner died within a year; the second, Emory Roy, was born in 1877 when his father was twenty-two years old and still living on the family farm. Three years later J.D.M. was "licensed to preach," but his family stayed at the Jackson Buckner homestead while he rode circuit around Iowa. Another son, Clyde, was born before J.D.M. received his first Methodist parish in 1883 and moved his family across the state line to a parson's house in Nebraska. Clyde would leave school to join the U.S. Army and fight Aguinaldo in the Philippines, would fall ill

<hr>

[9] Annual Address, 42nd Annual Session of Georgia Bar Association at Tybee Island, Georgia, 6/5/25, p. 8.

with tuberculosis while there and on doctors' advice would settle in New Mexico to make a living as a hunter and a guide for dudes, and to die unmarried in 1917, at the age of thirty-five. The third son, Arthur, born in 1887, would follow his father's calling, and like his eldest brother would finish his career in the East, where the two men, ill and prematurely aging, would draw close to each other toward the end of their lives.

The Buckners were wretchedly poor: at no time during the first thirty years of his ministry did J.D.M. Buckner make as much as $900 a year. When Emory was repeatedly ill with stomach disorders at the height of his career, Dean Roscoe Pound of the Harvard Law School, who had known him from Nebraska days, said it was because he had never had enough to eat at home.[10] As a young man in New York, behind the gaiety and gallantry, the cheerful and selfless pitching in at progressive civic activities that made his contemporaries suspect political ambitions, Buckner was eaten by a hatred and fear of poverty which came out in many of his letters to Frankfurter. When he did begin to make money, in reaction to his upbringing, he was "hopelessly improvident," as Grenville Clark put it; he was immensely generous both to people he knew and to people he didn't know; and his life was rarely free from financial troubles. He grew up, too, with a firm distaste for the soil. His wife was to become the best gardener in Nantucket, with baskets of flowers all over the house in seasons when others were struggling to protect a few surviving blooms, but Buckner never took any interest in it. A favorite family story tells of the afternoon when he looked out his window to see his wife sweating in a very hot sun, wearily planting seeds. He said, "Why don't you hire a gardener and tell him where you want them to go?" She looked up scornfully and said, "When you go golfing, why don't you take the pro with you and tell him where you want to put the ball?"

Liquor and tobacco were anathema in J.D.M. Buckner's home; and while he was a constant reader he liked to say that he had read only one novel in his life. Though they lived into the 1930s, and ended their days in the relative metropolis of Lincoln, J.D.M. and Addie never saw a movie in their lives; Addie, particularly, disapproved. It was a blow to them when their sons came home to visit and smoked in their parlor; Emory, in fact, smoked four packs a day.

[10] Lumbard to author, 1964.

Neither brother, however, ever had the courage to drink in their parents' presence; when Emory felt the need for such sustenance he would go up to his room and take it from a flask in the suitcase.[11] The home was a hive of Bible reading. "Ruth attended Sunday School for the first time this morning," Emory would write Frankfurter the week his oldest daughter turned five. "By the time I was her age it had already been a life's work."[12]

There was no whiff of Puritanism about Emory Buckner. He loved to dance. Elihu Root, Jr. remembered long evenings at roadhouses in the 1910s, when "Emory never wanted the party to be over." After an office outing at Lake Mohegan which he organized while U.S. Attorney in 1925, the office newspaper reported, "If there was a member of the fair sex at the outing who did not become a dancing partner of the Chief, why, she didn't dance, that's all."[13] But Buckner was in his own mind, always, very much the parson's son. Biblical reference came to him automatically, especially in the courtroom (though its use was more likely to be ironical than exhortative). His nephew James remembered that when Buckner came visiting home he would sometimes do a little lay preaching at a Sunday meeting. Though his voice and manner were flat, with none of the oratorical flourish cultivated in the pulpit by his younger brother, the oral tradition of the rural ministry was in Buckner's bones. He gathered information best by listening rather than by reading; he would let the briefs in his cases go to appellate judges without much picking of nits over the language or the argument, but he mapped his oral presentations with the precision of a cartographer.

Most important of all, of course, was Buckner's inheritance of moral obligation to his profession. "Buck," Grenville Clark said, "was rather particularly strict and scrupulous. He had extremely high standards and sentiments about having the truth come out."[14] As U.S. Attorney he told his young assistants that "a prosecutor should never . . . offer evidence as to the admissibility of which there is the slightest doubt. A district attorney should impress a jury as a governmental officer whose stern if somewhat reluctant duty it is to convict

---

[11] James N. Buckner to author, 1967.
[12] Buckner to Frankfurter, 12/17/11.
[13] *Scraps*, 6/20/25.
[14] Clark to author, 1964.

offenders. He is not a mere contestant. He is defending society."[15] As a private lawyer representing defendants, he refused to call to the stand, or enter any affirmative defense for, a client he believed to be guilty. "Clients," he told a meeting of the Association of the Bar of the City of New York, "are not entitled to have lawyers who disbelieve their stories."[16] In the last year of his life, Buckner wrote in a lesson for the young men of his office: "There is a lot of bunk going around, and has been ever since I have been a member of the Bar, that every man is entitled to a defense (which of course is true) and that has carried with it a connotation (which is not true) that a member of the bar has a right to represent anyone under any circumstances. . . . The law is not yet a common carrier and everybody is not entitled to a ride on a lawyer's back by paying his nickel."[17] On one occasion when an opponent's cross-examination revealed to Buckner (but not to the defense lawyer) that one of Buckner's witnesses was lying, Buckner himself undertook the man's destruction on redirect examination, and the next week prosecuted him for perjury.

He was much more tolerant with the outside world than he was with himself or his employees. While he was on the government's payroll to enforce the prohibition law, it was unthinkable that he himself could break it—and equally unthinkable that anyone on his staff would touch a drop. But he raised no objection to his former associates' and partners' drinking at the firm dinners he occasionally attended while in office—or to his political colleagues' drinking at the Republican dinners where the best hooch was served, by courtesy of the prohibition agents. Nor did he demand that others meet his own standards in choice of clients; though he condemned William Fallon and Leonard Snitkin, whom he considered jury-fixers, and he occasionally got annoyed with what he considered the self-hypnosis of Lloyd Paul Stryker, he respected Martin W. Littleton and Max Steuer, who put their cleverness at the service of people Buckner considered indefensible. Justice Aron Steuer remembered that his father and Buckner "were on first-name terms at a time when first names were much less common than they are today."

[15] *Scraps*, 4/17/25, 5/2/25.
[16] "The Trial of Cases," address, 1/31/29, p. 8.
[17] 21 *Bull* 44, 2/3/40.

"Buckner," said Livingston Hall, who worked some years at Root-Clark before going on to a professorship at the Harvard Law School, "was one of the smartest men God ever made—but I never saw him use it to harm anybody." The man who roused Buckner's greatest fury was the pious fraud, the Tartuffe, who exploited an asserted purity to harass others. This attitude, too, derived from his father. In 1923 Buckner wrote Roscoe Pound about a "pretty courageous thing which happened several years ago when my father alone of all the preachers in Aurora locked horns with the blackguard travelling Evangelist who took it upon himself to attack in the manner usual to his ilk a young woman high school principal who protested to the ministers of the town against the Evangelist's vulgarity. My father and the business men opposed by all the other preachers succeeded in running him out of town though as a result ten or a dozen of my father's members left his Church."[18]

Established in a Wall Street practice, Buckner kept on the wall facing his desk a big portrait of his father, a large, strong man with a round face and a firm jaw. Behind the desk was an equally large portrait of Elihu Root. Buckner liked to say that with the client facing Root and himself facing "the parson" he never had any trouble about fees. He spoke often of his father, and once said to his oldest daughter, "Rudy, if my father had been a butcher rather than a minister I'd still be proud of him." Once he had the opportunity to express through actions his admiration for and devotion to his father—when the Reverend Buckner, sixty-seven years old, was forcibly retired against his wishes by the Nebraska Conference of the Methodist Church, ostensibly on grounds of age and general unsuitability but actually because the bishops regarded as heretical his publicly proclaimed refusal to accept every word in the Bible as the Word of God.

This refusal had come as a kind of revelation to J. D. M. Buckner, who while his children were young had believed and preached a fundamentalist doctrine. His conversion to a more liberal position began about the time his oldest son went to college, and was accelerated by the theological modernity of his youngest son, who was preaching uncomfortably Unitarian doctrine to the Congregationalists of Davenport, Iowa, and was indeed looking to transfer to the Unitarian ministry. By the spring of 1922, the Reverend Arthur

18 Buckner to Pound, 5/15/23.

Buckner had made a first step by moving to a Congregationalist church in Chamberlain, South Dakota, which had sought him out in Davenport. His father felt a need to make public declarations, and started with a letter to the Omaha *World-Herald* on May 3, 1922, attacking William Jennings Bryan for his insistence that American schools should not teach anything that denied the truth of the Biblical version of Creation.

In early June he followed up with a letter under the heading "A Good God," which he sent to four Nebraska newspapers. Its topic sentence was: "When I read in the Bible anything which reflects on the goodness of God, I do not believe it. . . ."[19]

It was from a professional point of view a poor time for J. D. M. Buckner to tempt his superiors. After eleven years as pastor at Aurora, Nebraska, he had decided to move to another church, and was dependent upon the Nebraska Conference of Methodist ministers to supply him with a new assignment. On June 14, 1922, Bishop Homer C. Stuntz wrote him that his letter "is certain to have the effect of making your appointment more difficult next fall." Hoping to avoid a publicized battle, Bishop Stuntz decided to dispose of the Buckner problem by having the Conference retire a man who, at the age of sixty-seven, was subject to retirement by mandate of the Committee on Conference Relations. This action was taken on September 9, 1922. On September 10 Emory arrived in Omaha to help his father.

The opening gun was a pamphlet by J. D. M. Buckner entitled "How I Lost My Job as a Preacher," which Emory had printed in an edition of eight thousand copies and distributed around the country. The following January a lightly edited version of it was printed in the monthly magazine *World's Work*. Emory wrote religious authorities around the country to raise support for his father's position, and helped with the preparation of magazine comments which appeared not only in religious periodicals but in *The Outlook, The Nation* and *The New Republic*—ultimately, indeed, in *The New Statesman* of London. He wrote a series of nine "memoranda" presenting his father's case, had them printed and sent them out broadcast around the country. The ninth of these memoranda was later used at the Harvard Divinity School as a model for the presentation of theological argument. So large a fuss was kicked up in the press that *The Outlook,* hailing the

[19] *Outlook,* 11/8/23, pp. 424-425.

Reverend Buckner as "a circuit rider who without college or seminary education worked out his own freedom from a religion of fear,"[20] considered the incident "A Victory for Religious Liberty."

The campaign was estimated at the time to have cost Emory $15,000; and this figure did not include any losses of income from his virtual retirement for five months from the practice of law. The Root-Clark office newspaper in February, 1923, reprinted a long editorial from the Omaha *Daily News* beginning with the words: "Any dad who can get his son to plugging for him as Emory R. Buckner of New York plugs for his dad is lucky." The office paper commented that "We apologize to the younger men in the office for printing so much about one whom they have not even met; but he was once a valuable member of the office and had much to do with its early history."[21]

Buckner was unable to get his father restored to the good graces of the Nebraska Conference, but Arthur Buckner on departing for a Unitarian parish in Maine was able to arrange for his father to replace him in the Congregationalist Church of Chamberlain, South Dakota. After two years there J. D. M. Buckner returned to Nebraska, to become a free-lance minister in Lincoln, preaching often at the chapel of the university.

In the fall of 1928 Emory wrote Frankfurter a description of a visit to his parents in Lincoln: "I found the parson going very strong. He is seventy-three and says there is nothing wrong with his age except the almanac. He is very well and has not only the mind but apparently the physical strength of twenty-five or more years ago. Unfortunately, just a year ago my mother had a slight 'stroke' when in the best of health, and has been slowly creeping back to normal health since. She has not yet arrived but is sufficiently there to be gay and happy again. Too high blood pressure. Of course the parents have no background of 'examinations,' and she had no idea that she had a blood pressure and probably only the vaguest notions of just what blood pressure is. She is sufficiently recovered by now to re-enter with substantial zest the 'retired' life they hit upon some three and a half years ago when father left South Dakota where for two years after his forced retirement he was in charge of a Congregational church. It is a great pleasure to see them having so brilliant a sunset of their lives after a cloudy

[20] *Outlook,* 1/10/23, p. 66.
[21] 4 *Bull* No. 5, 2/3/23, p. 1.

four o'clock. They dash around in a new Buick, father is forever preaching, lecturing, conducting weddings, funerals, with mother always with him, or generally so. . . . Every Sunday my father publishes a little sermonette in the best paper in Lincoln which has a state-wide circulation, so he is preaching to many times more people than ever before."[22] A fact which Buckner left out of the letter was that he had supplied his father with the new Buick; indeed, he bought his father a new Buick every two years from 1922 until the parson died in 1934.

3

There had been little of this prominence or controversy when Emory was a boy; his family had been isolated as well as poor. Still, news from the larger world filtered in to Hebron, Nebraska; and one day in the spring of 1892 the Reverend Buckner heard of a new occupation which seemed to make sense for his son. A relative of one of the more prosperous members of his congregation had just completed a six months' course in shorthand at a business college in Lincoln, and had instantly been hired at a salary of eighty dollars a month, which was more than the Methodist Church was paying its minister in Hebron. Nothing would do but Emory must go to Lincoln for the summer and take the first half of that course; and somehow thirty dollars was found for the tuition. Many years later, an interviewer for *Success* magazine reported that every time Buckner saw his father he gave him thirty dollars, and quoted Buckner as saying, "It has become a kind of ritual between us."[23] In Lincoln that summer, the fifteen-year-old Buckner lived with a dentist's family, earning room and board by taking care of the horse and buggy, mowing the lawn and performing houseboy's chores.

The first experience of the business college, however, was something less than satisfactory; and the summer following his high school graduation Buckner went instead to a teachers institute. That fall he was hired to teach in a one-room schoolhouse with less than a dozen pupils, miles on horseback from Hebron. The next year his father was transferred to a larger church in the town of Guthrie, then the leading city of Oklahoma Territory; and Buckner taught eighth grade in a more established school. Among the other teachers was a girl from

22 Buckner to Frankfurter, 11/25/28.
23 Amber, "I Shall Keep My Oath," *Success*, 7/25/25, pp. 66-67, 116-117, at 116.

upstate New York named Wilhelmina Kathryn Keach, whom Buckner and all his friends were always to call Sofy (though his family called her Minnie).

During his summers in Guthrie, Buckner worked on stenography at the business college, but both the parson and his son determined that Emory must go to a university. Some money had been saved, finances were looking up, and in the fall of 1896 Buckner entered a "college" in Lincoln—actually a preparatory school which prepared for entrance to the University of Nebraska, which the high school at Hebron had not done. While at Guthrie, however, Buckner had made an impression on some important people, and before he could enter the university he received a job offer from Oklahoma—to be court reporter for the District Court of the Territory, at $1,500 a year with three months off each summer. It was an irresistible job, worth taking and worth keeping. In the 1898 elections the Oklahoma Territory went Populist by a big margin, and the Buckner family was known to be Republican. The new judge, Buckner once told Frankfurter, said to his young reporter, "I don't think I can keep you, because you're not a Pop. Do you think I could persuade you to become a Pop?"

Frankfurter chuckled, recalling the story. "Do you know what Emory said? He said, 'It's an experiment well worth trying.' And he kept the job."

For three years, Buckner traveled a circuit of four counties reaching down to the borderline of Texas; two places on the circuit, he later wrote, could be reached only by stagecoach.[24] It was undoubtedly in this period that he determined to become a lawyer. But he had made a commitment to himself and to his father that he would go to college; and Sofy Keach had made the same commitment. In the fall of 1900, both of them left their jobs and went up to Lincoln to matriculate at the University of Nebraska. During the course of their freshman year they were married. For Buckner, at age twenty-three, the decision to go to college meant seven years at school, at a time when an A.B. was quite unnecessary for entrance to law school, and law school was not required for the practice of law. (Indeed, several of the judges for whom Buckner had labored in Oklahoma did not have degrees.) Buckner later said the insistence on college was his

[24] *Scraps,* 3/21/25.

father's.[25] But in New York, despite his extra efforts for his A.B.,
Buckner would apologize to friends who had gone to college in the
East for the inadequacy of his academic background—apparently
with some reason.

Little recollection or documentary evidence survives to tell of
Buckner's four years at the University of Nebraska. He and Sofy
Keach were married in May of their freshman year, and he had to
work to pay their bills. Nevertheless, he joined Alpha Delta Phi,
managed the football team, served as a private in Company C of the
Cadet Battalion, belonged (with his wife) to the English Club, and
was a member of the all-victorious Nebraska intercollegiate debating
teams of 1903-4. The class yearbook, *The Sombrero,* described him
as "This original and versatile gentleman, court reporter, interstate
debater, football manager and literatus . . . one of the few married
men of the University. He loves his wife next to his pipe."[26]

Scholastically, Buckner was one of only three men in the class
of 1904 to be elected to Phi Beta Kappa. In 1933, writing to Roscoe
Pound, he recalled that fourteen girls had also qualified. "You made a
speech at the induction ceremonies," he wrote, "referring to this dis-
parity, and remarked that the mysterious and cryptic 'S.P.' on the
key stood for '*Sedeant Pueres*' or, paraphrasing a topical song of the
period, 'Let the Boys go 'way back and sit down!' "[27]

Pound was then dean of the Nebraska Law School, but urged
young Buckner to go East. "I shall never be able to express sufficient
appreciation for your steering me to Harvard as against Nebraska,"
Buckner wrote Pound thirty years later, "and also as against Columbia,
which back in 1904 had a very considerable vogue among us out
there."[28] In 1916, urging Pound not to worry his own work would
suffer if he became dean of the Harvard Law School, Buckner recalled a conversation from that spring of 1904: "I was discussing
with you Harvard Law School and the courses taught there with a
catalogue in my hand which I was scanning with eager anticipation.
My perplexed and ignorant ambition prompted the inquiry to you,

---

[25] *Success,* p. 116.
[26] I am indebted for this information to the University Libraries of the
University of Nebraska, and especially to Frederic S. LaCroix of the Social
Studies Division, who looked up the relevant publications.
[27] Buckner to Pound, 2/11/33.
[28] Buckner to Pound, 1/9/35.

'Where is Blackstone?' to which you eloquently replied 'Rubbish.' "[29]

Going to Harvard was a great gamble. Nobody believed that Sofy could get a teaching job in education-saturated Massachusetts, and Emory could not be certain of the market for part-time male stenographers in Boston. On her graduation, Sofy was offered a job as a high school principal in rural Nebraska, and a family story says that she sat down and wrote her husband a note which she gave him at dinner: "Dear Emory, I've just gotten a job as principal of a high school. I'm going to work until you can send for me. Love, Sofy."

In late September, 1904, Buckner went off alone to Cambridge with his suitcase and his typewriter. The money to pay his tuition had been raised in Lincoln, much of it, apparently, by Pound. He found an attic room in a frame house at 28 Mellen Street, only a couple of blocks from the new law school building. At twenty-seven, he was the sixth or seventh oldest of the 288 men who registered at the law school, and he was one of only two who were married. He was not, however, as he and Pound had feared, an isolated Westerner.

"Harvard Law School," Buckner wrote Pound a few years later, "has changed very much in the twenty years since you attended. . . . More than sixty per cent of the students at Harvard Law School come from other colleges than Harvard; practically every state is represented; the condition precedent of a college degree is rigidly adhered to; and it is a matter of common knowledge, that as a general proposition the young men who come from western and southern colleges are generally among the pick of these institutions."[30]

Moreover, Buckner found that the market for student stenographers was strong. While at law school he took dictation from fourteen or fifteen professors, plus President Charles W. Eliot and Dean James Barr Ames of the law school.[31] Perhaps his most interesting customer that fall, however, was a visitor to Cambridge: Henry James, who had returned to America in August for his first homecoming in twenty-one years, and was staying with his brother William. He was in process of arranging a lecture tour for himself, and also of composing the lecture, which he would later publish as *The Lesson of Balzac*. William James had been among the first professors Buckner worked for, and he recommended the young Nebraskan to his brother.

[29] Buckner to Pound, 1/7/16.
[30] Buckner to Pound, 4/2/10.
[31] Alva Johnston, "Courtroom Warrior—II," *The New Yorker*, 3/19/32, p. 25.

The night after his first session with James, Buckner dined with Frankfurter, whom he had met during his first weeks in Cambridge, and told him, "James talks just as he writes—the sentences come out of his mouth on clothes hangers." Buckner also brought Frankfurter a moral problem that fall: James had taken the entire working period reading him the final draft of the Balzac lecture. "Should I charge him," Buckner asked, "for listening to the lecture he gets paid five hundred dollars to give?" Frankfurter replied, "Of course you don't charge him"—but, of course, James paid.

A favorite story from those months dealt with James' initial discomfiture at Buckner's speed: As a court reporter, Buckner was used to taking down statements much faster than anyone else James had ever worked with. James commented, and Buckner said cheerfully, "You whistle down brakes, and I'll throw on the sand." The railroad lingo flabbergasted James, who thereafter would take part of their time to learn from Buckner Western locutions which long residence abroad had kept from him. He does not seem, however, to have been entirely enchanted with Buckner's approach to the English language. In his graduation talk at Bryn Mawr in the spring of 1905, an ill-tempered tirade about American abuse of English which he permitted to be published once, in a small edition, under the title *The Question of Our Speech,* James expressed particular displeasure about the "r" sound which had deprived Americans

of the power to emulate the clearness of the vowel-cutting, an art as delicate in its way as gem-cutting. . . .

[T]he letter . . . gets terribly little rest among those great masses of our population who strike us, in the boundless West perhaps especially, as, under some strange impulse received toward consonantal recovery of balance, making it present even in words from which it is absent, bringing it in everywhere as with the small vulgar effect of a sort of morose grinding of the back teeth. There are, you see, sounds of a mysterious intrinsic meanness, and there are sounds of a mysterious intrinsic frankness and sweetness; and I think the recurrent note I have indicated— fatherr and motherr and otherr, waterr and matterr and scatterr, harrd and barrd, parrt, starrt, and (dreadful to say) arrt (the repetition it is that drives home the ugliness), are signal specimens of what becomes of a custom of utterance out of which the principle of taste has dropped.[32]

[32] James, *The Question of Our Speech,* pp. 28-29.

To Buckner as an individual, however, James was both courteous and kind. They had made arrangements by mail for Buckner to resume his work for James, at the end of the lecture tour, and on June 1, 1905, the novelist sent a letter of apology:

I have been waiting to write to you till I should be sure, and now, alas, this certainty (of the next fortnight) has taken the *wrong* form! That plan I told you of, so many weeks ago, for my being in Cambridge again from about this moment and again getting at work with you, has had to give way to all sorts of hindrances, complications that have come up since then, and for which I didn't, couldn't then make allowances. I shall not get back to Irving Street till about the 14th or 15th, and then have some 20 days before me of extreme interruptedness. But I shall at that time want immediately to see you and shall be better able to tell you how the last weeks then stand with me. I feel as if I had trifled with your expectations, but perhaps you are too busy (I *hope* you are) either to desire [?] or to mind [?]! I hope you are full of prosperity. Yet you see how I *need* your alliterations. Your Balzac lecture has had high success. You shall hear me again, and I am yours very truly,

HENRY JAMES

His return to Harvard further delayed, James presently invited Buckner to make his first trip to New York, to work with him at a friend's house on Sligo Square. After a few weeks' financially profitable experience in the big city, Buckner returned to Nebraska to spend the summer with his family. On his return to Cambridge the next fall, Sofy came with him; and they found an inexpensive apartment some distance from the law school, on Ellsworth Avenue.

In his first year at Harvard, Buckner had taken the standard program of Contracts, Criminal Law, Property, Torts and Civil Procedure. In the last of these, he had received from no less an authority than Dean Ames the almost unheard-of mark of 88. His average of 80 placed him in the top half-dozen of his class, and he was inevitably invited to join the *Law Review*. He replied by mail from Nebraska that he couldn't afford the honor; and when he returned to Cambridge, Grenville Clark, who was on the *Law Review* in the class ahead of Buckner's, tried to talk him into changing his mind. Especially now that his wife was with him, however, Buckner simply could not take that kind of time away from his stenography.

Despite the added distractions of a wife in the house and the need to generate more income through stenography, Buckner slipped only to a 79 average in his second year (though Ames cut him down to a 77 in Trusts, and John Chipman Gray gave him only a 74 in Evidence; interestingly, considering how little attention he would pay to this subject later, he received from Professor Eugene Wombaugh the astonishing mark of 91 in Agency). In his final year the distractions were even greater, for his daughter Ruth was born on December 13, 1906, the only child born to a law school student during Buckner's time at Harvard (the third-year class in Property rose and cheered when Buckner entered the next morning). Nevertheless, only one of his five marks that year fell under 80, and his average for the year was 83. Over all, he chalked up an average of 81, and he ranked third in a class of about 190 (his future partners Silas Howland and Arthur Ballantine ranked fourth and fifth, respectively).

Buckner did not learn his rank in class until almost four years later, and then he wrote Frankfurter: "I was honestly and frankly surprised. Had I supposed I stood any such chance as that I would have cut a few dozen less lectures and done a few hours more work —with all my troubles I could have done it easily enough, except the last and curiously enough I guess my last was the star year. . . . Well, how unimportant it all seems, now that we look back on it, except for biographical reasons."[33]

Particularly after his wife's arrival, Buckner seems to have spent relatively little time socializing with his classmates. He saw a good deal of Frankfurter and Frankfurter's roommates (first Sam Rosensohn, who was to be in the early 1910s Buckner's closest friend in New York, and then the future philosopher Morris Raphael Cohen). He knew his future partners Elihu Root, Jr. and Grenville Clark, but they were a year ahead of him—and, besides, they were part of what he and Frankfurter called "the Gold Coast set," who made both of them uncomfortable. Howland, equally poor, son of a professor at Drury College in Springfield, Missouri, was a good friend: "We hatched our partnership," Buckner later wrote Learned Hand, "years ago in Cambridge."[34] The Buckners and Howland also saw something of Ballantine, who was socially well connected (his father was president of Oberlin) but economically restricted. Ballantine's com-

[33] Buckner to Frankfurter, 9/23/11.
[34] Buckner to Hand, 10/8/13.

petitiveness bothered them, however. More than three years after graduation, Howland "raised the roof with delight" at learning that he had finished "one two-hundreth of a per cent ahead of the man who threw him down." Describing an evening with Ballantine in New York, Buckner told Frankfurter that "he still has this curious Ballantine streak."[35]

Though he had little time for extracurricular doings, Buckner was sufficiently popular with his classmates to be chosen to deliver the toast to Dean Ames at the annual banquet given the faculty by the third-year class. "I propose a toast," he said, "to one who is gentle without weakness; courteous without suavity; whose professional work stands a monument to stalwart individualism; whose private life breathes an inspiration to humanism; who aids and counsels with *heart* was well as purse and mind; no task too difficult for his careful pains; no one too humble to call them forth; his personal contact the most prized advantage in our course; and when we take from here the parchment evidence of our work, its greatest value will lie in the autograph of

James Barr Ames."[36]

Buckner's future as he finished his work at the Harvard Law School was open, but by the same token indeterminate. He cannot have been sure he wished to gamble it on New York—he did not take the special course in New York practice which was offered third-year men who were planning such an adventure—but in April of 1907 he came down to see what might be available to him at one of the growing downtown law firms, which had just taken up the habit of paying their clerks. (Smaller firms still did not pay, the theory being that the young assistant was really gaining more in education than he was giving in services. Even in the larger firms the custom was only about ten years old. Henry L. Stimson remembered with amusement the managing partner of Elihu Root's law firm calling out, "Where's that *paid* law clerk?"[37]) He returned to Cambridge with encouragement but without any final arrangements. His professors and his friends urged him to try the gamble, and several of them loaned him money to carry him through his first years. "I

---

[35] Buckner to Frankfurter, 9/23/11.
[36] Sending his words to Frankfurter, Buckner added a little nervously, "I hope on rereading they will not prove conventional or 'flourishy.' "
[37] Morison, *Turmoil and Tradition*, p. 64.

could never have gone to Harvard or NY," he wrote Pound in 1914, "without the band of optimists who backed their credulity with cash."[38]

A few days after the end of term Buckner was back in New York, he had a definite job offer, and he had decided to take his chances in the city. He and Frankfurter indulged in the first of the many all-night talks which were to cement their friendship, during the course of which they apparently took apart a number of their law school contemporaries. Buckner the next day was apologetic: "I am not always so acrimonious and gossipy as last night. I feel the iron in my blood on this stupendous undertaking and it may have made me a bit sarcastic on some of our friends. Fat men are generous, above all, owing to their sloth and general good nature, the nerves being so comfortably embedded in adipose."[39]

Frankfurter (after "fifteen or twenty minutes in the Hornblower office," as Buckner later put it in a note to Mrs. Frankfurter[40]) had joined the team of young men Henry L. Stimson was putting together in the U.S. Attorney's office. In doing so, however, he had taken a salary cut from $1,000 to $750 a year (which, he later said, made him feel better about it, because it meant nobody could accuse him of self-interest in leaving his first employer[41]). He thought Buckner should join him in practicing law specifically in the public interest ("without having a client," as he put it[42]); but Cravath, Henderson & DeGersdorff had spoken to Buckner that afternoon in terms of $1,000. Buckner was a married man with a child and with debts, and $1,000 would be little enough in New York.

From the Harvard Club, Buckner wrote Frankfurter: "I have definitely decided on the CH & DG office—if they'll have me and consequently will not take any time of your busy, however courteous, chief. . . . My summer address is David City, Nebraska."[43]

Never again after that summer would Buckner have a home address in the West.

---

[38] Buckner to Pound, 10/29/14.
[39] Buckner to Frankfurter, "Tuesday," 1907.
[40] Memorandum to Marian, 2/20/35. The "Hornblower office" was Hornblower, Byrne, Miller & Potter. Among the others taken by this office from the Harvard Law School class of 1906 was Elihu Root, Jr.
[41] *Felix Frankfurter Reminisces*, p. 40.
[42] *Ibid.*, p. 39.
[43] Buckner to Frankfurter, "Tuesday."

CHAPTER TWO

Apprentice Prosecutor

1907-1910

Buckner was not a member of the bar when he reported for work at Cravath, Henderson & DeGersdorff on October 1, 1907; with the full consent of his new employer, he had put off taking the New York Bar examination until later that fall. Nothing a Cravath clerk would be asked to do during his first year would require certification as a lawyer—or, indeed, any great exercise of trained discretion. The "Cravath system" of breaking in law clerks did not assume that the new men were ready for much. Robert T. Swaine, an Iowan who came to Cravath three years after Buckner and stayed to become senior partner, described the firm's procedure as follows:

> At the outset of their practice Cravath men are not thrown into deep water and told to swim; rather, they are taken into shallow water and carefully taught strokes. The Cravath office does not follow the practice of many other offices of leaving small routine matters entirely to young men fresh from law school without much supervision, on the theory that a man best learns how to handle cases by actually handling them.[1]

After three years as a court reporter and more than six years as the head of his own household, Buckner must have found the Cravath arrangements rather babyish. His own policy in later years would be to delegate to the young men in his firm (and especially at the U.S. Attorney's office) as much responsibility as he thought they could possibly manage, and to build up in their minds the

[1] Swaine, *The Cravath Firm*, II, p. 4.

22

value of their own initiative and their own sense of care and thoroughness in the work they were given. He disliked the term "law clerk,"
and coined the now universally accepted word "associate" as a substitute for it. Practice was doubtless closer to Cravath's practice than
theory was to Cravath's theory, because both offices were facing
similar problems in usefully employing large numbers of brand-new
lawyers, but the spirit in Buckner's firm was far closer to young
men's dreams of importance and, in some ways, equality.

His first days in New York Buckner stayed at the Harvard Club
and looked for an apartment where his family could live. On a
thousand dollars a year plus borrowed capital, he had little choice
in Manhattan, and he never thought to look elsewhere. ("It would
have meant much to me," he wrote to a young man he was hiring
in 1920, shortly after he had moved his family to University Heights
in the Bronx, "if when I struck town someone could have gotten
hold of me and told me of a certain place I have since discovered."[2])
What he came up with was a mean, dark flat at 40 West Ninety-
third Street, in a five-story walk-up brick tenement. Its advantage
was its proximity to Central Park, less than a block away, where
Sofy could escape with Ruth.

Everything considered, the first experience of New York must have
been greatly unlike what Buckner was hoping for from his "stupendous undertaking." After his admission to the bar in January, 1908,
he did have one or two chances to see the inside of a courtroom for
Cravath. Elihu Root, Jr. many years later remembered that

I heard Emory Buckner handle his first case . . . I was up in the Municipal
Court answering calendar. Rubbering around before court opened I spied
Emory not far away. . . . They called the case on which Emory was in
court, and he answered, "Ready for the defendant," but the plaintiff did
not answer at all. The judge peered around the court with a surprised look
on his face expecting something to happen, and nothing happened. Then
I saw another barrister nudge Emory in the ribs and heard him say in a
raucous whisper, "Ask to have it dismissed." So the great future barrister
piped up and said, "Would Your Honor dismiss the case?" The judge said,
"Why, of course," and called the next one. And that all goes to show that
however good you are you need to know your way around.[3]

[2] Buckner to Cleary, 2/17/20.
[3] Root, "Early Recollections," 26 *Bull* No. 4, 1/27/45, p. 2.

Buckner stayed with the Cravath firm only five months. His departure seems not to have left any hard feelings: twice in the future he personally (and not his firm through other intermediaries) would be retained by Paul D. Cravath to handle matters in which Cravath was personally involved—once with regard to a civic organization which had been pounced on by the police because of its promotion of birth control, once with regard to a suit brought by a lawyer who had done a piece of work for Cravath and Cravath's client Jacob Schiff, and had not been paid.

2

It seems likely that from the day of his return to New York (a day concluded by dinner with Frankfurter), Buckner had been under pressure from his friend to join the U.S. Attorney's office—and that Stimson had been under pressure from the indefatigable Frankfurter to hire Emory Buckner, who came, like Frankfurter himself, highly recommended by Dean Ames. Unlike the romantic bachelor Frankfurter, Buckner was unwilling to move without a raise; and Stimson finally offered $1,200. "He used to say," Frankfurter recalled, "that five dollars a week had changed his whole life."[4] Buckner reported for work at the old Post Office Building on March 1, 1908. He used his small increase in salary to escape from West Ninety-third Street to the more pleasant environs of Columbia University and an airier apartment on Morningside Drive West; it was not enough to enable him to begin repaying any of the debts he had assumed when he first made his plans to come down to New York.

Stimson by then had been U.S. Attorney for two years, and had revolutionized the job. It was, and still is, a rather anomalous position. In each of the federal district courts, the U.S. Attorney is the government's lawyer, charged with prosecuting those accused of federal crimes, suing for federal claims of all sorts, and when necessary defending the government against suit. His position is to a degree independent of the Department of Justice; he is appointed directly by the President and confirmed by the Senate, and can be removed only by the President. Prior to Stimson's regime, the U.S. Attorney for the Southern District of New York had remained in the private practice of law, and had worked for the government on a con-

4 Frankfurter to author, 1964.

tingency basis, splitting recoveries from litigation and fines assessed by the courts (mostly for customs violations). The post had been one of the most cherished political appointments of any administration, and the income from it had been estimated as high as $100,000 a year.[5] To earn this money, the U.S. Attorney did not actually appear in the court for the government—he left the trial of cases to a small group of juniors whose salaries were appropriated by Congress rather than taken from his contingent share. In important cases ("extraordinary matters") he was empowered to hire outside counsel to handle the government's case.

Stimson—and Theodore Roosevelt, who appointed him—would have none of this. Their first reform was to put the position on salary, at $10,000 a year; their second was to establish a rule that the U.S. Attorney would try the more important cases himself (this rule was broken instantly upon Stimson's departure, to permit him and the young men who left with him to continue the prosecutions they had begun while in office). Their third reform was to give the U.S. Attorney a completely free hand in adding staff to the reorganized office, without reference to either civil service principles or political expediency. Stimson decided he wanted full-time people, and recognized that his salaries would not make it possible for him to recruit from the ranks of proven lawyers in New York. He wrote around to the law schools asking for the names of recent graduates who had just started their New York careers—it was by this route that Dean Ames supplied the names of both Frankfurter and Buckner—and he built up a young staff which by his retirement in 1909 numbered sixteen lawyers, more than half of them young. In the process, he fought off the politicians, who had their own candidates.

Though Buckner's day-to-day work at the beginning was mostly in the trial of petty counterfeiters, smugglers and postal thieves, he was soon embroiled in what had turned out to be Stimson's enduring crusade in office: the effort to make the American Sugar Refining Company—the "Sugar Trust"—obey the law. The first round in this war had been fought before Buckner's arrival, when the company and several railroads had been convicted under the Elkins Act for complicated and concealed rate rebates designed to enable the Trust

5 Morison, *Turmoil and Tradition,* p. 94.

to undersell the beet-sugar farmers of the West. When Buckner arrived another, even more spectacular case was building. This one had started with a tip from a former employee at the company's Brooklyn docks, that the scales which were used to weigh in the sugar for the purpose of computing duty (at about 1½ cents per pound) had been rigged to cheat the government.

Two "Special Agents" of the Treasury had been sent over to investigate, and had found that company checkers sat in the booth with the customs inspectors while the sugar was being weighed. At all seventeen scales, in all seventeen booths, there was a hole in the beam of the scale that ran to the desk of the company checker. From one of these holes—the first one they examined—the inspectors withdrew a steel corset stay twisted at the end to form a hook. Manipulated by means of a rope, this hook would catch on a lever to reduce the reading on the scale by about 10 percent.

On the basis of this discovery, the U.S. Attorney for the Eastern District, in Brooklyn, had secured a criminal indictment against employees of American Sugar Refining. But one of the two Special Agents was reached by the company and would not testify to what he had seen, and the other on closer examination turned out to be a notorious liar who could easily be impeached on the stand, and the prosecution lapsed. Stimson, taking over the problem, realized that the company would need weight records not only to calculate customs duties but also to pay its suppliers and operate its refineries—indeed, the suppliers in self-defense must have had private weighers working on these shipments. Stimson set Winifred T. Denison, chief of his Civil Division, to find out what could be proved.

Many years later, retelling the story for the young lawyers of Root, Clark, Buckner & Howland, as a cautionary tale on the value of concrete evidence, Buckner wrote that Denison "asked me to assist in the preparation of the case. He was occupied in having an elaborate investigation made of the books of the private weighers and the books of the government weighers both of which had to be filed at the Customs House. This job was immensely laborious and occupied the attention of a squad of fifty accountants whom he was supervising. I suggested to Mr. Denison that the seventeen stanchions with their holes be removed from the docks and brought into court as exhibits. I also suggested that we employ the Fairbanks Company to build us a model scale in the courtroom in front of the jury box, bore a hole in the left-hand stanchion and do some experimenting with the corset wire. Miraculous to say the experiment showed that the insertion of a piece of thin steel into the model scale erected by the Fairbanks Company corresponded pretty closely to the ten per cent difference in the weights which had been revealed by the elaborate tabulation.

"As can readily be conjectured, the judge and jury were tremendously interested in the seventeen uprights with their telltale holes and the experiments made in actual weighing by the model scale, all over the strenuous objection of the late John B. Stanchfield, at the time the leading trial lawyer in New York City. The amount involved was only $150,000 as the shipments selected for the test case were small. . . . The jury promptly found for the government."[6]

In the end, various civil suits against the Sugar Trust would recover more than two million dollars, which the Attorney General described in his annual report to Congress as the largest sum "ever secured by the government on a claim of that nature."[7] Throughout these suits, Stimson and his successor, Henry A. Wise, reserved the government's right to follow up with criminal prosecutions. Stimson left office with Roosevelt in March, 1909, and took Frankfurter with him back to his private practice; another laborer in the sugar fields, Francis William Bird, later an important figure in Buckner's life, had left for private practice two months earlier. All three men, however, continued to help Wise as Special Assistants in the preparation and trial of the civil actions against American Sugar Refining, and Frankfurter found a way to secure new criminal indictments against employees at the docks and executives of the company (including one of the directors—"the real culprit," Frankfurter said many years later, "a pious fraud and amateur astronomer in Montclair, New Jersey; speaking to the grand jury, I used the phrase 'distance deludes discovery and disinfects dividends'; Emory loved it"). In November, 1909, Stimson and his team of assistants won four convictions, including one of the treasurer of the company (its president had died by a shot from his own gun in a "hunting accident" while the civil cases were pending).

[6] 21 *Bull* 143-144, 4/13/40.
[7] *Turmoil and Tradition*, p. 103.

Frankfurter recalled that Buckner made the opening statement for the government in the criminal case, and that his mature style was already present. A short, pudgy man, with a high shock of brown hair lengthening his rather square face, Buckner breathed amiability and forthrightness, the breezy, no-nonsense manner of the West. He started, Frankfurter remembered, with the sort of throwaway line that was to be one of his assets in the courtroom all his life, alerting the jury to the fact that the government's most important single witness, the Special Agent, was a "confirmed liar." But if they heard a man say it was raining outside, he suggested cheerfully, and they looked through the window and saw the rain, they would believe him even though they knew he was a liar. "It was," Frankfurter recalled, "as homely as that."

The departure of several senior men with Stimson had meant a promotion for Buckner, and a raise to $2,000, which in June, 1909, he rather optimistically described to Roscoe Pound as "a living wage." Still, he wrote, "It takes a long time in New York to get 'out of the woods,' as you know. . . . I have no definite plans for the future, and do not know whether I shall remain here or carry out the notion I have always had of returning to the west—a notion I find diminishing the longer I stay."[8] The shifts at the office also gave Buckner a new and congenial boss in Goldthwaite H. Dorr, who became chief of the Criminal Division. Though Dorr was by some years Buckner's senior in legal experience (and in other experience: he had fought in the Spanish-American War), the two men were the same age, and they and their families had become friends.

"In those days," Dorr recalled almost sixty years later, "you had a pretty good vacation at the U.S. Attorney's office. I had a little cottage at Point O'Woods, on Fire Island, and in the summer of 1908 we invited the Buckners out to the Point for a visit. We went sailing. He never had any instinct for it or interest in it, and he started the practice of reading aloud while sailing—he read delightfully. That's what he'd do when we went sailing. They'd been having a hot summer in New York and that visit meant a lot to them, it was the first break they'd had.

"The summer of 1909 my wife and I took the same cottage, and we'd had so much fun the year before we thought it would be an

[8] Buckner to Pound, 6/4/1909.

awfully good thing if Buck and Sofy and their little girl came down. We had a nice little girl, a college sophomore, to help out with our own child, and it was pretty crowded. We got a catboat, Buck always described it as a family boat, which of course it was—it had a flat bottom—and we'd all pile in.

"It was a wonderful summer. I used to run into people who never saw Buck again in their lives who would remember him from that summer. We'd go sailing—he always took a book—and we'd go swimming. He wasn't much for swimming either, but he was pretty fat even then, and he could float. We would take the boat down to a place where nobody ever came, and strip and go swimming—at a decent distance apart, of course. One Sunday Felix came down. Buck and Sofy were at their best, very relaxed, lots of good talk, good reading, very intelligent people.

"When we came back from the Point that year, we thought this reading aloud was a good thing, and we formed a little group, with Harold Deming[9] and his wife and sister, and Felix, too. We were what was called in those days cultured people—terrible thing to call anybody. We cared about books and art. We used to read mostly plays, assign parts—it's curious how one could always assign parts according to the characteristics of the people in the group."[10]

One of Buckner's customs-fraud prosecutions was to have an interesting sequel. The accused were proprietors of a cheese-importing firm called A. Musica & Sons, who were bringing in from Italy, it developed, much more cheese than they were declaring for customs purposes. The fraud was not a complicated one in essence—it involved simple bribery of customs agents, one of whom got as much as $500—but the cover-up work of fake invoices and inventories had been done with genius.

"It was a wholly statistical case," Buckner wrote in 1940, "with some little corroboration of furtive visits of government customs employees. . . . Feeling that the jury would be completely lost in the mass of figures, I prepared a set of tables showing these discrepancies in a very simple and convincing way. The trial fell into certain different episodes, and at the end of each episode, having placed in evidence all of the primary evidence, that is to say the documents and

---

[9] Another Stimson assistant.
[10] Dorr to author, 1966.

books, I offered a summary in evidence to show what it all meant. I
was amateurish enough to head these different schedules 'Act 1,
Scene 1,' etc. Violent objections were made to these summaries by
defendant's counsel, the late Mr. Rushmore, and Mr. Louis L. Dela-
field, but the judge said he found them very helpful for himself and
thought the jury would find them helpful also though he would
instruct them to disregard the captions. I should have known better
and not put the captions in, but it was the way I viewed the case
as a gradually unfolding criminal course of conduct. Without them
the defendant would not have pleaded guilty in the middle of the
trial but might well have been acquitted. His name was Philip Musica,
who became extremely well known several years later as Donald
Coster."[11]

This telling was a little incomplete, for Musica's guilty plea was
part of a deal, by which the charges against his father were dismissed.
And when he re-emerged twenty years later as Coster, claiming a
German background and a Heidelberg Ph.D., he not only became
well known, as president and largest stockholder of the old drug
house of McKesson & Robbins, which he had purchased, but he
became on the recommendation of his investment bankers a corporate
(never a personal) client of Root, Clark, Buckner & Howland.
McKesson went into receivership upon the discovery that Coster,
still talented along the lines he had pioneered as Musica, had
invented some $20 million of its assets through fake invoices and in-
ventory receipts. Fortunately, from Buckner's point of view, the
McKesson & Robbins business had been transferred to Sullivan &
Cromwell some years before. Though Buckner had never met
"Coster" as a client, the newspapers could have had an embarrassing
amount of fun with the swindle if his firm had continued as counsel
for the company.

"Most remarkable thing in legal history," Dorr said, "that a man
you had sent to jail would come back to your firm as a major client
—and apparently a very desirable client."

3

The year with Stimson was immensely important in forming Buckner's personal and professional attitudes. Many of the matters he

[11] 21 *Bull* 145, 4/13/40.

worked on involved criminal behavior—clearly criminal behavior, on any standards—by men who were presumably leaders of the community: like Charles W. Morse, who owned half a dozen banks and swindled their depositors by lending himself the banks' money, or the directors of American Sugar Refining and the New York Central Railroad. Any tendency toward success worship that might have been developed by an ambitious young man in the Gilded Age was wiped out by the experience of the United States Attorney's office under Stimson, and Buckner's Republicanism became that of Theodore Roosevelt and Felix Frankfurter. Unlike Frankfurter, he was to remain a Republican all his life, but his basic belief was in nonpartisan government, where a voter owed his allegiance primarily to individual leaders. "You and I have so often said," he wrote Frankfurter in 1933, "that if we could pick the judges we could let almost anybody write out the reforms for criminal and civil procedure. And, of course, that is true of all public officials. It is 90% personnel and 10% 'constructive reform.' "[12] In 1930, when Buckner was one of the more prominent people in New York, he was canceled out of the Republican Party's list of radio speakers because his speech included a compliment to Al Smith. He wrote about the incident to Stimson, then Hoover's Secretary of State, and Stimson replied, "I am disgusted . . . I am going to make a similar statement in my speech, and I should like to see them stop me!"[13]

Watching Stimson, Buckner acquired passionate views about how a government law office should be run. Frankfurter nearly sixty years later remembered "a bitter cold night, when Chief Flynn of the Secret Service was going to raid some counterfeiters. Stimson sent Tommy Thacher[14] along to make sure they didn't overstep the search warrants." Stimson was, as Franfurter put it in his reminiscenses, "incredibly effective and wholly scrupulous. . . . If you read some of my opinions with regard to criminal prosecutions," the Justice added, "that's where it all comes from. In one opinion I actually said this, that maybe this was a bias derived from having served under a

[12] Buckner to Frankfurter, 2/11/33.
[13] Stimson to Buckner, 10/27/30.
[14] Thomas D. Thacher, then one of Stimson's young assistants, became a federal district judge, Solicitor General of the United States, and a judge of New York State's highest court. In his private practice, he was a partner in the firm still known as Simpson, Thacher & Bartlett.

United States Attorney who observed these standards and won his cases."[15] Though Buckner believed that no amount of formal rule observance was significant unless the chief prosecutor was a man of probity—and disliked certain constitutional restraints, especially the Fifth Amendment privileges—when he came to be U.S. Attorney himself in 1925, he modeled the rules of his office on Stimson's.

At that time, writing in the new "inside" newspaper of the U.S. Attorney's office, Buckner gave his staff a credo which he felt he had inherited from Stimson:

Civil office in time of peace is the greatest honor which can be conferred upon a citizen by his country. This honor carries with it the heavy responsibility of a trustee. . . . Our client and ward, the government, is inarticulate. It is deaf and dumb. However real, it cannot express itself. Public officials who happen to be our superiors are not the government. Individual citizens are not the government. When it is our duty to speak and we do not speak, the government is betrayed by our silence, because it cannot speak for itself. When it is our duty to act and we do not act, the government is betrayed by our sloth or timidity or personal ambition, because it cannot act for itself. To permit any consideration such as personal ambition, future law practice, future public office, criticism or praise of the community, hostility or commendation of friends, to enter our mind is to soil our conscience and smudge the right hand which we held aloft in pronouncing our sacred pledge. Public opinion is not the government.[16]

Perhaps most important of all, the Stimson office gave Buckner a long-cherished experience of working in a loyal fellowship of bright, energetic and often playful young men, who were in and out of each other's homes as well as offices, drank and sang and danced together, wrote doggerel verse and parodies, read plays to each other as well as observing each other's courtroom appearances. "The entire organization," Buckner wrote of his days with Stimson for the benefit of his young assistants in 1925, "was not as large as our criminal division or our prohibition division. An adequate lunch in Child's in those days cost 15¢. The whole situation was vastly different, but equally thrilling."[17]

For twenty years Buckner was to be a significant employer of young men fresh out of law school—often a dozen of them a year

[15] FFR, pp. 48-49.
[16] *Scraps*, 5/21/25.
[17] *Scraps*, 1/1/26.

for his own office, and scores of them when he was U.S. Attorney. Through parties, lunches and dinners, bull sessions over a bottle of good bootleg whiskey in his own office, intraoffice newsletters and just the inspiration of his own conviviality, he tried to duplicate for these young men the joys he found in Stimson's office—partly to recapture his own delights, but mostly out of a flowing, natural generosity. "The great thing he did was, he made you feel you were supposed to help the other fellow," said Ethan Alyea, who came from law school to Buckner's office in 1922 and stayed to become a partner. "It wasn't something to be proud of that you found something wrong in another man's work. Don't talk about it—tell him quietly."[18]

Neither in Stimson's office nor in Buckner's did this affection for the young men and their sports mean that the boss pretended to be one of the boys. Sitting in on the poker games in his office (which he vastly enjoyed: all sorts of wild-card games), Buckner was still the boss, and asserted his authority by insisting that the stakes never rise above nickels and dimes. The distance of a generation was then recognized as meaningful; men did not by their actions lie about their age. Recalling their association with him, only the men who were roughly of his law school generation speak of "Buck" or "Emory"; to the men who entered the law as his employees, it is always "Buckner," and sometimes, even now, "Mr. Buckner." In Buckner's correspondence with Stimson twenty-three years later, on the emerging scandals in the New York judiciary (scandals serious enough to command Stimson's attention while Secretary of State), it was "My dear Buckner" and "My dear Chief."

4

While Buckner was on Fire Island with his family and the Dorrs in 1909, the "good government" forces of New York were plotting the overthrow of Tammany in the city elections that fall. Stimson was involved, as the candidate of choice for Mayor if the coalition of the Republicans, the Citizens Union and Hearst (then a separate force) could be made to jell. In the end, Hearst withdrew, and the mayoralty race became three-cornered: William J. Gaynor for the Democrats (an extraordinarily attractive, indubitably honest and frequently liquored candidate, nominated when Tammany feared a

[18] Alyea to author, 1966.

strong opponent), Otto Bannard for the Republicans and Hearst for himself. The preliminary work bore fruit, however, in that both anti-Tammany slates nominated the same men for subsidiary offices; and fusion carried the Board of Aldermen and elected Charles S. Whitman as District Attorney.

Not long after the election, Whitman asked Buckner to become one of the Assistant District Attorneys of New York County. These appointments were wholly political, with salaries to suit their status; from $2,000 a year as an assistant to a federal prosecutor, in December, 1909, Buckner went to $7,500 as one of ten assistants to a county prosecutor in January, 1910. He wrote Roscoe Pound, who had become a professor at the University of Chicago: "An inexplicable miracle has transpired in my appointment as Asst. Dist. Atty. It gives me a great opportunity and with my first check I shall begin devoting half my salary to the payment of a heavy indebtedness. You will come just as soon as I can possibly reach it. . . .

"I haven't yet awakened from the wonder of my new job. I am the youngest of the full assistants, younger than many of the deputy assistants—and the youngest at the bar of anybody in the office. Do I need tell you I'll strain every nerve to make good? Happy New Year to you!"[19]

Probably the most plausible reason for Buckner's appointment is that Whitman wanted somebody respected in the federal courts. In 1908 the Supreme Court had upheld an injunction by a federal district judge in Minnesota, restraining that state's Attorney General from enforcing its railroad rate-regulation statutes,[20] and in New York as elsewhere the district judges were rather frivolously exercising their new powers (some of which Congress was about to take away). A commercial-fraud investigation launched by Whitman's predecessor had been stymied by a temporary injunction from Judge Learned Hand, and Buckner seems to have been put on this problem upon his arrival at the office. He had come to know Hand well enough while a federal assistant to write the judge a private letter in early February, 1910, explaining the damage the injunction might do if Hand made it permanent;[21] and Hand presently quashed it.[22]

[19] Buckner to Pound, 1/6/10.
[20] *Ex parte Young,* 209 US 123.
[21] Buckner to Hand, 2/3/10.
[22] *Ex parte Tracy,* 177 Fed. Rep. 532.

The deputy assistant who worked most closely with Buckner in the Whitman office, serving under a younger man, was William Dean Embree, a fellow Nebraskan, son of a railroad station agent, who would later become a partner in Milbank, Tweed, Hadley & McCloy and a president of the New York County Lawyers Association. "The reason Emory was appointed," Embree said more than half a century later, "was that Whitman had gone to Stimson, and asked for the best man he could get, and Buck's stock was high."[23] Felix Frankfurter was more cynical. "I told Buck," he recalled, "that Whitman had every community represented on his staff—a Greek, a Pole, a Jew, of course; and he thought the bar should be represented, too."

Frankfurter's judgment was a little unfair; several of Buckner's colleagues in the Whitman office would make distinguished careers. Among them were James O'Malley, a future judge of the Appellate Division; Isidor Wasservogel, later to be a distinguished if difficult Supreme Court Judge;[24] Charles C. Nott, later a General Sessions judge; and Charles Albert Perkins, who would serve a short term as District Attorney, by appointment. Among the deputies were Embree, Lloyd Paul Stryker (son of the president of Hamilton College, where the Root family was closely connected, later a dramatic and well-publicized defense lawyer), George W. Whiteside (later an important New York trial lawyer, counsel for American Tobacco and a regular companion of Buckner's at a Friday lunch table in the Bankers Club) and Morris Koenig (brother of the Republican county leader and later a General Sessions judge).

Many of these men, of course, maintained an outside practice, too—not until Thomas E. Dewey became DA in the 1930s was the part-time prosecutor abolished in Manhattan. And those who put the most time into their work for the DA's office usually considered it a steppingstone to a judgeship or to political advancement. Whitman, Buckner soon learned with great distaste, had been running for Governor from the moment he became District Attorney.

A Quaker, Amherst graduate, sanctimonious, formerly a magistrate by appointment from a reform Mayor and then a General Sessions judge, Whitman made no distinction between his holy crusade against

[23] Embree to author, 1964.
[24] In the New York system, the Supreme Court is the trial court of original jurisdiction for more important cases.

the city's crime and his personal ambitions. He planted newspaper
publicity and fawned on publishers, and would organize trials to make
the publicized opening and closing statements in cases he had not
prepared and knew little about. Frankfurter would later use Whitman
as his example of the "politically minded district attorney—one of
the great curses of America." To prove the point, Frankfurter told a
story which he said Buckner had told him, about the aftermath of
the fearful Triangle Fire of 1911:

> Whitman came in this morning mad as fury, and he called in the head
> of the homicide division and said, "What's happening in the Triangle
> case?"
> This was only a few days after it happened. "Well, boss, we're not
> finished with the investigation, but very soon we'll have the case before the
> grand jury."
> "Well, get an indictment! We can always *nol pros* it [i.e., decline to
> prosecute]. Here, look at it!" and he held up an editorial in the Hearst
> New York *American*. "You go and get an indictment. We can *nol pros*
> it if we can't maintain it. You can always *nol pros*."
> Whitman was getting indictments because Hearst's *American* was
> yelling blue murder![25]

In such an office, inevitably, a man would be valued primarily by
the contribution he seemed to be making to the boss's political ambitions—which meant that politics was incessant within the office itself.
There was none of the camaraderie of the Stimson office, and a great
deal of jockeying for position. At the beginning, Buckner was too
absorbed by his new situation to pay much attention to atmosphere.
He had a heavy burden of swindlers and petty criminals to prosecute,
and he was readjusting his home life to his new salary. He paid off
his old debts within a year, and then the Buckners moved down
from the little apartment uptown to much more spacious and expensive quarters at 780 Park Avenue; they also hired a French maid.
Soon Buckner would be living beyond his new salary, and feeling
poorer at $7,500 a year than he had at $2,000 a year.

5

Buckner's repayments of his debts to Pound extended far beyond
the mere matter of money. The Nebraskan, who turned forty in
1910, had become nationally known as early as 1906, when he

25 FFR, pp. 45-46.

delivered a chilling speech to a convention of the American Bar Association on "The Causes of Popular Dissatisfaction with the Administration of Justice"—a speech so highly critical of contemporary procedure that the routine resolution to have it printed created an uproar at the convention. Doubtful about "liberty of contract" as a guiding principal and disgusted with what he called "mechanical jurisprudence," he was the leading spokesman for what he called the sociological approach to law. Though he was clearly an outstanding scholar, the fact was that he had never taken a law degree— he had left Harvard after only one year—and in the opinion of the established leaders of the bar he was a meddling upstart. Buckner and Frankfurter launched a campaign to get Pound invited to Harvard Law School. In February, 1910, Buckner wrote Professor Samuel Williston at Harvard:

"Frankfurter and I on at least a dozen occasions have wondered why Pound was not brought to Cambridge, and a few days ago we agreed to write you a note calling him to your attention. Not that he needs calling to your attention and not that we have taken upon ourselves the nomination of professors—but only to remind you of him at this important time. You probably know something of Pound's early history. He graduated from the University of Nebraska when scarcely out of knickerbockers and took a Ph.D. degree in botany when, I believe, only nineteen years of age. His law teaching history for the past ten years you know. It has been brilliant. Dean Ames told me once that the reason his one year at Cambridge was not more distinguished was because his primary interest at that time was botany. The people in Nebraska and in Chicago think him a perfect wizard, and this accords with my own view. His case is the exceptional one of combining rare legal ability and scholarly attainments with a touch of the pedagogue, and students in the Law School at Lincoln used to tell me he was an excellent teacher. He is too good a man to be anywhere except at Cambridge."[26]

[26] Buckner to Williston, 2/16/10. Buckner sent a copy of this letter to Pound with an apologetic covering note:

"I trust you will not think me officious for what a friend of mine and I have written to Professor Williston. Felix Frankfurter is a very brilliant young man of the class of 1906 and has read many of your essays. When are you going to collect them into a book?

"I hope you will get a call to Cambridge, and if you do I earnestly hope you will go and if you are in a mind to decline I should like to submit a brief." (Buckner to Pound, 2/16/10)

Pound apparently gave Buckner a modicum of encouragement, but said he thought an invitation to Harvard was unlikely. Within six weeks, however, the invitation had been sent. "I do not flatter myself," Buckner wrote, "that I had any serious part in bringing about the offer, unless, perchance the mere stirring up which my friend and I have given Williston and Beale and others has resulted in the investigation of yourself, which, impartially conducted, could have but one result."[27] In his sesquicentennial history of the Harvard Law School, Professor Arthur E. Sutherland credits the appointment exclusively to Ezra Ripley Thayer, who succeeded Ames as dean of the law school. The invitation to Pound appears to have been concurrent with Thayer's installation as dean.[28] It is by no means unlikely that Buckner's letters—from a well-regarded recent alumnus who had known Pound well, to powerful members of the faculty—played a role in Harvard's deliberations.

As promised, Buckner now submitted his brief: "The service which you could render to the profession by wielding an influence on eight hundred college graduates a year can hardly be overestimated. These men, after graduation, scatter over the whole country and your influence at once becomes national instead of parochial. I feel very strongly on this point as there is an especial need of men like you, who bring to the law more of the sociological and humanitarian spirit than anyone I know. . . .

"I do not know that it is improper for you to consider the situation from a purely personal standpoint. . . . The school has the best library, I understand, in the country, and is only waiting for more books to be printed or discovered in order to purchase them. The school is now elegantly housed in two handsome buildings, and the mere material equipment is perfection itself. The members of the faculty appear to be broad-minded and congenial, and the fact that they have invited you after a very careful survey of all your work is an evidence of a very desirable catholicity of spirit. No one teaches over six hours, I think, and there is, therefore, great opportunity for

27 Buckner to Pound, 4/2/10.
28 Sutherland, *The Law at Harvard*, p. 238. Sutherland gives March 28 as the date of Thayer's appointment, May 9 as the date of Pound's. The Buckner letter demonstrates that the offer to Pound was made during the last week in March, and that Buckner was close enough to the situation to be privy to the news.

that constructive research for which you are so admirably equipped and of which the profession is sorely in need. The life at Cambridge will please you tremendously; the breadth and liberality of the town and university are in marked contrast with the well-meaning but irritating narrowness and provincialism of Lincoln, for example. . . .

"I suppose I am considerably influenced as a mere question of pride, pride in you as a Nebraska man and as a fraternity brother."[29]

Pound did heed the call to Harvard, and was immensely happy there. "Few of [my old friends at the bar] appreciate what a glorious place this is," he wrote Buckner a year and a half later. "I don't see how one could ask anything better."[30] But Buckner and Frankfurter were not through with him. In the fall of 1911 Frankfurter had gone to Washington with Stimson, who had been made Secretary of War, and was reveling in his daily proximity to the seats of the mighty. The two friends discussed what use might be made of Frankfurter's new influence, and the result was another letter from Buckner to Pound:

"My intimate friend Frankfurter is now Solicitor for the Bureau of Insular Affairs, War Department. He would like to see you on Supreme Court, and you bet we all would. It probably will be impossible to pull it off with Taft and Wickersham,[31] as you are not a metropolitan corporation practicing lawyer. He has . . . had Holmes' secretary mention it to him. Holmes thinks you are great. I wrote Frankfurter we ought to stir things up a little anyhow, because a little agitation might put you in the candidate class, and it would make it easier for us to pull it off with Wilson, La Follette, or Roosevelt—who knows what's going to happen?"[32]

Pound replied: "I appreciate your letter very much, but must confess the matter looks chimerical. Still, you might retort that I said that about coming here!

"I sat next to Mr. Wickersham at a seance after the dinner of the Illinois State Bar Association a year ago last June and we swapped and capped quotations from the *Inferno* all the evening. Really I formed a very good impression of him. He seemed modest, scholarly

---

[29] Buckner to Pound, 4/2/10.
[30] Pound to Buckner, 11/20/11.
[31] Attorney General George W. Wickersham.
[32] Buckner to Pound, 11/14/11.

and zealous to his duty."[33] Pound appended a list of seventeen judges and leading lawyers he knew well in the Middle West, and Buckner sent longhand letters to fourteen of them, passing Pound's note along to Frankfurter so he could write from Washington to the three federal district judges on the list. Nothing came of the young men's efforts. Buckner wrote in January, 1912: "Apparently we didn't even reach the stage of eastern newspaper 'mention,' but still it did no harm. Perhaps we can do more with TR or Wilson. I hear nothing but extravagant praise for your work."[34]

A third time, successfully, Buckner intervened in Pound's career. Early in 1915, by which time Frankfurter had joined Pound on the Harvard Law faculty, Buckner formed a group to promote Pound as the successor to Dean Thayer at the Harvard Law School. "Of the great opportunities that stretch ahead the next ten years," he wrote, "I do not even need to speak. They must be patent to you. These opportunities will absolutely be lost if some 'successful practicing lawyer' or some old dodo of a Back Bay judge is chosen. . . . You must accept the Deanship."[35] Pound was chosen, hesitated, accepted.

One of his first actions after telling President Lowell he would accept was to write a note to Buckner, who responded:

"Congratulations *ab imo pectore!* Congratulations first to the country, second to the school, third to yourself! . . . Now that the common peepul have established you and Felix within the walls of Troy as stool pigeons I tremble for the future of the Codfish."[36]

[33] Pound to Buckner, 11/20/11.
[34] Buckner to Pound, 1/24/12.
[35] Buckner to Pound, 1/3/15.
[36] Buckner to Pound, 1/7/16.

CHAPTER THREE *Assistant to Whitman*

1910-1912

People v. *O'Reilly,* Buckner's most important case while an Assistant District Attorney and the source of the first significant public attention paid to him, came in the spring of 1911, almost a year and a half after he joined the Whitman office. It was a case that put an end to a great public scandal highly derogatory to the reputation of the bar, and the victory was the more gratifying because it was unexpected, both inside and outside the District Attorney's office.

Dan O'Reilly, the defendant, was himself a former Assistant DA, the son of a judge, sufficiently prominent that a former chief of police testified as a character witness in his defense: "I have known the defendant since he was a baby; I knew his father when he was on the bench; I know others who know him." While still in his early thirties, O'Reilly had made a reputation in the courts by managing the defense of Harry Thaw, who had shot the architect Stanford White in the restaurant atop the old Madison Square Garden on Madison Square, in what may still rank as the murder of the century; O'Reilly had been the only one of the lawyers in his first trial that Thaw retained for the second. After Thaw's conviction and flight, O'Reilly solidified his reputation around town by living with Evelyn Thaw, whose affair with White had been the proximate cause of her husband's troubles. The prosecution of O'Reilly would be unpopular with politically important people; and his offense, while very serious, was not uncommon at the bar in 1911.

41

The origin of the case against O'Reilly was a minimal assault and substantial robbery of Aaron Bancroft, an aged Wall Street broker. Bancroft was carrying from his office to the vaults of the Produce Exchange Safe Deposit Company a red envelope containing about $80,000 worth of endorsed and negotiable stock certificates. In the corridor leading to the vaults he was jostled by a man who knocked the red envelope and his hat to the floor. Another man came along and helped him pick up envelope and hat; but the envelope Bancroft had when this courtesy was completed, while apparently identical to the one he had taken from his office (complete to his name and address), did not contain the stock certificates.

As the police were regarded as both inefficient and unreliable in any matter involving money, Bancroft told his attorney, William M. Sullivan, to hire the Pinkerton Agency to get the securities back and (as an afterthought) to catch the thieves. George S. Dougherty, director of the Pinkertons' New York office, put the story on private ticker services all over the country to alert bankers who might otherwise purchase the stolen goods. Meanwhile, the thieves had gone up to Boston to try to peddle the certificates through a lawyer they knew there, and Dougherty in two days could report no progress; at which point Sullivan paid Pinkerton for what they had done and discharged the agency. He began negotiations instead to secure new certificates from the corporations whose stock was involved, and he applied to an insurance company for a policy which would reimburse the corporations for any losses they might suffer through the reappearance of the stolen pieces of paper. He found that the premium for such a policy would be between six and seven thousand dollars.

O'Reilly's role in the case began when he was approached by an ex-convict named Frank D. Plass, keeper of the New York rooming house where the two thieves, Chester Yates and Charles Ross, had lived in the weeks before the robbery—and undoubtedly a co-conspirator (he had traveled with them to Boston). O'Reilly called Dougherty at Pinkerton's to say that he might be able to arrange the return of the securities to Bancroft if he was prepared to pay a price. Dougherty referred him to Bancroft's lawyer, and O'Reilly visited Sullivan's office, bringing with him one of the stock certificates as a kind of bona fides. The arrangement O'Reilly said he had made—and the story is a plausible one, though Sullivan denied it under oath—

was that Bancroft should retain O'Reilly to act in the broker's interest, at a nominal fee of $50. In return, he would arrange the return of the certificates at a price of $5,000, which he would pay to his "contact." Bancroft would save time and nuisance, and the money involved would be less than the insurance premium.

Sullivan notified the police, took cash from the bank, and met Plass at O'Reilly's office. The three men got in a cab near City Hall and, with the police trailing the cab, rode around town, Sullivan first checking off the certificates he was given against Bancroft's list of what was missing, and then handing over six bills—five one-thousand-dollar bills to Plass, and a fifty to O'Reilly. Three certificates were missing, representing three hundred shares of American Smelting & Refining Company, worth about $20,000: Plass and O'Reilly had been double-crossed by Yates and Ross. Nevertheless, Sullivan took what he had and went off. Plass and O'Reilly moved on to a bank where O'Reilly had a safe-deposit box; and Plass changed the five thousand-dollar bills and, he said, gave O'Reilly $833 as his one-sixth share of the deal. Then Plass and O'Reilly went over to the Men's Bar of the Biltmore Hotel and drank a convivial pint of champagne. The police had lost the cab on its way uptown.

The charge against O'Reilly was Criminally Receiving Stolen Property, and the major witnesses against him were Plass, who had turned state's evidence, and Sullivan. It was a stickier case than it seems in a brief telling, because to the extent that O'Reilly had been retained by Sullivan he had a possible technical defense; and Sullivan was not believable when he said that it was only an accident that he had given the fifty-dollar bill to O'Reilly and the five thousand-dollar bills to Plass. On the key question of the $833 allegedly paid over to O'Reilly, there was the fact that O'Reilly had been with Plass at the bank while he changed the money, but beyond that the evidence pitted the word of a lawyer and a former Assistant District Attorney against that of an unsavory ex-convict who had much to gain by playing along with the prosecution. There was no question in anyone's mind that the recovery of stolen property by just these means was then a regular occupation of the Pinkerton Agency. Dougherty had since resigned from the agency to become Second Deputy Police Commissioner (in which capacity he was again to have trouble with Buckner thirty months later). Under cross-examination by O'Reilly's

lawyer, Abraham Levy, Dougherty said, "In speaking about the
defendant's connection with this matter I said that everything that
O'Reilly did in this matter was fair and square and above board. I
said that to the District Attorney; and that was my honest belief
and it is now."[1]

It was also clear enough that O'Reilly was being prosecuted (by
the police and Whitman, if not by Buckner) less for what he had
done than for his failure to deliver the missing three hundred shares
of American Smelting. Inspector John H. Russell, chief of the Police
Department's Detective Bureau, testified on direct examination that
"I told him that if the matter was not straightened up, the 300 shares
of Smelters were not returned, I was going to submit the entire
matter to the District Attorney."[2]

Buckner, less than four years out of law school and new to the big
city, was personally horrified by the idea that lawyers were acting
as fences—and officially protected fences, at that—for the city's
thieves. Dougherty's cheerful statement at the beginning of the cross-
examination, that he had never seen anything wrong with what O'Reilly
had done, was a pressing danger to the prosecution. Buckner handled
it on redirect calmly but with great force:

Q. Referring to Mr. Levy's question whether you did not tell me that
O'Reilly's conduct was perfectly square in the matter wasn't the full statement that O'Reilly told you that the nominal fee of $50 took care of him
and that you said being a lawyer I suppose he knew, and didn't you say,
"To tell you the truth, Mr. Buckner, I suppose it was perfectly legitimate"?

A. Yes, I did. I based my opinion on O'Reilly's legal opinion to me.
I told you that the arrangement was that O'Reilly was to receive a nominal
fee of $50.

Q. Didn't you also tell me in that conversation that you yourself never
thought for a minute that $50 was all Dan was getting out of it?

Objected to; objection overruled; exception.

A. I am not so certain about that, no.

Q. Didn't you say something in words to that effect when you were
talking about this $50 retainer which Mr. O'Reilly got?

A. I might have suggested that, but I did not know it to be a fact.

[1] *People* v. *O'Reilly*, printed transcript, p. 126.
[2] *Ibid.*, p. 137.

Q. What I am asking you now does not carry any testimony on your part that you think the defendant got any more money, but didn't you state to me when we were talking about this $50, that of course you did not think that the $50 was all Dan was really getting out of it; I am just asking for that conversation, is that right?

A. Yes, I gave that as my opinion.[3]

Not the least of the threats to the People's case was the talent of defense counsel Abe Levy—"very formidable," Embree recalled. "Summing up, he always had a spell of emotion that never did him any harm with the jury—'All that I have, all that I am, I owe to this great city and great nation. . . .' We saw cases going out the window." Levy's defense, apart from the prearranged boost from Dougherty, consisted of detailed cross-examination of prosecution witnesses, character witnesses for poor O'Reilly and a long spell on the witness stand by the defendant himself. He took O'Reilly page by page through the testimony of the prosecution's witnesses, having him gladly affirm that which was not inconsistent with his story and sadly deny what might put him in the clink. Buckner in his summation turned this tactic against Levy by adding up exactly 105 places in the record where O'Reilly had contradicted other witnesses. That many denials—the People's brief on appeal enumerated fifty-five of them for the benefit of the higher court—could not be legitimate.

Most important to the mood of the case was Buckner's cross-examination of the character witnesses and of O'Reilly himself, all of it designed (as Levy later complained in his brief on appeal) to portray O'Reilly as a wastrel, an adulterer and a lush. The fact that O'Reilly owed the butcher and the grocer was repeatedly brought out, as were the fifteen judgments for debt that had been taken against him in recent years, five of which were still outstanding. One of O'Reilly's friends, a Wall Street banker, was called in his defense, and Buckner pinpointed a meeting of the two men during the time of O'Reilly's negotiations with Sullivan. He then asked, "Do you remember his telling you that he had been out all night before with the keeper of Barnum & Bailey, and took an elephant around to various cat houses?"

In his two-day cross-examination of O'Reilly himself, which vir-

[3] *Ibid.,* pp. 128-129.

tually ended the trial, Buckner saved for the last the questions that
would destroy completely O'Reilly's claim that he had never had
any real connection with Plass, and was actually representing Bancroft. He drew from O'Reilly the story of the night three days after
the taxi ride, when O'Reilly and Plass had gone carousing together
in various low-life joints in Harlem. It was with this testimony in
their ears that the jury went out.

They returned in one hour and twenty minutes, with a verdict of
guilty. The *Times* noted the next day that it was a surprise:

> [G]eneral opinion around the Criminal Courts Building was that the
> case would result in a disagreement. . . . The verdict was credited in great
> part to the address made to the jury by Assistant District Attorney Buck-
> ner: "What is of more danger to this community than to see this attorney
> at the bar, an associate of thieves, a thieves' broker? This lawyer took
> stolen goods useless to the thieves and by his genius changed it to $5,000.
> Two million people living in this county are crying for justice, and it is now
> up to you to give them justice."[4]

O'Reilly got five months and was, of course, disbarred; and other
lawyers who had been acting as fences found other ways to make
a living. The two crooks, Yates and Ross, pleaded guilty and received
sentences which look monstrous today: four to nine years for Ross,
a first offender, and twenty-one years for Yates for his second offense.
The DA's office felt indebted to Plass, but there was some feeling
on the bench that he might be the worst crook of the lot, and no judge
could be found who would agree to give him a suspended sentence.
At about the time Buckner left the Whitman office, Embree successfully moved dismissal of the indictment against Plass.

2

The O'Reilly case was important because, as a future generation
would say, it "made law": up to then, criminal lawyers had been
sure that behavior like O'Reilly's was unpunishable. Another satisfying
case for Buckner was the manslaughter conviction of a gangster
named "Biff" Ellison, though dawdling by police and previous prosecutors had allowed six years to pass since the killing, with the inevitable disappearance of evidence and witnesses. Yet another would

4 *New York Times,* 5/25/11, p. 1.

be the conviction of a lawyer who had collected $4,500 on a client's injury claim, and had turned over only $300 of it to the client. Moreover, Buckner was learning to play office politics successfully. When Whitman was out of town, as he increasingly was, making speeches on crime and virtue, Buckner, though the least experienced lawyer in the office, often found himself "Acting" rather than "Assistant" District Attorney. He had become sufficiently well known to be invited along with Isador Wasservogel (his most frequent rival for the "Acting" post) to dine with John D. Rockefeller, Jr., Abraham Flexner, Jerome Greene and City Commissioner of Accounts Raymond B. Fosdick to discuss the "social evil"—i.e., prostitution. "We had ice water," he wrote Frankfurter, "but the dinner was excellent. I daresay that while the pious JD insists on Baptist beverage his wife secures a continental cook. Wass and I are brought in because he apparently labors under the delusion that we are the best trial men and he has asked Whitman for permission to draft us for his sex cases whenever he wishes."[5]

But Buckner found the routine of the Criminal Courts Building increasingly dull and distasteful. Moreover, in that age of Edwardian extravagance, he felt poor. The Buckners spent the summer of 1911 in New Hampshire, in a house they rented on the estate of some wealthy friends, and Buckner wrote about the experience as part of several long letters to Frankfurter, who had recently left New York for Washington.

In a letter written from the Harvard Club the night of his return from New Hampshire (he had left his family in the country for another month), Buckner recommended Jane Addams' *Twenty Years at Hull House* ("Make all haste to get that book and read it all—not felix it"), and added: "It was particularly inspiring, because I have been a little more fretful over wealth this year than ever before— because possibly the B——'s were under our nose with all the power to command those things which we wish and need so badly and of course some of which we feel we have more capacity to enjoy."[6]

Five days later he went into greater detail: "I found to my surprise (and I confess to my great satisfaction) that we were to be on a much more independent basis than I had supposed would naturally

[5] Buckner to Frankfurter, 11/28/11.
[6] Buckner to Frankfurter, 9/18/11.

be the case. In fact I found Helen (who is boss) quite imbued with
the idea of landlord and tenant—the fact that the tenants were friends
and congenial was a mere incident—by applying my (to you) well-
known psychic seismograph I soon discovered that we were not
to depend on them for rides, or horses, or vegetables, or what not.
We at once took the cue, and it all worked out very well, everything
considered. . . . [T]his English status of landlord and tenant . . .
results in the expense being greater, but that is much better than being
the beneficiary of a philanthropist—subject to two observations: it
depends upon how hard it is to meet the extra expense, and it depends
upon who the philanthropist is. With this family in mind the last
contingency applies and it is time to evoke Rule XXVI of Rules for
Conduct in Life, which is, as you well know, 'Well, business must
be business, *especially* between friends.' "[7]

Nor were these nagging jealousies restricted to the country: "P——
and wife took me out to dinner Thursday for reports on summer. I
was just thinking (as I think too often of late) on the rottenness of
being poor, for I really should have been taking them but had no
money either in pocket, bank, or elsewhere, when he spoke of the
theater and said there was a show in town he heard was good called
'Dis— Dis—' I supplied Disraeli and he said, 'What does that word
mean?' Just at the moment I was wishing like mad I could buy Sofy
the extremely stunning and becoming gown which Mrs. P—— wore
—and the antithesis was so ludicrous I almost laughed, though there
was nothing to laugh about."[8]

Frankfurter answered unhappily. "Seriously," he wrote, "I am
much perturbed by the depth of the seam of poverty reflections in your
present mental outlook. The thing is deeper and, what's worse, more
permanent than you think. . . . I am keenly anxious that you should
get some of that out of your system. If you'd take their money away
there wouldn't be a figleaf left on them." Frankfurter felt that Buckner was forgetting too easily the real poverty of two years before,
when his salary had been one-sixth of what Whitman was paying.
"[H]arrowing worry," Frankfurther wrote, was now removed "permanently." Buckner should remember that "life has more zip for
you, as it is, as well as more gray hairs."[9]

[7] Buckner to Frankfurter, 9/23/11.
[8] *Ibid.*
[9] Frankfurter to Buckner, 9/26/11.

For the assorted nuisances of the District Attorney's office Frankfurter could offer less consolation. Buckner wrote of his problems in preparing a criminal libel suit against a German immigrant socialist who had been printing pamphlets about the personal dishonesty of the leaders of a large corporation. The case had been prepared by the counsel to the corporation, Howard Gans, whom Buckner respected, but Gans had gone to Europe and "in place of his coruscating mind I have his clerk. Sparks never yet came from bone. I dislike the case and think it will prove to be a lemon. I asked this clerk about our various witnesses. 'Have they anything on Francis?' (Francis is a newspaperman and a sort of detective who got the technical proof of publication by posing as a magazine writer who wished to write up a story of defendant and his courageous campaign against the trust.) 'Oh, no, nothing that amounts to much. The only thing they can say about him is that he has been living with Evelyn Thaw the last year. He took her up shortly after she and O'Reilly fell out, but that's nothing.' 'Anything against Sully, the chairman of the Executive Board?' 'Oh, no, he is under indictment for land frauds, but he is absolutely innocent and the indictment will probably never be tried; a mere charge proves nothing.' 'Anything against Stadler, the president?' 'Nothing except he and other directors back in 1899 paid dividends out of capital in order to boost the stock and sell out their pool, but later when they were sued they settled and paid back half a million dollars into the company; everybody did those things then, and besides, suppose he did do that twelve years ago, is he to be hounded forever after, and at a time when the company is honestly run?' About this time I asked, 'By the way, have you ever tried a criminal case?' 'No.' . . . I am doomed to try a crazy man, who tells at least half the truth, and who has the spirit of a missionary. Judge Crain called him up to his desk last month on an interlocutory matter while I was away and said kindly to him, 'Why don't you stop these circulars and let these people alone and we shall drop the indictment.' But the red-headed Teuton with the fervor of Stein and and   (supply the proper German heroes) replied with a wild gesture, 'No, Judtch, not if you send me to the electric *shair*!' "[10]

Buckner won this libel case (he noted in passing that as a result of his work Gans had been able to put in a supplementary bill for $2,500) after a trial held in the criminal part of the Supreme Court

[10] Buckner to Frankfurter, 9/23/11.

rather than in the Criminal Courts Building, because Buckner had maneuvered it into the better court. Presently he and Embree were to maneuver Justice Samuel Seabury into the courtroom where they worked, to assure themselves competence on the bench in the cases they tried. But being an Assistant DA in those days was, in the words of Judge Jonah J. Goldstein (later to serve twenty-five years on the criminal courts bench), "a whore's game." And Buckner found Whitman increasingly intolerable. Nearly a quarter of a century later he was to recall to Frankfurter a meeting of the Legislative Committee of the Citizens Union which they had both attended, where Whitman came to appeal for additional staff. "You turned to me," Buckner wrote, "and said, 'What about it?' I whispered, 'He has men enough to man the office but he is not man enough to men the office.' We, as usual, were in agreement but it did no good."[11]

In an October letter to Frankfurter, Buckner vented his grievances at bitter length:

"Keitel [the libeler] will get a jail sentence—six months or so—next Monday morning. I have tried since two murder cases, with conviction in one and plea in the other at the end of my case. I am planning to appear in every case, with Embree preparing half of my cases and Morris Moskowitz the other half, and each assisting, taking as much active part as I feel the case justifies. But I have little hope this will impress the chief, for though in Part V [of the criminal courts], which is analogous, there are two experienced trial men dividing the calendar, and next month there will be three, making one-third each, yet the chief feels that every full assistant in the office is ducking work, and he thinks trial work the easiest thing in the world, so I can hardly expect to receive any appreciation by going the next morning into an important case after I have burned the candle at both ends for two or three weeks preceding. But such is the view point of the next governor.

"Absolutely under the belt, I am informed that he is working day and night for the nomination. He has Abe Gruber absolutely backing him (in the dark), and I do not see why he can't get it. He makes a splendid wooden horse because he has so many people fooled including your friend Schiefflin, etc., etc., *ad glorificandum.* DeFord

---

[11] Buckner to Frankfurter, 2/11/33; Whitman is not mentioned by name, but is inescapable in context.

is already beginning to work for the [interim] appointment [as District Attorney] by Whitman when elected, and thereafter for the nomination. He readily realizes that Whitman won't have anything to say but will appoint whom they tell him to, so he has contributed to Hearst's campaign fund, to Shearn's fund, and others, I guess, is speaking on the fusion platform, and spends a social hour or evening every week with Gruber. All this is below the surface and only comes to me by my trusty emissaries. Wise [Stimson's successor and Buckner's former chief] is not in the running, and the only pledge that has been made to him by the organization is to head the delegation to the national convention and by delivering his vote to Taft to insure his reappointment, which I am informed he wants, and will insure in that manner.

"All new appointments to this office are made on strictly organization lines, and the policy in the beginning of representing everyone with the hope of a successful coalition for renomination has now been changed to a policy of cementing the organization for the gubernatorial nomination. All in the name of the people of the county and the state of New York. It makes me put my lunch.

"McGuire is absolutely incompetent for this office, but he is chairman of the speakers' committee of the new fusion movement which is now having a healthy recrudescence, and therefore he can have anything in this office he wants. Wasservogel is on the joint committee, and he can have anything he wants. December 1st will therefore mark my exit from S[upreme] C[ourt]. Mark my word and mark it well. January 1st at the very, very latest. The fact that notwithstanding three weeks Keitel case we disposed of eight homicides in one way or another: trial, plea, recommendation, but not a single acquittal, and the fact that the cognate Part V running full blast on homicides alone has dispose[d] of only about six with one or two acquittals, goes for naught. The fact that the press this morning recorded a juror's protest in open court against McGuire's cross examination goes for naught. . . .

"Nothing has happened to me and Keitel caused quite a little talk in the office, notwithstanding it was not a public case and I never had more than a dozen auditors. The Scheftels case is on. The hog had to give Pit [Wolcott H. Pitkin] the technical proof and Smith the examination of the suckers, but he opened and will close, which is about all the papers will notice. Of course H.L.S. [Stimson] was surprised. How should he know better? If it comes up again, tell him not to take your word but to ask me, Pit, [Daniel D.] Walton, [Robert P.] Stephenson, and the rest of them. Tell him to ask the lawyers who have had dealings with him and find how he is liked."[12]

3

The immediate cause of Buckner's decision to leave the DA's office was a peculiarly trivial case he later loved to talk about as "the shooting showgirls." It was not amusing to him at the time, however, and the letters he wrote about it to Frankfurter in November and December, 1911, are the most complete documentation he left to tell of his feelings about any of the cases he tried during a quarter of a century in the courtroom.

The complaining witness, victim and villain of the piece was a distasteful older sportsman, lecher and fool named W. E. D. ("Billy") Stokes, who raised horses at a farm in Lexington, Kentucky, and owned considerable real estate in New York, including the then fashionable Ansonia Hotel on Broadway in the seventies. Though he was married and had a young child, he had acquired the habit of helping along occasional young ladies who would otherwise be dependent on their own talents for their support. Among these in 1906 was a Midwestern girl named Lillian Graham, who had come to New York at the age of sixteen (she said) to Seek a Career on the Stage. Their relations flourished. In 1907 Miss Graham visited Stokes in Kentucky, breaking off an engagement with a touring troupe for the purpose; and presently she settled in the Ansonia. Stokes prudently secured from her a written statement that she had already had relations with other men, to mitigate possible future damages.

For four years, Miss Graham was in and out of suites at the Ansonia, where her status was that of a tenant whose rent bills were allowed to mount. Twice Stokes sent her off to Paris, whence she would bombard him with letters asking for more money. She had some theatrical engagements, for which she admitted she was never paid more than $35 a week (Stokes said $18). He rather disapproved of her being on the stage. They exchanged an odd correspondence, in which he wrote of "slightly damaged widows" whom he was entertaining.

[12] Buckner to Frankfurter, 10/28/11.

When Miss Graham returned from Paris in 1911, Stokes was no longer particularly interested in her, and she found an apartment of her own. In early May of 1911 she acquired a roommate, Ethel Conrad, nineteen years old and a good friend of one of the city's more prominent strikebreakers. Miss Conrad, who had been born in Venezuela, was made of somewhat stronger stuff than her new roommate. She carried a gun, and had once used it to extract from an upstate storekeeper a written statement of retraction of a letter he had sent concerning her relations with her strikebreaking friend. (The statement of retraction was introduced in evidence, and Miss Conrad told the story of pulling the offending letter from her handbag and reading its deplorable contents to the storekeeper. On redirect examination, the situation subtly changed: "I forgot to say that I pulled out a revolver with the letter."[13]

The ladies' story was that Miss Graham had given Stokes $1,700 of her inheritance from her sainted mother, to invest; and that Stokes still owed $500 of it. The state's story was that the ladies had decided they could extort up to $25,000 from Stokes, either on the basis of the letters he had written Miss Graham or, if necessary, at gunpoint. The campaign was launched on the morning of May 31 by an alleged attempted suicide by Miss Graham, who supposedly swallowed a quantity of carbolic acid and left a note about "this man Stokes, who has ruined my life from the time I was sixteen years old, an innocent child."[14] The note also urged Miss Conrad to see to the posthumous publication of her correspondence with Stokes.

Naturally, Miss Conrad, after determining that Miss Graham's dose was not fatal and making her comfortable, took this document to Stokes to solicit his help. "Mr. Stokes," Buckner explained to the jury in his opening statement, "gave Miss Conrad thirty dollars to obtain a nurse for Miss Graham. All this happened in the morning, but where do you suppose the two girls were the afternoon of the same day? They were in the sporting goods department of a large Broadway store, buying *two* nurses." And Buckner displayed a blue and a white revolver.[15]

Stokes had always been conscious of danger in the letters he had written to Miss Graham, and he decided he had better get them back.

[13] *New York Times,* 12/11/11, p. 3.
[14] *New York Times,* 12/8/11, p. 7.
[15] *New York Times,* 11/24/11, p. 4.

Apparently he entrusted their recovery to Miss Conrad (whose career as an "illustrator" he had promised to further). She accepted $200 from him for Miss Graham, who was to use the money to return to Europe, and on June 7 he went up to their apartment, possibly to enjoy the company of Miss Conrad, possibly in hopes of acquiring the letters.

The girls were waiting for him with their guns, and a dozen wild shots produced a number of holes in the plaster at heights ranging from six inches to three and a half feet, plus leg wounds and shock for the gallant Willie Stokes. The porter came, detectives arrived, and somehow in the excitement most of the letters Stokes had written disappeared. A few survived to be introduced in the trial, together with some dozens Miss Graham had written to her "dearie," entice-ments to compromising replies ("I do want you, and if you will be devoted to me alone, I promise not to make any trouble for you"). The indictment was for attempted murder, on the strength of the testimony of the Wanamaker saleman who had sold the girls their weaponry, who said he had told them to "fire two feet below what you are aiming at."

The case was popular with the public and the newspapers. On the morning Miss Graham was to testify the crowd brushed aside the court attendants opening the doors and rioted through the courtroom, knocking copies of grand jury testimony off the prosecutors' tables. After the room was cleared of all those who did not have seats, reporters estimated a crowd of five hundred milling grumpily in the halls. Extra interest was added by Miss Graham's quite unexpected claim that she had armed herself in fear of Stokes, because her sister (wife of another man about town) had warned her that Stokes was the murderer of a gambler named Al Adams, who had been shot in the Ansonia a few years back.

Trial began on November 21, 1911. In late October Buckner had written Frankfurter that the case "seems impossible to win from general impression, but I haven't begun working on the material as yet."[16] After the first day's testimony he wrote Frankfurter: "The Stokes case is an interesting study in trial psychology. It seems easy after Keitel so far as work goes, but fairly bulges with dynamite on questions of tactics. I shall hardly win it. Stokes cannot make a

[16] Buckner to Frankfurter, 10/28/11.

friend on the jury and the girls are well trained—helplessly huddled together, occasionally weeping, in striking and unfortunate antithesis to Stokes on the stand—strong, positive, dominating, powerful, rich, conceited—no one cares much what the result is, except the man trying it."[17]

After a weekend's thought on the question, a juror announced that on reconsideration he knew his mind was already made up, and asked to be excused. The rule that the withdrawal of a juror creates a mistrial was not yet in force; by consent of counsel, a new juror was substituted in the box. Buckner read him the transcript of Stokes' direct examination, and defense counsel read as much of the cross-examination as had been completed; and the trial proceeded. After going through direct, cross and redirect, however, Stokes collapsed of "kidney poisoning" (at the horse show) before the recross could be completed. "I certainly am playing in bad luck," Buckner wrote Frankfurter. "Stokes is seriously ill and can't come to court for 4 or 5 days, and though they got all through, except a little *re*cross, it gives them sufficient predicate to demand completion of S before proceeding. It looks as if the case were hoodooed. Breaks stop momentum."[18]

The next week, however, the girls' lawyers agreed to strike Stokes' redirect and recross and continue with the case. And once Stokes was no longer in his line of sight, Buckner cheered up. On Friday, December 5, he wrote Frankfurter: "I thought we had a splendid day today, but apparently the defense thinks they did too so there is barometric error somewhere. Moore and Jordan [defense counsel] present a beautiful demonstration all the time of what not to do. If a witness is apparently wrong about something and flatly contradicts Stokes, although on that particular point the error of the witness is inconsistent with *both* prosecution and defense, they raise a great hullabaloo, just because it *is* a contradiction.

"They were also very cheap in claiming that Stokes was shamming illness, and the doctor's certificate in due medical parlance said 'acute indigestion and auto intoxication,' so Moore in loud voice protested because the affidavit showed clearly that Stokes was suffering from self-indulgent drunkenness. This is sample. If Stokes were less of a

---

[17] Buckner to Frankfurter, 11/25/11.
[18] Buckner to Frankfurter, 11/27/11.

burden around my neck and the defendants men instead of women, we would pull it over—even as it is, maybe so. I anticipate the girls will go on the stand and weep and faint and tell dramatic and salacious stories and create an atmosphere of sympathy and prejudice which may be absolutely fatal."[19]

The girls did take the stand, and their lawyers elected to make a positive defense, opening the door for Buckner to introduce on cross-examination dozens of Miss Graham's money-grubbing letters. He scribbled to Frankfurter from the courtroom on the narrow stiff notepaper supplied to DAs for preserving their interviews with police officers: "This is my field day. Best yet. Goes to prove eminent cross-examination is always possible with trumps up sleeve and when too much fabrication is attempted. If girls are acquitted or disagreement will be because jury won't convict non obstante evidence. . . . I begin to feel the case *may* be won, at any rate the performance was just what you would have it. . . . My nerves are like mandolin strings —'Were they men they would be convicted.' " While Miss Graham was testifying, a large box from a florist was delivered to the witness stand; and she left carrying her flowers.

On December 12, three weeks after the trial had begun, the defense summed up. Jordan urged the jury to "think of your own daughters." The *Times* reported that defense counsel wept, the girls wept, the jurors were moist and Buckner himself had a handkerchief to his eyes (which seems unlikely). Moore for Miss Conrad made much of "the large check trousers, the little green hat, the olive-colored waistcoat and short tan overcoat Stokes wore on the night of the shooting. . . . 'Are these,' he asked, 'the proper clothes for a million-aire hotel owner to be wearing in the street?' "[20]

Frankfurter came to New York for the weekend and stayed over Monday morning to hear Buckner begin his summation in the case, which ran through the lunch break. Buckner reminded the jury of their pledge "to try these women just as if they were men," and bluntly attacked Miss Conrad: "A new actress has taken the center of the stage and is in the glare of the calcium. This personage is Miss Conrad, the most remarkable woman I have ever met, and I hope I shall never meet another like her."

[19] Buckner to Frankfurter, 12/5/11.
[20] *New York Times,* 12/21/11, p. 3.

Buckner ridiculed the inconsistencies of the defense and struck heavily at the justification argument: "They have blackened Stokes' character in every possible way to prove that they might have reason to shoot him, and as a roué and a libertine he should have been shot. If that is a fact, if that is the law, let us go up to the Ansonia now and finish the job these girls left undone."

But Buckner did not wish to rest any of his chance for conviction on the jury's view of Stokes. "It makes no difference," he said, "whether you like Stokes or not. I don't like him. I'm glad he isn't my father. My father is a preacher of the Gospel, and stands for everything Stokes is against. Stokes isn't Joseph, although his coat is of many colors and his other clothing of many more colors."

When Buckner finished, Justice Marcus threw out the attempted murder charge, which was supported only by the salesman's recollection of his advice on aiming the gun; but he echoed Buckner's summation in telling the jury how to consider the surviving second-degree assault charges. The jury was out fifty-three minutes, and returned with an acquittal. According to the *Times,* the girls had hysterics in the courtroom. Miss Conrad shouted to her brother, "Tell mother we are free! Tell mother we are coming home!" Her brother shouted back, "Ethel, how can I tell mother if you won't tell me the telephone number?"[21]

Buckner was devastated. He wrote Frankfurter the next day: "Well, after a few more days when I have regained a sense of proportion, I suppose I shall not be prepared to say that the verdict was raw, under all the circumstances. My case was mathematically perfect up to the time of the shooting. As to that I am not entirely positive it was just as Stokes said, though I didn't believe the girls either. I was much disappointed in myself in the forenoon. It was the tragedy of watching the clock. After lunch with only a short space to cover and with the jury refreshed and with my poise regained I spoke for one hour the best I shall talk for some time to come. I am quite ashamed that you were there in the forenoon instead of the afternoon. Ask Sofy. In that last hour there wasn't a juror who let his eyes wander. I (foolish man! !) thought I had every one of them, and Judge Marcus said to me immediately after: 'That is what did it! You will get assault in the second degree!' And the newspapermen

21 *New York Times,* 12/16/11, p. 1.

and many spectators (most of whom hate Stokes and wanted an acquittal) said there would be a verdict with a recommendation, or at the very worst a disagreement.

"But why should there have been a verdict? If all this sentiment was in the air that the girls were guilty but ought to be acquitted anyhow —at least guilty of tricking and trapping and attemping to blackmail —even if the actual shooting were a free-for-all fight in which Stokes started to take the gun away (as it may have been)—how could I expect that such sentiment would not be in the jury box as well as outside of it? . . .

"I cannot find much regret in my heart except in its reaction upon me. It sort of takes my nerve away and makes me lose confidence in myself. I find myself hating to take up the next case—however small and routine. You will be interested in Marcus' statement to me while the jury was out that while he charged vigorously for conviction he didn't care what they did except for my sake, and he also told me that I must quit taking my cases so much to heart as it would tear me to pieces. I told him I couldn't help trying a case clear to my toes."[22]

Back in Washington, Frankfurter read the verdict in the news-papers and sent a telegram of consolation. Buckner two days later was still inconsolable: "I went to the office early yesterday morning and your thoughtful telegram reached me late in the day. I am of course very much disappointed. I grant every argument you would make were you here, but I feel chagrined and in a way rebuked that twelve men could have listened to me the way those men did for the one hour after lunch and yet be against me all the time. In that hour I changed scores of doubting Thomases in the courtroom (so I am told by reporters, lawyers and others), and it is rather singular that I could have won the jury outside the box and not inside. . . .

"Apparently (from the way the jury are now loosely talking) I never stood any chance, *de hors* the evidence. It was Stokes, Stokes, Stokes. I wrote Olcott (Stokes' attorney) a note saying among other things if I had won S would have thought me the biggest man in the world; now he will be enraged at my refusing to defend him. I told Olcott when he reached that rage stage to tell him for me that he was an old man of the sea around my neck and throttled me with his legs

[22] Buckner to Frankfurter, 12/16/11.

and particularly with their intervening premises—to say nothing of the load imposed by the sex and age and apparent poverty of the defendants. . . .

"Perhaps my disappointment is selfish and personal—realizing the need for me in NY to gain as speedy a footing as possible. I feel too the rebuke of the jury, but possibly that is only meant for Stokes. I am wondering how I can live through civil suits and defendant's causes if I take so hard the impersonal client's defeat.

"My summing up was wholly extemporaneous (even as to the 'phrases') as Embree and I only had time to draw up the skeleton of presentation. The only prepared part was the last six or eight minutes, so I wouldn't wholly be without carfare to get home after a night's debauch. It is comforting to know you have a little solid ground to stand on at the very end. Even that was changed in delivery, but I enclose it for your amusement. You may throw it in the waste basket after reading and I assure you I have no other copy. . . .

"Well, sufficiency! Sorry you are not here for dinner to-day. We could at least eat the 'funeral baked meats' together with Sofy, who by the way doesn't feel half so bad as if it were some other kind of case which *had* to be won. . . . Sorry not to have had our usual inspiring session on your last trip. I was too much engrossed in my absolute determination to win (though I didn't let anyone know that). . . . Sam [Rosensohn] is coming up for a little while this after-noon but says not for the purpose of condolence as he won't give it. In a way the DA's office secured a conviction—of Stokes."[23]

Buckner never lost his disgust for Stokes (some years later he would represent Mrs. Stokes in a nasty divorce case), but when he told the story in later years it was for entertainment, and he enjoyed expanding it beyond the end of the trial. Even before they were tried, Miss Graham and Miss Conrad had gone on the stage as a duo—Buckner at the trial had displayed a poster advertising the forth-coming presentation of *Those Two Girls*. Their acquittal, and the public fuss surrounding it, persuaded Oscar Hammerstein that they could sell tickets, and he headlined them in his theater for a week as "The Shooting Showgirls." They re-enacted their cannonade of Stokes for the paying public in a performance long remembered for ineptitude by those who saw it. After their first night, Buckner

[23] Buckner to Frankfurter, 12/17/11.

recalled, someone asked Hammerstein if he would give them a second week. "Not," he replied, "if they shot at William H. Taft."

Buckner also enjoyed noting that Miss Conrad's histrionic talents, which he had celebrated in his summation, turned out to be real if specialized. A decade later she was making her living as the star of one of those I-was-a-sinner-before-I-found-Jesus shows that delighted the expanding population of California.

4

"For reasons which I now find inadequate from—for want of a better word I shall call 'a spiritual'—point of view," Buckner wrote Marian Frankfurter in 1935, "I had become dissatisfied, and about the turn of the year 1912 I reached a decision to take the plunge into private practice, as in those days I could not hope to get a job in a law office at anything like the equivalent of my very high salary."[24]

Indeed, the plunge looked dangerous and even irresponsible to many of Buckner's friends. "We on the staff were greatly concerned," Embree remembered. "We feared for two reasons—first, we were fond of him; second, we were apprehensive about his financial success. He had given hostages to fortune—a wife and a small child. He said to me, 'Bill, I'm an optimist. Out in Nebraska we used to describe an optimist as a fellow who jumps out of a balloon without a parachute expecting to land on a haystack.' "

In looking for someone to practice with, Buckner inevitably thought first of Frankfurter. They seem to have talked about it during Christmas week when Frankfurter was in New York, but there is no letter from Buckner to Frankfurter on the subject. Frankfurter's reply survives, however—an effort to talk Buckner out of the project, followed by a graceful declination:

"I had meant to say a word specifically in regard to your recent chafing against your present job and the reference to our possible practise. I know, or I'm gradually getting to know, as you probably would have it, that pain cannot be argued away, satisfaction cannot be persuaded into a man and, above all, jars to one's self-respect cannot be stoically suffered. I have a very live sense of appreciation of what it means to follow the leadership of the uninspiring—it's a terrific oppression, particularly to one of your sparkle and pent-up

24 Memorandum for Marian, 2/30/35.

Utica. But I do insist that the margin of independence is ample to tide you over, and somewhat inspirit the mere prudential considerations. Or, if you will, the prudential considerations are so strong that to submit to them *cheerfully,* despite their crushing potency, is to ennoble them. But I cannot hope to convert you by reiteration—you know my gospel on this score and if it have truth it must make its own way without frequent nursing.

"If I am ever to practice law, doing it with *you*—as I have not infrequently told you—would bring the maximum possible enjoyment. You also know, however, my passion for the practice has always been a pretty tepid one. . . . I have none of Sam's [Rosensohn's] fire and flame for the mere intellectual problems of the profession; I can't quite become a crusader for the rule in Shelley's Case or shipwreck a friendship (as he almost did before I knew him as well as I do) through disagreement on a picayune point in pleading. Nor does the conflict of the courtroom call the ego's all-consuming ardor, which lifts you to the pitch of *'Was schert mich Weib, was schert mich Kind'* —the jury is wine to your lips; for me they are twelve torturing nuisances. But of course I can get ample fun out of much of it. The prospect is more inviting if you promise me that I'll never see a client—even if we get one. I don't deny the great disciplinary value of getting and keeping clients—but there are other things I'd rather do. Yet there are worse things than practicing law—particularly if you see to it that I'm kept busy, say two-thirds of the time, arguing cases before the C[ircuit] C[ourt of] A[ppeals], especially as now constituted and occasionally running the gauntlet of Holmes' questions, while you do the jury skit to crowded houses."[25]

Twenty-three years later, next to Frankfurter's phrase "the jury is wine to your lips," Buckner penciled the comment: "Not on your life! But neither is it hemlock."

Later that month disorder in Cuba threatened to become true anarchy, and President Taft considered sending an American expedition to intervene under the terms of the Platt Amendment. Frankfurter offered Buckner another way out of Whitman's office: "I had a long talk yesterday with Mr. Stimson [Secretary of War] as to the probable personnel to be sent down if occasion calls for it. I told him that while in New York the other day I sounded you as

[25] Frankfurter to Buckner, 1/6/12.

to your willingness to be one of the men to go down for the very important work of reconstruction that will have to be done. He was very warm in his approval of the suggestion, and wondered whether you could be persuaded to go. I told him that you were worried about tearing away from the place where you had roots—or rather where you had not—but I rather thought that the more venturesome sportsmanship of Sofy could be pressed into patriotic service. I only write you so that you may turn it over in your mind, and be ready to act in case the emergency arises. . . . Tell Sofy this is the most delightful time of the year in Cuba, and Ruth would bring back joys and wonders untold."[26]

But before February was out, Buckner had found the partner with whom, failing Frankfurter, he would enter private practice. His choice was Silas Wilder Howland, his close friend from law school days. Like Buckner an extrovert and a friend of club-car laughter, he was also a sportsman and athlete. He shared none of Frankfurter's and Buckner's political interests. Lacking the lightning flash of verbal reaction that was always at Buckner's command, he disliked courts—after a certain point in his career he could not be persuaded to enter a courtroom—but he liked law as law, enjoyed entertaining and managing clients, and in the opinion of competent judges possessed the most powerful intelligence in what was to become a very large and very brilliant office. From law school, Howland had gone to the New York firm of Byrne & Cutcheon (which Harrison Tweed has amusingly remembered in several memoirs as an office of late hours and ferocious discipline). He had escaped to be counsel for the receiver of two bankrupt railroads in Chicago, and returned to New York as house counsel for the Texas Company (Texaco), at a salary roughly the same as that which Buckner was being paid by Whitman.

About a decade later, Howland was to receive an LL.D, *honoris causa*, from Drury College, and Buckner was to write a mock citation suitable for delivery on the occasion:

. . . his capacity for comradeship, his sagacity without craft, his benevolence without sentimentalism, his dispassionate judgment without lack of sympathy, his golf score of 75, his premiership at chess, his supremacy in tennis, his mastery of the cue, his clean but deadly blade at bridge, his

[26] Frankfurter to Buckner, 1/17/12.

masked and Corsican strategy in poker, his wizardry with ivory cubes, his pre-eminence at the corporation bar, his courageous challenge of the eighteenth amendment, jeopardizing his own safety for the liberties of his countrymen and rivalling John Hampden in defiance of a sovereign's tyranny. Drury College honors herself in thus honoring her most distinguished son. . . .[27]

Frankfurter reacted to Buckner's announcement with a touch of feline jealousy: "I'm amazed at Si's readiness to leave the manna of the oil fields. What a mask everybody wears—I thought he surely was anchoredly content. He is of course fit to the notch for all professional potentialities. I'm with you, too, in the belief that he has improved lots. The soft glow of romance may have weaved her warmth into all his fibres. Yet I'm not sure that I should want to practice with him. On the whole, I think I could, with little misery—but there isn't that anticipated joyousness that one spontaneously demands (to hold to our exacting standard) of professional matrimony. I say this, of course, with no thought of affecting your own possible decision—the practical uncertainties of my own doings of course forbid that and, as I said, it's largely a survival of an old (though justified) attitude. But you'll want to know. Tell me of your interview with him."[28]

By April Buckner's plans were firm: he and Howland would open their office in October. They were by no means certain, however, how they would support themselves. Buckner especially was living up to every penny of his income—was, indeed, by the evidence of some of his letters, in debt. Nobody could see how the new firm could from the beginning generate $15,000 a year to split between the partners. Howland had one certain corporation client: the American Malting Company, which would pay the firm a fairly modest annual retainer. Though he was as eager to leave Texaco as Buckner was to depart from the aura of Whitman, Buckner persuaded him that he should arrange a slow exit, working half-time at their offices to help meet the bills of his new offices. For Buckner himself, as for any trial lawyer, the practice would be whatever could be got to come in the door. Frankfurter, still a touch disturbed at the need to split his friend's loyalties with Howland, wrote encouragingly:

[27] 4 *Bull,* 6/2/23, p. 1.
[28] Frankfurter to Buckner, 2/13/12.

"I rejoice beyond the telling that your plans have reached the precipitation point. It has long been apparent that you had gotten beyond the possibility of self-adjustment under Whitman, and 'the remedy of self-help' was the only possible outlet. I'm very happy that it is definite and near at hand—the summer will dance by all too quickly and Part IV will become a memory, and with it all, as time will efface the neutral smallness of W, worth the having had.

"Si is far and away the best of the possible alternatives. He shows up well in his letter—I like his deference to your independent wishes as to the retention of the Oil Company connection. He'll soften and expand under your daily contact and conflict will suppress into gradual extinction some of his absurd tho offending pettiness. He needs a little revaluation of things and the last two years have made me increasingly feel his capacity to secure it. Lucky he to get it under such auspices! I am really quite content, beyond considerations of expediency, at your undertaking with him—even tho I have a notion twenty years from now Si and I will be talking in foreign language to one another. But then ———— twenty years!

"Despite T D's [Thacher's] gloominess I'm cheerful as to the outcome—if you're reasonable in your outlook. It's a slow investment enterprise and I don't expect a bumper crop until at least the second year. You know my observation of New York practice—and your concurrence—as a slowly acquired momentum which, in the case of men of your ability and personality, is gradually increased in geometric progression. I'm sure you'll get participating trial work from an unexpectedly large number of sources, some commercial work from Malt Co. and like sources, some little references . . . and Si should get corporate drippings from the overfed board of Byrne & Cutcheon. I'll bet cheerfully—to the full extent of other people's checkbooks we can chain."

Frankfurter then devoted a paragraph to listing wealthy mutual acquaintances who might be persuaded to give the two young lawyers some money to get started—"idle fools," as he described some of them, "who waste their sportsmanship on steel when they have a chance to stake it on gold. . . . [W]e'll have a meeting of the Ways and Means Committee when we get together in a fortnight. By that time you have a budget speech outlined that will make Gladstone's human efforts in that direction look like a table of logarithms."[29]

[29] Frankfurter to Buckner, 4/20/12.

The only one of Buckner's letter to Frankfurter which survives from that spring of 1912 is one in which he notes that he has kept a copy for himself. And little of Frankfurter's voluminous correspondence was devoted to Buckner's private problems. Frankfurter had been badly bit by the Washington bug in that season when Roosevelt was mounting his challenge to Taft, and he wrote Buckner long and rather self-important letters on the agonies of his personal decision-making:

"I have been beating myself out these last ten days in the hot furnace of upright thinking—I have sought to forge Truth in the flames of mind as well as conscience. . . . And I suppose, however awry my perspective as to the specific issues—Taft or Teddy and all the implications thereof—since my relation to them involved the most relentless kind of clear thinking and plain speaking, with the Devil temptingly throwing all possible deflecting personal or rather human considerations into the game, the issues were really magnificently challenging as a test of manhood. I feel I made an honest stab—at least I didn't blink at facts, and honesty to the facts compels me to disclaim even a remotely or vaguely accusing sense of self-deception. As for the rest, whatever the pain, it was and is richly prized as the test of things, and whatever of disappointment, time and an increasingly rational faith in the worthiness of events will take care."[30]

Frankurter analyzed Taft: "[H]is is the tragedy of a good safe judge, *i.e.,* the ability to choose one of two arguments presented to him—requiring no initiative—and the social interest to derive from that pursuit the most satisfying exercise of his highest powers, finding himself the political head and the national leader of the biggest of modern democracies. He has no appreciation of the significance of his job, no directing zeal for or understanding of its potentialties. Government as the biggest organized social effort for the courageous but intelligent grappling of social problems is not a living, dynamic thought with him, the marrow of his bones. The symmetry of our Constitutional system, the beauty of our laws, kindles his imagination and measures his scope. Law is concerned with the procedure of life—he thinks it's Life itself. His is the tragedy of honest unfitness."[31]

By contrast, Frankfurter felt that Roosevelt "deeply sensed the times when he conceived the President as 'the steward of the public

[30] Frankfurter to Buckner, 3/4/12.
[31] *Ibid.*

welfare.' . . . To a striking degree among our public men Roosevelt
realizes the affirmative demands of the Presidency. He sense[s] the
problem of the day and his stirring sympathies strive to be translated
into ameliorating action. . . . Of course, Roosevelt's main contribution
is moral rather than intellectual. He is keen to scent a wrong, far less
resourceful to suggest a remedy. . . . But he *has* got the right sympathies, the deep driving force, the desire and the ability to turn governmental machinery to social uses, the realization that evils are not
inevitable and that it is the business of statesmanship to tackle
them. . . . No one else, I think, is comparable to him in fitness and
likely fruitfulness of achievement."[32]

But Frankfurter was working for Secretary of War Stimson in Taft's
cabinet, and Stimson had endorsed the re-election of Taft. Stimson's
decision had been by no means a foregone conclusion. Roosevelt
had arranged Stimson's nomination for Governor of New York in
1910, and had campaigned for him so vigorously that the candidate
himself was put in the shade. In the conservation controversy between
Secretary of the Interior Richard A. Ballinger and Roosevelt's old
friend Gifford Pinchot (a controversy which provoked a Senatorial
investigation during the course of which Louis D. Brandeis as counsel
for the Pinchot forces was to uncover an embarrassing deception by
Taft and his Attorney General, George W. Wickersham), Stimson
was publicly on Pinchot's side—indeed, before accepting Taft's nomination as Secretary of War he had insisted that Taft know of his
support for Pinchot.

"By this time," Frankfurter continued in the same letter, "you'll
wonder how Stimson can differ from all this, and as between Taft and
Roosevelt side with Taft. As a matter of fact he would agree substantially with my basic criticisms of Taft. Of course, most of my
data come from him. He admits '[Taft] is not a popular leader,' that
'he does not realize the potentialities of his job,' that 'he lacks
initiative tho he is responsive when you get at him,' that he makes
break after break 'because of political amiability,' and that 'it was a
crime to take him from the bench.' . . . I think the answer is to be
found in Stimson's deep sense of personal loyalty and in the influence
of environment or contiguity. Loyalty to his assistants, his associates,
to his chief is one of the fine traits about him—he has it to such a
degree that it frequently lessens the acuteness of his judgment both

[32] *Ibid.*

in the appraisal of men and the significance of the personal elements
to larger causes."[33] Frankfurter would maintain this patronizing attitude toward his revered chief throughout this period of their one
serious disagreement: "Poor old Stimson!" he wrote in another letter.
"The iron has gone into his soul. He's as calm as ever, more so, but in
deep anguish. I have stopped talking politics with him."[34]

Frankfurter was shaken by the need to decide about his job in
the Taft administration. "Feeling as I do, I debated for days whether
to yield to my surface desire and resign. I told him [Stimson] plainly
I was for T.R. so my conscience was at ease; and I finally concluded
. . . that I could reconcile my ardor with my continuance at the job
with perfect propriety and probably sound sense. Since then I was
immensely glad to have [George] Rublee bring me a message from
the Colonel, *sua sponte,* to stay at my job, and Mr. Brandeis the
other night was strongly of the same opinion. Of course it tries my
patience and tests my spirit—for I now have the discipline of getting
my stimulus largely out of my work instead of the inspiration of
leadership. But it's a discipline of rare value."[35]

A postscript on the letter asked Buckner to have copies made of
the description of Taft, and to send back the letter as a whole so
Frankfurter could read it aloud to some friends. "If you think this
does show I'm losing my perspective by all means and in the name
of friendship, say so." Buckner agreed with Frankfurter's politics—
indeed, that fall he was to be one of very few people in the country
for whom support of the Bull Moose turned out to be, briefly, of
practical utility. But he was far more tolerant. A few months before,
Senator Elihu Root had been the guest of honor at a dinner at the
Harvard Club in New York, and at the request of one of the group
had "talked on insurgency. . . . He has," Buckner reported, "a fine
think box. . . . Root's plea for *time* element in reform," he added as
a postscript to the letter, "was reinforced by saying insurgents were
like the small boy who planted a bean and dug it up every day to see
if it were growing."[36] By contrast, Frankfurter would report a Root
speech to Buckner as "empty, jejune and dispiriting."[37]

In the instant matter, Buckner did feel Frankfurter had gone over-

[33] *Ibid.*
[34] Frankfurter to Buckner, 4/20/12.
[35] Frankfurter to Buckner, 3/4/12.
[36] Buckner to Frankfurter, 11/26/11.
[37] Frankfurter to Buckner, 3/12/12.

board, and told him so, tactfully: "Your long letter on the political situation received, much prized, and will be carefully treasured. Your remarks on Taft and Roosevelt are exactly right. . . . [O]ne wonders a little upon reading your letter why you should be so 'het up' and why quite so fulminant, and why so obvious a stand, for you at least, should only have been reached after such travail of soul as evidenced in the extravagance of the initial and concluding portions of your letter. . . . [A]fter all, you know, you are not deciding a third term for yourself, or intervention in Mexico, or a veto on the Arizona constitution, but the fairly simple problem of whether you personally favor Taft or Roosevelt for President, with the accompanying question of good taste and honesty: Can a minor federal office-holder, whose functions are wholly non-political, continue to serve the government when he personally favors a change in the Chief Executive? That seems fairly simple to me; but I am not in the atmosphere. . . .

"You know," Buckner added, "Sofy charges both of us with too much strutting before the epistolary mirror. She says when I bring home a shorthand copy of what I think a clever note I have written you, that it is out of vanity and a love for putting one's own record into a phonograph and inviting in the neighbors. She points out that writing with any such use in view is inimical to pure correspondence —intimate conversation; that if one wants to write a magazine article one should write it; but if one wants to write a letter one should write as if talking. . . . To what end should you wish me to return your letter, she asks. Valentine and Denison [the two men to whom Frankfurter said he wished to read it] are both in Washington, and can be told, and have been told, the obvious. You have scarcely reached the point yet when your views must always be carefully prepared for public consumption. Therefore, though she thinks your letter excellent—freer than usual from linguistic parade—she thinks it excellent discipline to ask you to ask yourself a question or two. She, however, as usual, is prepared to relent, and will completely surrender, if you wish it, when you come. She invites you to dinner either Wednesday or Thursday, at which time you can fix it up." To remove what sting might be in the letter, Buckner added in a postscript: "I am taking home a shorthand copy of this note!"[38]

[38] Buckner to Frankfurter, March ?, 1912.

This letter provoked from Frankfurter an epistle to Sofy in what Buckner had once called his "linguistic lingerie."[39] It began: "If one were to attempt to define the distinguishing characteristic of your friendship—as elusive a quality to be yoked to mere words as the unique fragrance of a particular rose—I should say that your affection was so thoroughgoingly sincere as to compliment me with your robust criticism." Presently, Frankfurter's crisis passed, and though he was still suffering crises of political self-flagellation as late as August, by the end of the summer he was sufficiently resigned to inactivity in the election that his letters to Buckner deal almost entirely with Buckner's problems—problems which had turned quite unexpectedly interesting. Only five years out of law school, Buckner had received an assignment which would take him away from District Attorney Whitman and all his doings, and would briefly make the name Buckner one of the most publicized and important in the political life of New York.

[39] Buckner to Frankfurter, 6/22/11.

CHAPTER FOUR   *The Aldermanic Investigation*
1912-1913

Late at night on July 16, 1912, before a curious crowd in Times Square, a small-time gambler named Herman Rosenthal was gunned down as he stepped out onto Forty-third Street from the Metropole Café, one of the city's more glamorous restaurants. Normal public interest in this sort of occurrence was heightened because Rosenthal had recently complained to the newspapers that he had been regularly paying a share of his profits to Lieutenant Charles Becker, chief of a new "vice squad" that operated out of police headquarters itself, and Becker had double-crossed him. The day after the shooting District Attorney Whitman revealed that Rosenthal had been scheduled to visit with him that morning, to lay his evidence on the table. For many weeks, the case dominated the front pages of the newspapers—Whitman's arrest of Becker, his tracking down of the four gunmen, his race to take custody of the killers and possible witnesses before the police did something unspecified to them.

Becker would die for this crime in the electric chair—the first member of the New York City police force ever to be executed—after his plea for commutation of sentence was turned down, ironically by Whitman himself, who had ridden to the Governor's mansion on the publicity from this case. The lieutenant was no loss: he had been a brutal grafter, possibly a rapist and probably a killer. But nobody except the jury who tried him, and perhaps Whitman, has ever been really sure that he planned or participated in the Rosenthal murder. The coincidence of Buckner's departure and the Becker case left some of the men in the DA's office with the feeling that Buckner had resigned in protest against Whitman's prosecution; even Embree many years later thought Buckner might have believed Becker to be innocent.

Buckner was always noncommittal about the question of Becker's guilt. "I realized," he once wrote, "that the Becker prosecution was pretty thin on the evidence and there were many rumors about it. However, I had already left the District Attorney's office . . . so my information is very general."[1] He did have strong feelings, however, about Whitman's conduct of the case, and when it was about to come to trial he directed his own publicized investigation of the police force away from questions of vice and into neutral areas. Becker, he wrote Frankfurter, "is on trial for his life and is entitled to a fair jury, and one of the worst things in the whole case is the newspaper campaign which has been waged undoubtedly at the inspiration of the District Attorney, which has resulted in a very inflamed feeling against Becker. On the merits I do not wish to add to this, no matter how bad Becker may be."[2]

In the uproar following the crime, the newspapers revealed that, despite dozens of complaints about Becker that had been sent to him and to Mayor William J. Gaynor, Police Commissioner Rhinelander Waldo had not only affirmed his belief in Becker's honesty but had praised his administration of the vice squad in a message to the city's ten thousand policemen. This was preposterous naïveté, because everyone knew Becker was a crook—a dozen years before no less a publicist than Stephen Crane had written an exposé of the man's brutal extortions from prostitutes. The Rosenthal murder seemed to fit into a pattern of police scandals, including the employment of ex-convicts who used the camouflage of a uniform to burgle places they were supposed to protect. Whitman made daily announcements of what he was doing to preserve the city and catch the murderers.

Frankfurter broke into a letter on national politics to write: "But I'm talking of minor men and small issues—'the Eyes of the Nation' are now on Charlie. Lucky Charlie—Fate loves to play with him for

[1] Buckner to Robert Morss Lovett, 11/29/27.
[2] Buckner to Frankfurter, 9/28/12.

surely she does not mean to inflict him on us beyond his present office. That police situation needs ground-up work—uprooting, not Whitmanesque politics and Gaynor homiletics. When will a MAN arise who can mould and stir N.Y. to action. Not a big city in Europe has *that* kind of a situation."[3]

Seventeen years had passed since the Lexow investigation had dredged up for horrified public examination the sewer of the city's professional vice and the role of the police in maintaining it; obviously, the time had come to try again. The state legislature, which would normally have undertaken such a job, was not in session, but the three-cornered election of 1909 had produced a Republican-Hearst-Progressive-Fusion majority in the Board of Aldermen, the unwieldy, eighty-member predecessor of the modern City Council. With the city's executive and legislative branches in different political hands, the stage was set for a locally administered probe. Even Tammany could see no point in fighting the tide, and when Republican Alderman Henry H. Curran introduced a resolution calling for an investigation, it was passed unanimously. Eight other aldermen—five from the coalition and three from Tammany—were appointed to the new "Curran Committee."

Any legislative investigation is inevitably managed largely by its counsel, if only because lawmakers cannot devote all their time to such work. Curran, who "took his responsibility very seriously," as Buckner later put it,[4] solicited recommendations from the City Club and the Citizens Union, the purse and heart of the nonpartisan reform movement. Both urged him to hire Felix Frankfurter who in turn insisted that the man they really wanted was Emory Buckner, and got Stimson to second the recommendation enthusiastically. Curran offered Buckner a fee of $1,000 a month.[5] With this client in his pocket, Buckner on August 13 resigned from the DA's office, rented space at 32 Liberty Street, and, six weeks ahead of schedule, opened the new firm of Buckner & Howland.

During the week between the passage of the resolution and the appointment of a counsel, the newspapers had discussed a number of

[3] Frankfurter to Buckner, 8/2/12.
[4] Memorandum for Marian, 2/20/35.
[5] *New York Times*, 7/16/13, reports Gaynor's rejection of a bill for $566.63 for Buckner's fee from June 1 to June 17; 17/30 of $1,000 is $566.67.

names, and the day the committee met, the *Times* announced that the choice lay between Magistrate Corrigan and John Purroy Mitchel, the maverick Democrat who was president of the Board of Aldermen. Buckner was a complete surprise. The *Times* ran a description: "a short, stout, florid-faced young man, with an aggressive manner and a downright method of making his wishes known."[6] Asked about politics by the reporters, Buckner said cheerfully, "Being interested in Colonel Roosevelt, I, of course, have no politics."

Gaynor and Tammany knew that no such investigation could be free from politics. In approving the appropriation of $25,000 for the investigation, the Tammany-controlled Board of Estimate let it be understood that the counsel for the committee was to be part of the Corporation Counsel's office, where the administration could exert a degree of control over him. Buckner was offered his appointment on this basis, and on Curran's advice turned it down. Corporation Counsel Archibald R. Watson thereupon appointed a Democrat, William McMurtie Speer, and wrote him:

> The Aldermanic Committee have selected to serve as their unofficial assistant, rather than as counsel, a Mr. Emory R. Buckner, a young man of whom I hear nothing but good report. During the four or five years since his admission to the bar Mr. Buckner has occupied successively positions in the office of the United States Attorney for the Southern District of New York and of the present distinguished District Attorney of New York County. His former chiefs think highly of Mr. Buckner and unite in his praise.[7]

Buckner, Watson proposed, would serve as Speer's assistant.

The newspapers accepted Watson's analysis as correct, and downgraded Buckner's role in the forthcoming investigation. But the night the Watson letter was made public, the Citizens Union held a mass meeting at Cooper Union, and on the platform were the Reverend Lyman Abbot, editor of Roosevelt's organ *The Outlook*, Curran, Whitman and Buckner, who was introduced as the committee's counsel, and made a fighting speech built around reiteration of the words "since July sixteenth" and statements of the new hope that was coming to the city as a by-product of the Rosenthal murder. The resolu-

[6] *New York Times* 8/13/12.
[7] *New York Times*, 8/15/12.

tion passed by the meeting bears some marks of Buckner's com-
position: "Whereas the proceedings of the Grand Jury are secret and
cannot be known, the proceedings before the Aldermanic Committee
are published, and, as in the case of all such commissions, have as one
of their greatest utilities the germicidal effect of publicity with its
consequent enlightened public opinion." Curran announced that Speer
would have no function in the investigation, and Gaynor backed
away.

Much of the criminal activity of a big city—gambling, prostitution,
excise evasion, extortion—cannot survive without cooperation from
the police, and the creation of a police department free from
temptation has been a prime goal of civic reformers for a century.
The problems with which the Aldermanic Investigation dealt were not
new in 1912, and most of them are still unsolved today. The basic
reform—the appointment and permanent promotion of police officers
through Civil Service mechanisms—had already been instituted in
New York, though the patrolman's most likely promotion (to detective) was and still is at the discretion of the Commissioner, who
was and is also empowered to bust any detective back to patrolman
at any time for any reason. The investigation Buckner ran for Henry
Curran was extraordinary, however, in its concentration on organizational deficiencies rather than on scandal, on the administrative problem rather than on the exposure of malefactors. In midstream,
Buckner wrote Frankfurter a letter detailing the kinds of question
he hoped to answer:

"How do men get on the force? Are we using a character ex-ray
at the wicket gate? After getting on the force, how are men promoted? How can the best balance be struck between opportunities
for graft in promotions on the one side, and suicidal shackling of
discretion on the other? How can we strike the median line between
arbitrary power in a Commissioner on the one hand, with its political
possibilities with a bad Commissioner, and the cast-iron automatic
promotion system which would rob a good Commissioner of any
power, and remove the premium upon honesty and efficiency as a
basis for discretionary advancement? How preserve the balance between the right which a Commissioner should have to enforce discipline rigorously, and the right which an officer should have to
seek redress in the courts? What as to the effect upon efficiency,

morale, *esprit de corps,* when the officer is reinstated either by the courts, or in the discretion of a succeeding Commissioner? What is really the method of the Police Department in handling vice? Who is responsible? Who are the instruments? How are they selected? Is it true that out of a force of 10,000 men only 150 are making any efforts to enforce this law? Does the short-ballot principle of this centralized responsibility also centralize the graft and make it safe? Then, when we strike the Augean stables of the Detective Bureau we almost despair of finding the necessary river.

"In addition to all these, I am ambitious to study all sorts of bureaus in the department from a strictly business efficiency point of view. So you see how the problem has grown and grown, but the motif of the entire *opus,* in my mind, is the great fundamental question of the character and the spirit of the individual, and the character and spirit of the aggregation as the resultant of the action and reaction of the units."[8]

Meanwhile, Buckner had his own organizing problems, and political problems. To begin its work, the committee hired four assistant counsel and an investigator, and arranged for the members of the City Club and the Citizens Union to supply additional, unpaid investigators—young businessmen and lawyers whose employers would volunteer their services for the tedious work of plowing through the Police Department files. A first public hearing was scheduled, with Mayor Gaynor himself as star witness, for Monday afternoon, September 9. When the time came, however, Curran and Buckner were still closeted with the Mayor, seeking to lay out the ground rules for the meeting. The next day, when Gaynor took the stand in what is now the Council Chamber of City Hall, it quickly developed that the parties to the previous day's conference had not reached agreement.

Gaynor was a bearded, crotchety old man, aged beyond his sixty-one years by a slow and imperfect recovery from the bullet of a would-be assassin, a dismissed city clerk, in the summer of 1910. He knew more about police work than most mayors, having been Police Commissioner of Flatbush when that district was a town independent of Brooklyn, then itself independent of New York. Buckner started the hearing by attempting to determine the procedures by which Gaynor supervised the Police Commissioner and the work of the

8 Buckner to Frankfurter, 12/20/12.

department, and received the answer that there was an annual report, there were letters, and the two men spoke to each other fairly often.

"Do you have any system of reports other than letters or other than speaking to you?" Buckner asked.

"I know of no other way by which he could communicate," Gaynor replied acidly, "except by writing, or speech."[9]

Buckner produced some letters to the Mayor proclaiming that the Police Department was demoralized and the law was not being enforced, and asked Gaynor what he had done about them. "I have no recollection of what was done," Gaynor replied. "I only know the allegation was chiefly untrue; worse, it was untruthful." Buckner persisted, politely, and provoked an outburst: "I know I came in and took possession of a demoralized police force, as Mayor, and I went to work systematically to do the best I could to lick it into shape, and it took time: it all took time. I am not through yet. It would take all of my time. I suppose the decent people of the community remember what I have done to lift up the police force. Certainly those who have lived here for any length of time have taken note of it, and very well, too."[10]

Again Buckner persisted, to receive the reply, "I have answered that all I intend to. I have a commissioner at the head of every department. I appoint a man that I have thorough confidence in, and I guess the whole community say I appointed a good lot of them, too. This government, good or bad, is in my possession, and not in your possession or in the possession of anybody outside the Mayor's office—that community knows everything."

Gaynor rose from his chair as though to leave the hearing, then thought better of it—but the threat was there from then on.

By executive order, Gaynor in 1910 had tightened a number of the rules relating to police behavior while making an arrest. Buckner, perhaps unwisely, sought to probe his reasoning. Had not a number of policemen, for example, misunderstood Gaynor's restrictions on the use of clubs? "They do not club boys or defenseless people in this town since I have been there," Gaynor replied, "not after the

9 New York City Board of Aldermen, Aldermanic Committee to Investigate the Police Department, transcript, p. 2.
10 *Ibid.*, p. 8.

first month I was Mayor, nor smash in doors without a warrant, either."[11]

On the previous Sunday, Buckner said, a group of young men (from the Citizens Union) had investigated obedience to the law on Sunday closing of saloons, and out of 401 they visited they found 344 wide-open for business. Was there any relationship between this commonplace lawbreaking and Gaynor's rule that uniformed police were not under any circumstances to enter a saloon? Gaynor snorted, and vividly explained the reason for the rule: "Tom puts down a dollar bill on the bar and gets $19.95 change from that after buying just a glass of beer."

What did Gaynor propose to do about enforcing the Sunday laws? Finally, Gaynor said he didn't propose to do anything about it, because the law couldn't be enforced, and he blew up again: "All the clubs in the city are open and in full blast, aren't they, where the rich people go, and they swill wine and whiskey all day. . . . [Y]et they get up and twit me because somebody is drinking a glass of beer on Sunday."

"Our only interest in the excise question," Buckner replied rather feebly, "is the interest of grafting."

"I know your interest," Gaynor said. "Your interest is to make some scandal about it, but it so happens that I have lived here so long that you cannot do it a bit, a bit. [Applause] I believe you have been here three years, if I understand it. I don't twit you for that. I came here when I was a boy, too."[12]

Buckner did a little better, but not much, on questions relating to appointments and promotions on the force. Before Gaynor's appointment of Police Commissioner Waldo, a pudgy, well-to-do and ineffectual young man, the Police Department had conducted an independent investigation of applicants, and had taken full advantage of the gap in the Civil Service rules which permitted a hiring authority to choose any one of the three candidates who had stood highest on the examination for a job. Gaynor had insisted that the top man on the list be taken, and Waldo had closed down the investigations department, leaving all checking on personal qualifications to the Civil Service Commission. Why was that?

[11] *Ibid.*, p. 12.
[12] *Ibid.*, p. 38.

"Why, everybody knows," Gaynor said. "When I became Mayor, you could not get on the police force without paying for it. Don't you know that?"

"No," Buckner said, and the transcript reports "laughter among the spectators."

"You could not get appointed captain," Gaynor continued, "without paying from fifteen to seventeen thousand dollars. Don't you know that well enough?"

"I want it in the record," Buckner said.

"You could not get anything, either an appointment or a promotion, and I thought that everybody knew that I had laid down the rule that the first man on the list should be appointed throughout, doing away with the possibility of such iniquities. And yet you bring me here to catechize me about things like that."[13]

At no time would Gaynor give an opinion as to what changes in the administration of the Police Department might be desirable; he would not rise to the bait even when Buckner asked "whether three Commissioners in thirty-two months is a proper or improper term for a Commissioner."[14] Buckner remained courteous throughout, never answering Gaynor's sallies, sometimes expressing sympathy with or amusement at Gaynor's replies. When Gaynor broke into a question to denounce Lieutenant Becker, Buckner put on the record that it was the Mayor and not the committee who had introduced the notorious name—and Buckner himself did not mention it again.

Gaynor was a popular Mayor, and the crowd in the hearing room had been on his side. But the newspapers thought the young counsel had bested the old pro. An editorial in the New York *Post* said:

With high moderation Mr. Gaynor insisted only upon two things in the course of his examination before the Aldermanic Committee yesterday. One was that the counsel for the Committee, in framing his questions, should stick absolutely to facts. The other was that in framing his replies to such questions His Honor the Mayor should be allowed to wander absolutely away from the facts. Repeatedly Mr. Gaynor rose from his chair, a wearied and angry Titan, and threatened to leave the room unless Mr. Buckner got down to the specific matter at hand. As a matter of fact, Mr. Buckner's examination was admirably planned and executed. The

---

13 *Ibid.,* pp. 15-16.
14 *Ibid.,* p. 15.

one question that is uppermost in the minds of the people of this city, is Where does the primary responsibility rest for conditions in the Police Department? The general impression is that Mr. Gaynor has been his own Police Commissioner since his advent into office. But when Mr. Buckner, without wasting a moment, set to work, to clarify this important point, he was met with everything but the facts. The Mayor ran the whole gamut of Gaynorian emotions, now a touch of irascibility, now a flash of wit that would have been delightful on any other occasion, now a homily on men and manners quite in the spirit of Epictetus, now a very bald contradictory statement, and nowhere, really a sincere desire on the part of the Chief Magistrate of the City to help solve a problem that lies very close indeed to the welface of the city and to the heart of the great public. Mr. Gaynor's conduct on the stand yesterday gives rise to the solemn question, Must a Mayor be a mule?[15]

Buckner himself wrote to Frankfurter: "The examination was the most interesting and difficult experience I suppose I shall ever have. [Twenty-three years later, forwarding a copy of the letter to Mrs. Frankfurter, he penciled the word "Right!" in the margin opposite this statement.] One thing never occurred to me until the examination started, and that was the possibility of the 'Old Man' walking out under the claim that he was being badgered for partisan purpose. No matter how unjust the accusation would have been, people would have taken sides, there would have been a storm in the Committee between the Democrats and Republicans, and our whole inquiry might easily have blown up in the beginning.

"It was my job, therefore, to keep him there at all hazards, and yet get as much out of him as possible. His refusal to answer any [questions about his] opinions cut my plan half in two, but if I had insisted, I would have precipitated a storm. Howland and Sofy were perfectly delighted, which is good enough for me."[16]

The questioning had left Gaynor vulnerable from several directions. He had been pushed into expressing complete confidence in Commissioner Waldo, whose handling of the Becker situation indicated that his knowledge of what was happening in his department was something less than perfect; he had failed to check up on how the appointment-from-the-top-of-the-list system was actually work-

[15] New York *Post*, 9/11/12.
[16] Buckner to Frankfurter, 9/12/12.

ing or on what Waldo was doing in remitting the fines and dismissals imposed by former Commissioner James C. Cropsey; he had unwisely denied that burglary insurance rates had risen in the city during the previous year—a denial he would reiterate more forcefully the next week, eventually provoking the most bitter moments in the eighty sessions of hearings. But Buckner and the majority of the committee were wrong to be pleased; it was not in their interest, over the long run, to make Gaynor an enemy.

The next witness would be Waldo. Buckner recessed the hearings for two days while he and his staff searched frantically through police files and solicited tips from people who might know something. Frankfurter came by the office during this week, and was apparently handled rather brusquely; and he wrote Buckner a note about it which does not survive. Buckner replied: "Any disturbances which your p.s.[17] recorded the other day were due wholly to the fact that Waldo's examination was only thirty-six hours off, and I was wholly unprepared with a program or trial brief. I stood the reporters and crazy advisers at bay for three weeks, and I really believe that if you had been by my side at all times, you would have agreed with every move I have made."[18]

Waldo turned out to be an entirely hostile witness. He refused to waive immunity to prosecution for anything he might say to the committee, thereby setting a precedent for a number of police officials and patrolmen, whose refusals to waive immunity would bring them neither punishment nor rebuke from their employer. Buckner pressed him throughout the afternoon of September 12 on a number of appointments which had been made under his administration after his predecessor Cropsey had rejected the same candidates for falsely denying on their job application forms that they had ever been arrested. All these new patrolmen had been cleared by the Civil Service Commission, Waldo replied, and if Buckner had any questions on the matter he would have to ask them of James Creelman, head of that Commission. Waldo was asked to return for further questioning on appointments, promotions and remissions of fines, and agreed to do so. And between his first and second appearances he generously turned over to the committee an affidavit from Captain John

[17] Psychic seismograph.
[18] Buckner to Frankfurter, 9/18/12.

T. Reith, who swore that in 1907, in the administration of Police Commissioner Theodore A. Bingham, he had been passed over for promotion despite his leading rank on the examination because he had refused to pay off a pair of Tammany hacks who still held minor but not insignificant city office. Reith's statement was a little suspect: his affidavit was dated shorty after Bingham had started suit against Gaynor for libel, and his promotion to captain had come through only after he swore to the charges. Still, Buckner wrote Frankfurter, "I must step aside from the constructive inquiry to do something or other with this affidavit."[19]

Two days were wasted on this will-o'-the-wisp, and then Civil Service Commissioner Creelman took the stand. His position fundamentally was that the candidates for the force who had falsely denied that they were ever arrested had done so because they did not understand the question—one of them, for example, had been involved in an involuntary homicide charge following a traffic accident; another had got in trouble over some firecrackers in the street; another had been playing baseball where baseball was not permitted. Creelman, a former newspaper reporter, was a surly and angry witness. He believed that the police investigations bureau had shaken down candidates who had reason to fear the bureau's veto. By insisting that the department approve applicants despite trivial offenses his Commission had eliminated a source of bribery and contributed to cleaning up the force. Then Buckner came to the case of George Hammond, who had been arrested four times but had denied the existence of any arrest record. One of the other Civil Service Commissioners, Creelman replied, had personally gone up to interview the young man and to check his reputation in the neighborhood, and on the basis of the oral report from this Commissioner, Hammond had been passed.

Buckner read off the list of offenses for which Hammond had been arrested, then said, "Without at all questioning the seriousness or triviality of the petty larceny and violating the ordinance, do you think a man—"

Creelman interrupted: "I beg your pardon."

"Just a moment?"

"I absolutely decline to submit to any further examination if you

[19] Buckner to Frankfurter, 9/18/12.

keep inserting lies; you are not making a frank statement. You say, without considering the seriousness of the petty larceny, the man was discharged."

"Here is the affidavit."

"You mustn't lie here all the time."

"Here is the affidavit."

"I decline to submit any further to an examination by a liar. . . . If you want facts, I will give you facts, but you mustn't misrepresent facts all the time."

"What record have I misstated?"

Creelman shouted. "You are uttering a lie when you say, without considering the seriousness of petty larceny, that this man was arrested and discharged. The record you read shows that; then you proceed to put this lying question."[20]

In fact, though he did not know it, Buckner was near the bone: young Hammond was the son of a Tammany district leader. Not until several weeks later did this piece of information turn up, and by then it was too late for Buckner to do more than insert the fact in the record. For the moment, Creelman's violence was inexplicable.

"The day with Creelman," Buckner wrote Frankfurter, "was almost as interesting as the day with the Mayor. I wish you could have been there. I was not under perfect control when I gave him one indignant answer, but it was more effective than my usual good nature, and when he blew up the next time, I was smiling as usual. The general row and turmoil has not helped us, although it was all the fault of the witness; but Rule 25 of the judicial attitude is to blame both sides, and consequently I was not surprised to read the *Globe* editorial last night begging us to lift ourselves to a higher level, and commenting on the fact that the several hostile witnesses up to date had been insulted by the counsel for the Committee, and had given insults back in turn. Of course the thing which most of my friends have been most pleased about is the fact that the 400 pages of the record contain not a single insulting question. I realize, however, the importance of Rule 25, and therefore have paid no attention to the editorial.

"I see enough material ahead of us for three or four sessions, but in general must count upon daily evolution. I wish you were here

20 Aldermanic Committee, *op. cit.,* p. 393.

to see how little monomaniacal I am."[21]

Buckner and the committe now were given a brief breathing space. Becker's lawyer requested—Buckner thought legitimately—that all inquiry into Waldo's conduct of his office should cease while Becker was on trial for murder; and the state political conventions met to nominate candidates for Governor, requiring the attendance of aldermen. (Whitman was the leading Republican contender, but failed to get the nomination; he backed away gracefully, citing all the work in the DA's office in connection with the Becker case and its aftermath.) Meanwhile, publicity of varying value to Buckner continued to appear in the newspaper.

Mayor Gaynor wrote an open letter to Corporation Counsel Watson:

> When I was testifying before the Committee for the Alderman inquiring into police conditions, I was asked whether I did not know' that the insurance rate for burglary had been increased 35 per cent within the past year. I believe that I responded that I did not know it, and that I believed the questioner did not know it. Since then I have been fully informed by the insurance authorities, including the President of the New Amsterdam Casualty Company, that there has been no such increase, and, indeed, no increase at all, and that the lowest rate in the whole country obtains in the City of New York. . . . I was asked several similar questions, and Mr. Waldo was also. That is to say, questions are asked whether the witness does not know a certain thing, the question itself being false, and the object being to have the question taken as true by the newspapers and the public. Please object to such questions if they continue to be asked. You are the legal adviser to the Common Council and to the Committee, and you should see that such methods are not resorted to.[22]

Buckner bided his time in replying to this letter, and six months later called several insurance company executives to testify to the increased rates. Alderman Frank Dowling, the leader of the Tammany representation on the committee, then asked Buckner "to call the insurance man that the Mayor refers to in that letter."

"The committee can call him if it wants to and find out why he is not in harmony with ninety-nine percent of the companies."

[21] Buckner to Frankfurter, 9/25/12.
[22] Aldermanic Committee, *op. cit.,* p. 3688.

"Well," Dowling said, "if you want to hear both sides."

And Buckner replied bitterly, "Did the Mayor want to hear both sides when he called me a liar?"[23]

When summoned, Gaynor's source turned out to be the head of an insurance-industry rate-fixing committee that had been in existence less than a year, and his company turned out to have been in the burglary insurance business less than a year. But the declaration of war by the Mayor was itself immensely damaging. Indeed, with a meanness of which he was probably unconscious, Gaynor carried his opposition to Buckner a step further, holding up in an administrative tangle the payment of the committee's counsel fees. Buckner was eventually obliged to write Frankfurter, and ask if he could find some money for his friend to live on. Frankfurter arranged a loan from Winifred T. Denison, who had supervised Buckner's work on the sugar frauds case in the Stimson office and had already given him money to help start his office. "I hope the enclosed will bring relief," Frankfurter wrote. "Would *that* burden were not so insistent. His finances are not good and it had to be a time loan—I told him till your aldermanic argosy comes in. I suppose in this game of playing tag with the wolf, it's a question of passing it on for the moment—so some adjustment will come by that time."[24]

Frankfurter at this point gave Buckner his first dose of national publicity, a worshipful portrait of "The Investigator of the New York Police" which appeared, unsigned, in *The Outlook* for September 28, 1912.[25] Frankfurter closed his article with a little story: "Not so long ago, at dead of night—that solvent of truth—two young men were dreaming of youth. The long silence was at last broken by one of them: 'Buck, you seem to be thinking hard.' 'I was thinking,' replied the other, 'of the great fun in conducting a public office solely for the public welfare.' "[26] Buckner wrote a faintly embarrassed letter of delight about "the panegyric," and added: "The fillip at the end is good, but what I said was, 'It would be great fun,' as we were talking of the DA and his conception of his job. The way the thing stands it sounds as if I were bragging about the patriotic manner in

[23] *Ibid.*, p. 3689.
[24] Frankfurter to Buckner, 10/13(?)/12.
[25] *Outlook*, Vol. 102, pp. 225-227.
[26] *Ibid.*, pp. 226-227.

which I was discharging my own job as Assistant District Attorney—but this is what you call 'insectile criticism.' The article is perfectly bully and I appreciate it so much, although it is extravagant. It was just like you to pull the thing as a surprise party."[27]

Through October and November the committee hovered over a mass of detail about how the the police were appointed, assigned and disciplined, where the lines of authority ran, what men in different positions were supposed to do in searching out violations of the law and in dealing with complaints. The lieutenant who had headed the now abolished internal investigations bureau was called and complained of his fate (which Waldo was presently to make much worse). Many witnesses were fundamentally cooperative—most notably Raymond B. Fosdick, who had just resigned as Commissioner of Accounts after a municipal career which included an exposure of police-vice collaboration on Coney Island.

Frankfurter at a distance, reading the newspapers and occasionally catching up with the transcripts, grew a little restive and suggested that a dose of "social evil" investigation might brighten the proceedings. Buckner, however, was not displeased: the purpose of the committee, he felt, was to make recommendations; and he was building a factual record on which specific suggestions could rest. Indeed, as the complexity of the police job opened up before him on the witness stand, he was losing some of the uninformed Fusion faith in sharp solutions which had inspired the Citizens Union mass meeting at the time of his appointment. In any event, he planned to avoid attempting what he knew he could not do.

"We shall only be in session a few months," Buckner wrote Frankfurter, "and our primary purpose is a police inquiry; and while, to be sure, the social evil question, the gambling question and the excise question are closely interwoven problems of police administration, I do not believe that between now and February 1st our work can be so comprehensive as to assist us in formulating views. If it took over a year in Chicago on the social question alone, and took six or eight months in a small town like Minneapolis, it is hardly feasible for us to settle the problem after breakfast."[28]

Still, it was awkward to be running an investigation which turned

[27] Buckner to Frankfurter, 9/28/12.
[28] Buckner to Frankfurter, 10/30/12.

up so little that was wrong—especially in the face of an almost universal belief that a great deal was wrong. Several leads petered out rather disconcertingly—especially the discovery that Waldo on assuming office had remitted (with doubtful legality) a number of fines his predecessor Cropsey had imposed on most of the precinct captains. It turned out that the fines were for violation of an idiotic order Cropsey had issued, that whenever a job required both inside and outside duty, the inside work was to be assigned to the older men and the outside work to the younger men, regardless of any factors other than age. Cropsey was in process of revealing himself as a sadistic District Attorney in Brooklyn, and would presently move on to be a hanging judge; Waldo's remissions seemed fair and just. There was information here about the failings of the administrative system, and about the stupid brutality of disciplining policemen by fining them some days of their inadequate pay or by assigning them to posts as much as two or three hours' travel from their homes—but there was not the sort of revelation which the preliminary inquiry had indicated.

Then, on December 8, a brothelkeeper named Mary Goode, who had been arrested and bailed a month before for keeping a disorderly house, was informed that her case would come up for trial on December 12. It had never really occurred to Mrs. Goode—a trim and not unattractive lady in early middle age who claimed to be a college graduate—that there was anything wrong with her chosen profession, though she had been paying police protection and buying her beer from the approved source. (She didn't sell the beer, however, because only "quiet, respectable people" came to her brothel. And she rather disapproved of her competitors on the block—"nearly all foreigners. I was the only Irishwoman.")

Mrs. Goode's bad luck had begun with a robbery in the apartment she used as her place of business, and her subsequent indentification of Gyp the Blood, one of the Rosenthal assassins, as the robber. From the point of view of the grafters in the West Side police, she became hot. Thanks to the Becker scandal and the Aldermanic Investigation, the costs of protection were rising beyond the ability of Mrs. Goode to pay. And the police districts now needed some convictions for their records. Adding everything together, and badly miscalculating his risks, the Inspector in command of Mrs. Goode's precinct decided to turn her in and laughed when he saw her in the station house.

"Jail staring me in the face," as Mrs. Goode later wrote Mayor Gaynor, "no relative, no friend in the world to help me,"[29] she scattered letters of appeal broadcast through the city—to Waldo, to Mrs. O. H. P. Belmont (who was lecturing on the problems of young girls in the big city), to Whitman. Someone in Whitman's office tipped Buckner off, and on the night of December 10 he and an associate counsel went to interview Mary Goode at her home on West Sixtieth Street. (Immediately after he left, Buckner learned later with some dismay, some police officers visited her, too, asking what she had told the counsel for the committee.) On December 11 Mrs. Goode was on the stand at City Hall, by far the most spectacular witness the investigation was to command.

Mrs. Goode's great assets before the committee were that she was honestly outraged, she had a solution to the problem, and she spoke well. The police had picked her up too near midnight to take her to Night Court, and at the station house had charged her $100 bail, four times the previous maximum. "Who has heard of $100 to bail a woman out," she asked indignantly, "until Rosenthal was killed?"[30] Writing to Mrs. Belmont, she had proposed, in essence, the legalization of clean houses of prostitution: "We want to be put under a committee of citizens, or a vice committee. Something of that kind, where they won't be after you every minute for money, and then railroad you off to jail, and expect you are going to hide it."[31] Now she told Buckner, "There is not a Mayor living can stop the police from taking money, and there is not a D.A. can stop it either. Never."[32]

She would be happy, she said, to be segregated in a red-light district. "We always choose places where there are no families or children. We always go there of our own accord. Nobody has to ask us. In return for [supervision by a committee] we will help you with the streetwalkers, we will help you with the noise and disorder; we will tell you about young girls on the street who are working for pimps; and every pimp makes a thief out of every girl he has. They have to be a thief on the street."

Buckner said, "What do you mean by that?"

[29] Aldermanic Committee, *op. cit.*, p. 4232.
[30] *Ibid.*, p. 2188.
[31] *Ibid.*, p. 2185.
[32] *Ibid.*, p. 2187.

"They have to pick their man's pocket, and to take every cent he has got, if they take him to a room. That is the street girl. There is not a street girl in the City of New York today, Mr. Buckner, that is not a thief. If they are put into the houses, they will be taken care of. If they are diseased, they will be found out. They will be reported. If they are thieves, they will be reported. If they are under age, they will be reported. There is no graft, there is no exposure and scandal of the police. There was the Rosenthal case. Now it is me, and there will be another. . . . Now, you gentlemen have had committees all over the country, vice committees, you have had police officers, you have had everybody after the men who have lived off the earnings of the women. Have you accomplished anything? You never can accomplish a thing until we help you. We are the ones who can cure that evil."

Buckner kept her going: "What do you mean by that?"

"What we call the pimps. The man who lives off the earnings of the girls. In this city today there are hundreds, more than that—thousands of girls that are glad to be rid of a pimp, but they are frightened to death. If it can be left to me, in my house, if there is any girl in my house and there is a man takes her earnings and abuses her, I can hand him to you. I can give him to you. He don't dare touch me."[33]

It was great newspaper copy, but also something more—four men were to go to jail on the basis of Mrs. Goode's information. Buckner played it straight, stressing the question of police organization rather than the question of vice. An ex-Inspector had testified at a departmental trial, of which Buckner had the records, that he had been ordered by his superiors not to make any raids in his district. They denied it—but admitted that any such order would have been given orally. Why weren't these things in writing? In general, Buckner told reporters, "Our idea is to take the face off the clock of that department and let the public see what kind of works there are inside and how it runs. I want the public to hear something more about it than the click."[34]

The next day, the charges against Mrs. Goode were dismissed in court on the motion of the District Attorney, in gratitude for her

[33] *Ibid.*, p. 2188.
[34] *New York Times,* 12/12/12, p. 3.

cooperation; and the news brought Buckner another witness, George A. Sipp, a dashing gentleman with a military mustache, owner of a hotel in Harlem which had been used for prostitution, who was prepared to identify the people to whom he had paid his $100-a-month protection—and to whom he had refused $200-a-month protection, with the result that his place was closed down. He also had a fascinating story to tell about an attempt to operate another such hotel on a block across from Tammany district headquarters, where a competitor was already active—and of the police captain who told him that he'd have to give up the new place, because it infringed a patent. Again there were names and dates and places (the district leader was an ex-Sheriff and ex-Fire Commissioner); and again police inspectors and captains were to be convicted on the evidence that grew out of testimony before the committee.

"The investigation," Buckner wrote Frankfurter triumphantly at the end of that week, "has taken a sudden and violent boom at a time when sorely needed for financial and educational purposes.[35] The beginning of the present violent disturbance was Goode, and it ended last Wednesday with a Zipp! I got each of these stories myself by accident plus persuasion, without any detective bureau and without any expense. They have in one week changed the attitude of many people towards the investigation, and they feel we are now really 'getting somewhere.' Even lawyers and our friends, who ought to know better, appear to think that these little sensations are more worthwhile than the hard, steady plugging on fundamental questions of police administration.

"My own ambition is to have enough Lexow evidence to arouse and maintain public interest and approval in order to enable us to do hard work in the less feverish fields. The developments of the past week—unexpected and accidental as they have been—have also served, I think, finally to take us out of any danger of being classed a failure, no matter how little we do in the next three months. I have said this before, but I have never felt quite so secure about it as now. I must continue to keep a sense of proportion, to insist that I am not a vice commission, to emphasize that we are not attempting

[35] Curran was about to ask for an additional $15,000 appropriation to continue the work of the committee into the spring, and before the Goode testimony the betting had been against him.

to solve the question of prostitution, and to keep fairly well fixed to the problem of internal police administration. The suburbs of the social evil are attractive after a hard day's monotonous work upon files and documents—the penumbra of politics (showing, as last Wednesday, a definite connection between police and Tammany district leaders) throws about our investigation the thrilling combination of publicity and peril—and with it all I insist that what I want more than anything else to accomplish is to draw a huge chart of fundamental administrative problems."[36]

The next week Waldo came back to the stand—under subpoena now; he would not attend voluntarily. With Gaynor's support, he had been making it more and more difficult for the amateur investigators supplied through the City Club and the Citizens Union to locate the files they wanted to read. He had refused to supply the young reformers with more than one file at a time, and insisted that they could examine the papers only as his detectives brought the folders to a small room they shared with an attentive policeman.

Buckner interrupted the testimony of the witness on the stand when Waldo appeared the afternoon of December 27, and began by pleasantly assuring the press and the committee "that the Commissioner has always been most pleasant and most agreeable. This is simply a fundamental difference as to where the work is to be done, and that is a thing that the committee has got to decide. That's all." Then he asked Waldo to verify that the committee's investigators "are not permitted by you to go down into the Detective Bureau itself and make an investigation of the files as they are there now."

Waldo, grumpy on the stand, replied that "We have no record we want to conceal from you. We are willing to have you go through the records in any way that you want to, providing it is in an orderly manner, and providing that the records are protected from being upset. . . . But you cannot start in to tear them to pieces, and we do not know whether you put them back or not. Certainly, in view of the fact that you are employing a large number of young men who are not in the city service, [and] are not responsible . . . to me, to the committee, or to anybody else, and who are changing continuously."

"Well, of course," Buckner said, "they are drawing a good deal

[36] Buckner to Frankfurter, 12/20/12.

bigger salary than we could afford to pay, or the city could afford to pay, and they are amenable to the committee. That is the committee's business, I think."

"Naturally," Waldo said, "but I do not propose to have a number of young men go in, who are changing every day, and who are responsible to nobody in authority."

"I do not quite get the answer to the question," Buckner said mildly. "Are you willing that the committee itself, or any subcommittee appointed by the committee, or one of the counsel, Special Assistant Corporation Counsel, shall be permitted to go into the Detective Bureau itself, and, there, in an orderly way, direct an investigation into the files?"

"If you want to go into that research," Waldo began, but Buckner interrupted him. "That can be answered," he suggested, "yes or no."

Waldo bridled. "If you want to go into the Bureau and tear the files to pieces, it will take an order of court. If you want any file that is there, you can have it. Take it in the order of file number or any sequence that they are there."[37]

The next day Buckner wrote Frankfurter a summary of the situation: "The chamber was packed and packed as never before, as the public expected a spectacular fight between Waldo and myself. . . . I shall very rapidly empty the chamber during the next three or four weeks as well as be taken off the front page. An intelligent newspaperman could write brilliant reports on my gradual unfolding of the administrative system, but I do not expect it. They have acquired a cannibal's appetite for warm blood, and refuse to sit down at my table of cold meat and potatoes, although I assure them it is far more nourishing.

"The DA is getting very busy now on first-page work, such as 'Men higher up in the net,' 'Wide sweeping graft investigation to be begun'—which suits me exactly and in a way furnishes an excuse for us to hammer away upon our job. What annoys and amuses me as much as anything else is the clamorous editorial and personal exhortation to pursue the trail while it's hot. They do not seem to realize that 'there ain't no trail.' Flynn[38] failed; Burns failed; Whitman gave

---

37 Aldermanic Committee, *op. cit.*, pp. 2416-2417.
38 William J. Flynn, once briefly head of the Detective Bureau, who had been Buckner's first investigator and had resigned.

up hope; and I brought out yesterday that Fosdick[39] tried for months before Rosenthal was killed to break into the police graft and failed to get any evidence whatever."[40]

When the hearings resumed on January 2, 1913, Buckner had better tools to work with. With a grant from John D. Rockefeller, Jr., the Aldermanic Committee had commissioned a series of studies of police operations from the private, nonprofit Bureau of Municipal Research, and one by one the expert reports came in. Some of the authors testified at the hearings, on the administrative horrors of the pension plan and the physical horrors of the precinct houses (ill-constructed, ill-ventilated fire traps with dried tobacco juice caked in the corners). Other reports were printed and entered at the end of the record of the hearings. One explored the court decisions in cases where policemen had appealed against dismissals or other disciplinary actions imposed by the department—and found, dishearteningly, that the sympathetic attitude of the courts was not an example of judicial irresponsibility but a necessary remedy for arbitrary and unjust decisions by the Police Commissioner. Another report looked at the economic condition of one hundred policemen's families, and found that far from rolling in ill-gotten gains they were wretchedly poor—ninety of them in debt, eight "in absolute need," five receiving charity. The fringe benefits of the job did not come through (the police surgeons, for example, were too busy, or said they were too busy, to take care of policemen's families); the fringe disabilities were all present (the need to pay for uniforms and equipment, including the mattresses on which the policemen slept at the station houses; "extra duty . . . so excessive that the policemen see very little of their homes and families").[41] Yet another proposed a shake-up of the police school, a six-month rather than a four-week training period and a "less ambitious" curriculum.

On the general question of police responsibility, the Bureau observed rather sadly, "To make the policeman more anxious for truth than conviction is a matter of general morale which can be attained only after long effort by those in command consciously striving to create such a standard."[42]

---

[39] Raymond B. Fosdick, former Commissioner of Accounts.
[40] Buckner to Frankfurter, 12/28/12.
[41] Aldemanic Committee, *op. cit.,* p. 4490.
[42] *Ibid.,* p. 4617.

Most of the witnesses in the new year were men of distinction, whose part services gave them authority to recommend reforms in the department. Perhaps the most fascinating of all was William McAdoo, who had been Police Commissioner and was currently Chief Magistrate. He thought the Police Commissioner was underpaid. "You ought to give him a decent salary. He works harder than any Supreme Court judge. He is the municipal pincushion. Everybody sticks a pin in him for fun, and you pay him $7,500 a year."[43] He thought public attitudes were dangerous: "You cannot expect a policeman to be self-respecting if you do not respect him."[44] And he thought it a mistake to get too exercised about vice graft: "The London police were grafting from prostitutes in 1285, two hundred years before Columbus sailed for America."[45]

For its still significant good sense, its style and its influence on Buckner's final position, McAdoo's testimony is worth a chunk of quotation:

"Any young man of a certain age in Great Britain can apply to be a London policeman by simply writing a letter, and he goes up to London and they examine him physically and send him to school for six months, and I saw the school in operation myself, a hall not as large as this. It is all practical work. He lives there. They give him a room and he lives in the school, and he is under six or seven instructors in different branches, and his ability to write a fine letter and compose beautiful answers about the last Acts of Parliament is a secondary consideration. The main thing is, will he make a policeman, so they watch his habits, his personal habits; they study his character; they put him in a room and simulate a court scene and try him as a witness, and they teach him to keep up his voice. All the cops in New York whisper. They got that in the old magistrate's court. And they put hypothetical questions to him: 'What would you do if you were confronted with the following situation?' and they put their heads together and they select those that they think best for the police, and that is the way, in my judgment, they get good policemen. Of course, that cannot be done here and the civil service is not going to be touched. Its friends here need not get afraid of that, but it could be made practical and the standards could be

[43] *Ibid.*, p. 3896.
[44] *Ibid.*, p. 3914.
[45] *Ibid.*, p. 3907.

changed, in my judgment, to an advantage. I am not criticizing the
Civil Service Commission. They do the best they can, but the Police
Commissioner, if he were a permanent officer, would have more to
say about that.

"Now, coming back to the Police Commissioner, a thing I overlooked. There are three things essential to the honest policing of a
city like this, the absolutely harmonious cooperation of the following
officers: the Mayor, the District Attorney and the Police Commissioner. They should have no official secrets one from the other in the
enforcement of the law. They should cooperate heartily with each
other in its enforcement, and they should be willing to aid and help
each other. The greatest weakness of your present Police Commissioner is that he don't command the respect of the District Attorney.
If you are elected District Attorney, as I suppose you will be, after
this, and I am appointed a Police Commissioner, now let us see how
it works out. . . .

"You personify the majesty and power of the State of New York
in your office. You have a secret body behind you there with a locked
door; you can go in and tell them anything you want. I do not know
what you would tell them; you might indict me or grant me immunity
—I don't know what you will do with me. You are a good-looking
fellow, Buckner, I think I would trust you. I come down, pay my
respects to you; I am Police Commissioner, we are both sworn officers
of the City of New York to enforce the laws of the state and the
ordinances, the peace, the order and the good morals, and the honesty
of public officials depends on you and me to a large extent.

"Well, after I have gone out a fellow comes in and says, 'What
do you think of McAdoo?' 'Oh, he won't last a month. He is only
a fill-in. . . . The real man will be down in a month.' You say to
yourself, 'I need not waste any time with McAdoo. What is the
use of bothering with him?' So you go your way, and I go my way.
So the first thing we are divided, we are openly antagonistic; you
are bombarding me like it was in Mexico, and I am turning my guns
down on you, theoretically, of course.

"Why, the result is, the law is a farce. You ought to have a man
up there in my office advising me and helping me to enforce the
law. . . . Instead of that, why, you are telling everybody that I am
a joke or a fraud or a crook, and do not bother with me. Now, if I

went up there with ten years in the Appellate Division behind me, you would respect me, and we would get together. . . . Temperment-ally I might not like the cut of your gib, or something about you. But when you put your Police Commissioner in there with the power of office and a solid tenure, and a disciplined and united police force, there will be cooperation and adhesion, instead of conditions which we have witnessed in times past; long past, of course."[46]

Meanwhile, Whitman was prosecuting the men Mrs. Goode and Sipp had named, and getting convictions; and Waldo was behaving more and more outrageously. The former head of the investigations bureau, who had testified voluntarily, was dismissed on a charge of soliciting a bribe, the charge brought by a fellow policeman who had been Waldo's chauffeur and was now promoted to detective. Employees of the department were given orders not to speak with the committee's investigators unless they were subpoenaed to public hearings. Emboldened by their boss's attitude, the old-timers of the police fraternal organization held a banquet in honor of one of the men Whitman had indicted, and Waldo attended. Buckner took judicial notice of the phenomenon while questioning former Mayor George B. McClellan: "Did you ever hear of one of these organiza-tions giving a dinner at which a guest of honor was an indicted inspector," he asked, "at which the Commissioner was present?"

"I heard of it, yes," McClellan said. "Last Saturday night, I believe."[47]

The state legislature was now in session, and a committee chaired by State Senator Robert F. Wagner was charged with looking into the need for new legislation affecting the New York police. The aldermen suspended their hearings to prepare recommendations for Wagner, and submitted them on March 11. They were far less revolutionary than most of the committee's supporters, especially in the Citizens Union, had expected. The three major items were an eight-year term for the Police Commissioner, who could be removed by the Mayor for cause and after a public hearing where the cause was revealed; a straiter gate for applicants; and home rule for the city on the question of Sunday booze. Significantly, in the light of subsequent developments, the report was unanimous.

[46] *Ibid.,* p. 3910-3911.
[47] *Ibid.,* p. 3989.

The hearings proper ended on March 27, and for two months Buckner and the Fusion majority of the committee were engaged in writing a long final report for adoption by the Board of Aldermen. They came up with fifty-two recommendations for reform, including (in addition to their prior proposals to the state committee) an increase in policemen's salaries, revamping of the police school and the disciplinary machinery, reorganization of the Detective Bureau, a guaranteed rogues' gallery of all accused felons and ways to get the pictures around town when needed, vastly tightened control over the expenditure of money and the assignment of jobs. Recommendation No. 1, unfortunately, was the removal of Waldo—and in Buckner's first draft this request was to be made directly to the anti-Tammany Democratic Governor, William Sulzer.

At any time, this recommendation would have been a tactical error; in June, 1913, it was a strategic blunder. The committee, of course, had every reason to be annoyed with Waldo: he had been personally uncooperative, had persecuted their informants, and had made common cause with recalcitrant witnesses from his department. The evidence of his incapacity as an administrator was all through the record. But no doubt had been cast on his personal honesty, and it was questionable that a legislative body had or should have the right to cashier a member of the executive department on the ground that he was incompetent. Sixteen years later, as keynote speaker at the Republican Convention to nominate a candidate for Mayor to oppose Jimmy Walker, Buckner would say, "The one outstanding recommendation we made after the Aldermanic Investigation was that the Police Commissioner should not be interfered with by the Mayor."[48] But as Buckner and Curran handled their report, the outstanding recommendation was something else entirely, and not constructive.

The *Times* opposed Waldo's removal in an editorial, and added, "Judging from the first part of its report the city will gain no benefit from the labors of the Curran Committee."[49] The appeal over Gaynor's head offended the home-rule instincts of the Fusionists themselves, and had to be dropped within the committee; and the resolution that passed, by a 4-3 vote, was an appeal to Gaynor. This had

48 *New York Times,* 8/2/29.
49 *New York Times,* 6/4/13.

to be hopeless, not only because Waldo was Gaynor's man, but also because 1913 was a mayoralty election year in New York, and Gaynor was bound to see the resolution as the opening gun in a Fusion campaign to unseat him. As though to clinch this point, two days after the committee announced its recommendation on Waldo (but none of its other fifty-one recommendations) Whitman declared his candidacy for Mayor.

Meanwhile, the committee was unable to gather a quorum to consider its other recommendations; the Tammany members were boycotting, and one of the Fusion members was ill. (Buckner may have missed some of these meetings himself: his second child, Elizabeth, was born June 5, 1913, two days after the release of the committee's first report.) Finally, the full committee was scraped together, and by a 5-4 vote adopted the rest of the report for presentation to the Board of Aldermen. The Citizens Union and the Bureau of Municipal Research, the Federation of Churches and the Laity League endorsed the document, but visibly a tide was rising against the Waldo recommendation. Asked how he thought the vote would come out, Buckner said he did not know, and it would not make much difference: "A vote for the report cannot make the facts any more true. A vote against the report cannot make the facts false." But when the Board took up the document, Curran's first motion was to separate the Waldo recommendation from the others. It carried by a single vote out of seventy-seven. Then some Fusion aldermen who were suspected of Tammany connections left the chamber, Tammany leader Frank Dowling moved a reconsideration of the question, and the Board voted to consider the report as a whole, including the Waldo passages. The motion for its adoption thereupon failed, 29-45. Six weeks later, on Dowling's motion, the Board passed thirty-seven of the fifty-one other recommendations. By that time the mayoralty campaign was in the headlines, and nobody was paying much attention to last season's investigation.

Neither Whitman nor Gaynor, incidentally, was nominated by his party. Despite a nominating speech by Stimson, Whitman lost out at the Fusion meeting to John Purroy Mitchel, by a vote of 45-44. Tammany leader Charles F. Murphy dumped Gaynor in favor of Judge Edward F. McCall. Gaynor decided to run as an independent —with support from a number of Fusion stalwarts, including Jacob

H. Schiff, president of the Citizens Union. He was an odds-on favorite to win re-election without help from the politicians when he died aboard ship en route to a European vacation in early September. Buckner paid tribute to him, and claimed that in the months before his death he had been moving to put into effect most of the reforms suggested by the Aldermanic Committee to Investigate the Police Department.

CHAPTER FIVE *The Birth of the Office*

1913-1919

The firm of Buckner & Howland enjoyed an unexpectedly successful first year. In addition to Howland's part-time salary from the Texas Company and Buckner's fees from the Aldermanic Committee (which were eventually collected), there had been a merger of the American Malting Company and the American Malting Corporation, a stock issue for Texaco and several minor matters to be pressed or defended for the oil company and its employees. There were also incidental cases of the kind that were fun to talk about. An intraoffice interim history of Root, Clark, Buckner & Howland, prepared in 1924, offered from the Buckner & Howland archives

an illustration of the importance of acquaintance. [Mr. Howland's] former landlady of the old hall room days sent to him a woman who was rooming in her house who was in need of professional advice. This woman had been living with a man whose business was hawking grotesque glass eyes at Coney Island and other resorts. [He] was an alchemist as well. That is to say, he minted affection into loans and when no loans were forthcoming he deserted his benefactress. The firm prepared a summons, and as the partners were not equipped with a managing clerk's department, Mr. Howland and Mr. Buckner personally wandered through the rain under the firm umbrella until somewhere in the forties the purveyor of glass eyes was discovered and served. He later wrote the firm from Philadelphia a scurrilous and threatening letter and the firm hastily dropped the case, accomplishing nothing for the client. Mr.

Buckner points out that the firm did not have that capacity for sustained activity which was later furnished by the membership of Mr. Clark.[1]

But a highly successful first year gave Buckner & Howland no guarantees for the second year. Two major sources of revenue, the investigation and the Texas Company job, were irrevocably gone; and what might come to replace them was unknown. In the middle of a rather bleak summer, Elihu Root, Jr. came visiting with a proposition.

Behind Root's proposition lay the departure of Francis William Bird from the firm of Root, Clark & Bird. Buckner knew all three men; they had been at the law school in the class a year before his. Bird was the son of a wealthy and prominent paper manufacturer in East Walpole, Massachusetts. He had been Root's roommate at the law school; and he was, Clark said half a century later, "the most brilliant man of my generation." Bird had gone into the U.S. Attorney's office with Henry Stimson, and Buckner had worked with him on the sugar frauds cases. Clark had started as a junior at Carter, Ledyard & Milburn; Root, at Hornblower, Byrne, Miller & Potter. "After I'd been at the Byrne office two years," Root recalled in 1966, "I thought it was time to push off. I have a letter from my father saying one year was enough. I wouldn't," Root added, looking around his office at Cleary, Gottlieb where he was a "Counsel" in his later years, "want the young men here now to see it. I asked Bird to join me, and he told me Clark had already asked him. We opened Root, Clark & Bird on January 1, 1909. When we first got a client, we were $750 down—I remember the war dance when the first fee arrived."

In fact, of course, there was never any serious reason for worry at Root, Clark & Bird. Though the only guaranteed client at the beginning was the publishing house of E. P. Dutton & Company (through Bird's cousin George Dutton), Clark was the scion of a very-long-established New York banking family with infinite connections, and Root's father without thinking about it would in the fullness of time inevitably refer considerable business. Indeed, through Senator Root the young firm found itself involved from its first year with one of the largest clients in America: Andrew Carnegie.

"Carnegie had the utmost contempt for all lawyers," Clark recalled. "The only lawyer in the world he would pay any attention to

[1] 5 *Bull* 257, 9/13/24.

was Elihu Root. When we set up our little firm, Carnegie was active in setting up the Carnegie Corporation, to handle all his charities. And he was writing a new will. He told Senator Root to give the business to us. I drafted—I was a kid twenty-eight years old—I drafted the special act that is to this day the charter of the Carnegie Corporation, and I drew his will." Not that anybody drew Carnegie's will who wasn't named Andrew Carnegie—but the new firm got paid for trying to help.

Most of the Carnegie work was done by young Root. "We all helped each other, of course," Root said in 1966. "People did things differently for Mr. Carnegie. I have a handwritten note from him in my desk, from 1911, asking advice on a point of law. The way it's written, I think that funny old fellow was taking advice from two lawyers."

Also through the Senator, young Root became one of those regularly employed by the Interborough Railway Company for the defense of negligence actions, at a fee of $25 for a day in court. Bird's time in the first year was fairly completely taken up with his role as Special Assistant U.S. Attorney in the sugar frauds cases, but occasionally he undertook a job for fun—for example, the representation of the Pushcart Peddlers Association in an action to restrain the Police Department. Bird learned some words of Yiddish so he could address the membership of the Association: he was already looking toward a career in politics. Clark, whose combination of tenacity, austerity and cheerfulness gave him one of the most remarkable temperaments at the bar, specialized in collection work and in bankruptcies. He said years later, "When judges appointed receivers— patronage—we were beneficiaries from the two Hands, who had just gone on the bench."

In 1912 one of these bankruptcy cases, a real-estate firm with considerable mortgage holdings, produced a major job. Root, Clark & Bird hired two law clerks, Alfred C. Intemann and J. Lloyd Derby, and expanded its quarters on the tenth floor at 31 Nassau Street, taking Buckner's law school classmate Mansfield Ferry as a subtenant to help pay the rent and to handle some of the spill-over. All the secretarial labors were done by one lady Phi Beta Kappa from Cornell who had been a high school teacher before moving up to clerical work in a law office.

Bird during this period was in and out of the office. Having become in the sugar frauds cases an expert on customs procedure, he was appointed Appraiser of the Port of New York by President Taft; but as a Roosevelt man he felt uncomfortable in the job in 1912 and resigned to return to the law firm. His energetic activities on behalf of Roosevelt led to his election as County Chairman of the Progressive Party, and thereafter his interest in practicing law slackened substantially. He had decided he was going to elect a Mayor of New York, and he had picked his candidate—John Purroy Mitchel, then president of the Board of Aldermen, a fiery thirty-three-year-old Irish maverick Democrat. (Legend had it that Bird had never met Mitchel when he made this decision—that he walked into Delmonico's one evening, asked who that man was dining in the corner, received the information, and said, "I'm going to make that man Mayor!")

In the spring of 1913, Woodrow Wilson (who wanted to see an anti-Tammany Democrat become Mayor of New York) took Mitchel temporarily out of the hurly-burly of New York politics by making him Collector of the Port of New York; and Bird left Root, Clark & Bird to be Mitchel's adviser and liaison. He "found his duties as a Progressive leader," Buckner wrote Learned Hand, "entirely too exacting to permit him to practice law."[2] That summer, probably with some help from Buckner, Bird organized the opposition to Whitman among the Fusion leaders and won the mayoralty nomination for Mitchel. He probably bankrolled the campaign, too—Buckner called Hand's attention to a comment in the *Evening Sun,* about "the Bill-bird with a yellow beak and a green back."[3]

Buckner wrote to Frankfurter that fall: "Mitchel is certainly lucky. He ought to name his first son 'William.' William Bird, against all political advice, made his nomination possible; William Gaynor by his untimely death removed the factor which mathematically spelled defeat; William Sulzer [the impeached Democratic Governor, knifed by Tammany, returned to the political scene to run for the State Assembly as a Progressive] . . . now make[s] his election possible by putting into the campaign the Tammany issue, although all previous efforts to do so had produced apathetic results."[4] Bird would continue as County Chairman for the Progressives through 1914, when he

[2] Buckner to Hand, 10/8/13.
[3] *Ibid.*
[4] Buckner to Frankfurter, 10/27/13.

blocked the gubernatorial nomination of Whitman with the comment that he'd rather run for the job himself than support Charles S. Whitman. (The Republicans ran Whitman without Progressive endorsement, and he won easily.) Shortly thereafter Bird returned to Massachusetts to run a newspaper his father had bought him; and to die at the age of thirty-two.

With Bird gone (and Clark's wife so ill that he felt he would have to take her away from New York for an extended trip that fall), the young firm needed new partners. "We had a little more work than two men could do," Root said many years later, "and Emory and Si had a little less work than two men could do." Both Buckner and Howland had known Root and Clark, though not well, at the law school; all four men had been active in Harvard Club affairs; and "we used to see a lot of each other," Clark recalled, "at the old Underwriters' Lunch Club on Liberty Street—a kind of second-class cheap lunch club where young lawyers used to foregather." On September 1, 1913, Root & Clark at 31 Nassau Street became Root, Clark, Buckner & Howland; and the Buckner & Howland offices at 32 Liberty Street were closed.

"Ten years ago this morning," Buckner wrote under the heading "Cake and Candles" in the issue of the interoffice paper that appeared September 1, 1923,

R C B & H opened its doors to the unfeeling public. At or about nine o'clock that morning SWH and I walked in and joined ER Jr and GC and their young Associates, Messrs. Intemann and Derby. At about the same hour postmen were delivering to our competitors the engraved warnings usual under such circumstances—an irrational custom which no one has satisfactorily explained. At the same hour the stenographer–bookkeeper–file clerk opened up her new books. The student assistant–telephone operator–managing clerk–office boy enlarged his responsibilities. The outer office continued to accommodate the combined clientele although already housing the library, telephone, legal associates and managing clerk. We were in varying degrees a "long way under forty."[5]

For all four of the partners, the early years of the new firm would be forever a model of what a partnership should be. What Grenville Clark remembered best was "the absolute harmony and teamwork.

[5] 4 *Bull*, No. 35, 9/1/23, p. 1.

We all worked on each other's cases, and we always said what we thought. I remember I had a case—Redmond & Company against Powellson—equitable relief. It was a block of bonds sold at auction, with a requirement of posting 10 percent. Redmond never posted the 10 percent; didn't have to; had credit. But Powellson forced cancellation, and won in the lower court. I passed the brief around, and a note came back from Emory: 'You haven't done yourself justice. You're stale on it. It can't be amended, we'll have to start all over again—I'll help you with it.' We rewrote it and I won a unanimous reversal."

Elihu Root, Jr. remembered an occasion when "I'd gone up to Utica to try the Utica Pipe Foundry case. I found the lawyer on the other side was Theodore Letchworth, who had been editor of the *Law Review* the year ahead of me. It was the sort of thing that ought to be settled, and in fact we did settle it. Suddenly, Emory came posting up—he thought there was going to be a fight and he wanted to help. I remember a cold night sitting around after that in Clinton, New York [the Roots' ancestral home]."

All four men were unconventional. Howland when the office got to be too much would wander out and up to the Eden Musée to play a game against the chess automaton. Clark would work in great bursts of individual energy, throwing his big frame around his room impatiently. A note in the office paper in the early 1920's reported, "We were showing an important visitor over the office. On passing GC's room, the stranger saw someone on the floor and said, 'Ah! I see you are having the carpet repaired in that room.' 'Oh, no,' was our reply. 'That is Mr. Clark writing an important brief.' "[6] Root's life was full of outside interests—Greek and Latin, sailing, designing things for sailboats. At the end of the day, often enough, all four men would have a drink together in the office, and someone would usually join Buckner in the long walk uptown to Park Avenue which was the only exercise on his normal weekly calendar.

Of his three partners, Buckner was probably closest to Clark, whose austerity touched a deeper chord in him than could be reached by the lawyerly concerns or off-the-job sporting conviviality of Root or Howland. When Roscoe Pound retired as dean of the law school in 1936, Clark was among those proposed as his successor, and Buckner wrote Frankfurter:

[6] 2 *Bull*, 2/4/22.

"I am not sure G.C. would accept. If not, it would be for the same reasons that I think he *should*. But how can we go on and not be 'Root Clark?' . . .

"He is an 'abler' (for 25-28 years you and I have been groping in vain to find out just what 'able' means) man than anyone I have heard mentioned whom I personally knew. He is slow. Hugh Johnson [first administrator of NRA] was fast. I know, I know, I know —but just calling attention to it. He is a good judge of men. A Dean doesn't have to pick a faculty out of a circus crowd during the 10 minutes he is on the flying trapeze. He is sound. He is open minded upon everything and most zealous in a humble search for the right. When finally—and at long last—through, then he's through! His process of search being long in time and wide in scope would be called by some 'tact' and 'diplomacy'—not the words—his final adherence after he gets through would be equally erroneously called 'stubbornness' when it is conviction."[7]

2

When the new office opened, Buckner's newsworthy client (whom he cherished, though the job was "practically unpaid"[8]) was William R. "Daddy" George, founder of the "George Junior Republic," one of the educational experiments of the Progressive era, a boarding school in upstate New York where mixed bags of adolescents (including some referred by courts) made their own rules, elected their own officials, tried their own disciplinary cases. The movement had spread nationally, with half a dozen other Junior Republics scattered in various states, and an eminent board of trustees for the national association. George himself lived beside the New York property, and though no longer its direct supervisor was constantly in and out. One of the girls became pregnant, and said George was the father; and two others alleged certain lesser indecencies. Two investigations were launched, one by the State Board of Charities (which did not examine George or permit his representatives to question their sources), the other by a distinguished committee of the national board—Joseph H. Choate, Lillian Wald and Justice Samuel Seabury. Henry A. Wise, Buckner's former chief at the U.S. Attorney's office, was counsel for the committee.

[7] Buckner to Frankfurter, undated, 1936.
[8] Buckner to Frankfurter, 4/7/38.

Buckner was unhappy about his chances. "This damned fool Daddy George," Frankfurter remembered, "used to go into the rooms in the girls' dorm. Buck said, 'I'm afraid of the case because every man has internal evidence of what he was going to do.' " After Wise's examination of George, Buckner was even more unhappy, and wrote Frankfurter a letter of description:

"All day Saturday and Sunday and Sunday night I had the painful experience of sitting at the Bar Association and listening to Wise grill George before our committee. Although he thinks his examination *quasi* judicial, he in fact turned the proceedings into a veritable *auto-da-fé*. The boot, the screw, the dropping water, and all medieval accessories were employed. With it all, however, George acquitted himself pretty well.

"The most tiresome feature was the manifestation of a principle of professional conduct which you and I long since discovered in W's case, namely, a passionate stand for the universal democracy of facts. With him all facts are created free and equal. Against the feudal system of a sense of proportion and probative subordination, he has drawn the battle-ax of democracy and is the champion for the equality of every fact which moves or lives or has its being in the air or on the earth or in the waters under the earth. North is north; south is south; if where directions are in nowise involved one should say he stepped across the road south when in fact the direction was north, all proceedings must be instantly stopped until the great Commoner can spit the witness upon the needle of the compass, with this ameliorating proof, however, that at any particular latitude and longitude standardized variation must be allowed."[9]

The State Board of Charities reported first, recommending George's removal from any contact with the Republic, the abandonment of much of the experimentation in self-government, and the elimination of girls. Buckner made a statement to the press, pointing out that the eminent private committee was still weighing the evidence of its much more extensive investigation: "The enemies of Mr. George," he said, "are engaged in the unusual proceedings of trying to shoot an accused man while the jury in the case is out, and all because they are afraid a delay might mean the vindication of the defendant."[10] In early

[9] Buckner to Frankfurter, 10/27/13.
[10] *New York Times,* 12/18/13.

March, 1914, the select committee completed its report, and the newspapers carried an advance rumor that George had been exonerated. The story included the last paragraph of Buckner's summation for George at the hearings: "He was very fond of his boys and girls, and treated them just as if they were his children. Why, whenever he returned from a trip he would be greeted by crowds of them who called him daddy. I suppose that unconsciously he may have laid himself open to criticism, but after going through this whole investigation I am satisfied that he is not guilty of any actual wrongdoing."[11]

When the three "judges" submitted their verdict, however, George was considerably less than exonerated. He had not, the committee ruled, impregnated the young lady who started the fuss, but in the case of one of the other girls he very likely had, as the *Times* delicately put it, "made a physical examination . . . such as only a physician should have authority to make." This constituted "wilful misconduct . . . in pursuance of his theory, which we can not too strongly condemn, that being the head of the republic at Freeville he could treat and handle the grown women among the citizens there like children, and according to his whim and caprice and without regard to the rules and usages of common life and civilized society."[12]

A quarter of a century later, Buckner found the memory of the experience still distasteful. "Wise was the worst man in the world to choose to investigate 'Daddy George,' " he wrote Frankfurter in 1940, "and I leave for your own mental comment the 'Board' composed of Joseph H. Choate, Lillian Wald and Samuel Seabury in this particular type of case. As a matter of fact it is obvious that even Appellate Courts are limited in their capacity to find the real truth on a printed record, but it goes a long way if a man has the background to visualize the situation and appraise *character* and size up the testimony of an overzealous woman such as indicated in the George case. When I think of the real character of the late Daddy George and compare it to ribald things Wise said about him to me privately, it makes me quite indignant."[13] Still, at the time, thanks in large part to Buckner's continuing *ex parte* efforts with the trustees of the national association, George came out of the investigation

---

[11] *New York Times*, 3/2/14.
[12] *New York Times*, 3/4/14.
[13] Buckner to Frankfurter, 3/8/40.

spotted rather than destroyed. Meeting that May, the trustees confirmed his position among their number, rejected the State Board of Charities recommendations, and reinstated him as the guiding light of the Freeville Republic.

3

Root, Clark, Buckner & Howland was a general law firm, prepared to accept any business that came in the door, and it did not need a trial specialist. Root and Clark were themselves in court a good part of the working day. In 1930 Buckner told the Chicago Bar Association that "I have ever since I got out of law school done nothing else at all [but try cases]; I am so frightfully lopsided I practically have only one leg professionally."[14] But most of Buckner's time in the early years of the firm went into work on wills and estates and bankruptcies, fields which require appearances in court but are by no means a trial lawyer's practice. "If he had wanted to do it," Elihu Root, Jr. said in 1966, "Emory would have been a good business lawyer, but that wasn't the way he wanted it."

From 1915 on Buckner was the regular recipient of appointments by the Surrogate's Court as special guardian and as referee, and Learned Hand called on him with increasing frequency to protect public interest in bankruptcy proceedings. (One exchange of letters in 1916 reveals Hand's discomfort at the fact that a large piece of work Buckner did for him in this area produced no fee whatever.) The friendship between Buckner and Hand flourished, and was a great source of pride to the younger man. In 1918 Buckner wrote an enthusiastic "Dear Bee" letter beginning: "I don't know why they call you 'Bee.' Is it because you are such a worker? Is it because you are forever in the garden of law books, buzzing around, with feet always heavily laden with the pollen of learning, even though the honey you distil is not always sweet, but sometimes acrid with the tang and bite of criticism? Or is it because when annoyed you sting and sting hard? Or are you a queen bee swollen with the gestation of a myriad purple thoughts?" A postscript to the letter adds: "Your suggestions of possibilities of intellectual liaison quite overwhelm me."[15]

[14] "The Lawyer in Court," 13 *Chicago Bar Record* 100, p. 101.
[15] Buckner to Hand, 6/18/18.

In early 1914 Buckner was the source of an article on pension funds in the magazine section of the *New York Times* ("If the present direction and speed were maintained, New York would have to go into one of two things—the hands of a receiver or the business of counterfeiting"[16]). Frankfurter thought highly enough of Buckner's capacity in fiduciary questions to send Justice Brandeis to him with problems relating to the will of a widowed friend. Buckner wrote Brandeis a thoroughly lawyer-like reply.

In handling his own matters, Buckner could be remarkably sloppy about the legal as well as the economic consequences of his actions. (A favorite story around the office some years later concerned his tax audit, and the examiner's questioning of a deduction for a bad debt. "Oh, you don't have to worry about that," Buckner replied. "That debt's been bad for years."[17] A case growing out of this audit wound up in court, where Buckner lost it.) And he was at least as much a negotiator as he was a trial lawyer; he believed in settling, and he had a genius for handling his own client at those frequent moments when a man in a fight wants to strike as hard as he can rather than step back and size up the situation. Not infrequently, when a settlement seemed a reasonable result, a case would be maneuvered into his office and out of the hands of Grenville Clark, whose sense of humor deserted him whenever he discerned a matter of principle and who thus found negiotiating painful. "Grenny was an impossible man to settle with," Judge Joseph M. Proskauer remembered. "He was an indomitable hewer to the line. With Emory, you could give and take."

"The first thing Emory would do," Frankfurter recalled, "was search out the other man's lawyer and find out what they'd settle for. One case, a libel against a manufacturer's good name, he nosed around and found out they'd settle for little. Then he got the client in and he said, 'Mind you, we're sure to win. But sometimes judges go wrong. Then, of course, we'd be sure the Appellate Division would overturn. But the Appellate Division can go wrong. Even the Court of Appeals.'

"His client said he'd feel like a son-of-a-bitch if he settled this case. And Emory assured him—*he* wouldn't have to settle it at all. His

16 *New York Times,* 1/11/14, Section V, p. 101.
17 George Cleary to author, 1965.

lawyer would settle it for him. 'Let me be your son-of-a-bitch,' he said; and he settled it."

Over the years, Buckner argued scores of appeals with the same enthusiasm and the same quest for clarity that he displayed in a trial. But to an increasing extent with the passage of time, nothing interested him much except people, their character and actions, good or bad. If the people were interesting enough, he was quite satisfied to spend his time counseling them. Starting in 1914, he devoted many more hours than fees could justify to the establishment and maintenance of *The New Republic,* whose editors, particularly young Walter Lippmann, became close personal friends. (The financing of this venture, incidentally—wheels within wheels—came from Dorothy Straight, daughter of the traction manipulator whose multifarious misbehaviors in New York had been the largest single source of legal income for both Elihu Root and Henry L. Stimson.) Alexander Royce remembered a story of a little dinner at Morey's in New Haven after the publication of one of the first issues of *The New Republic,* when Buckner said to the assembled editors, "I see in this little magazine everything that anyone could ask for—everything except perhaps a little humility."

Buckner found his function as a lawyer most obvious and most rewarding, however, when he could deal with people in conflict. And the factual basis of the conflict struck him as ultimately far more significant than its legal ramifications. Trained as a common-law lawyer to the point where any other mode of approach to legal problems was quite outside his frame of reference, he once defined "law" as "simply some other set of facts which other courts have dealt with."[18]

His interest in people was in their relations with each other far more than in their relations with him. Every trial lawyer is inevitably a bit of an actor and a preacher, and in his courtroom appearances Buckner was doubtless satisfying the same drives from childhood that had given him an early interest in the theater and led to the play-readings with the Goldthwaite Dorrs and others. But he seems to have felt much less need than most trial lawyers to impress his ego on the situation. His vastly appreciated generosity to his young associates in the courtroom—his insistence on saying "My assistant

[18] *Scraps,* 5/8/26.

reminds me" whenever a matter he had forgotten was called to his attention (in contrast to the normal trial lawyer's impatient pretense of having known it all the time and being about to work up to it)— was made possible by the fact that his satisfactions came so often from observing and understanding rather than from imposing his personality. His hearty, open-handed, aggressively honest manner was never a device, because his interest in the other man's situation was so rarely touched with self-interest. Trial practice, with its unrivaled opportunities to watch and to control the relationships as necessary, was the only area of the law likely to satisfy all the elements of his temperament.

Buckner could not, however, go into competition with the Max Steuers and Martin W. Littletons and William Fallons and William Travers Jeromes of New York. He did not wish to represent people whose stories he did not believe; and though the divisions among lawyers were nowhere near so rigid then as they later became, it was not seemly for an aspiring Wall Street commercial law firm to feature a criminal law specialist among its partners. The firm did handle a very occasional plaintiff's case for personal injuries, but Root's and Clark's contacts were mostly on the defendant's side, and Buckner seems never to have had much interest in that sort of trial. There must have been, in the 1910s, at least some breach-of-promise work for victimized gentlemen—Buckner came to know enough about this problem to serve on the committee which in the 1920s secured the elimination of this cause of action in the law and of blackmail in lawyers' offices.

The year 1914 brought two major litigations, one of which later became important to the growth of the firm. The more significant at the time was a suit by the Boston Condensed Milk Company against the Sanitary Can Company for supplying cans which, the milk company alleged, spoiled the milk. Buckner tried it for the plaintiffs in federal court, and lost it. For the future, however, the more important case was a criminal action against the officers of a Florida bank, where the counsel of record for the defense was a trustee of the Flagler estate. As a result of Buckner's trips to Florida to work on this trial, the Flagler estate and later that of his widow became Root-Clark clients, as did the Florida East Coast Railway.

During those early years, however, cases were not easy to come by. Henry Mayer, who joined Root-Clark as an office boy during its first year and stayed to become one of the associates after his admission to the bar, recalled (in an *envoi* written on his departure for solo practice seven years later) a conversation "between Mr. Buckner and some other member of the firm. It was apparently about some unpromising prospective litigation. Mr. Buckner, as I recall it, remarked, at the close of the conversation, 'Let's take it—we don't know what March will bring.' "

Happy as he was with his partners, Buckner in the early years of the new firm was something less than pleased with what was, after all, his first experience in the private practice of law. In the fall of 1914 he closed out the last of his debts to Roscoe Pound.[19] In response to Pound's reply, he sketched some of the aspects of life as a New York lawyer that were bothering him after a year of Root, Clark, Buckner & Howland:

"You are indeed a good friend. You lend me money, reject interest, wait an unconscionable time while I am struggling with the heavy expenses of success—for *that* is what has been the trouble —and when finally I tardily reimburse you, you write me a note worth more than money. Well, it's all very interesting. Why can't you shuttle a little less rapidly when you shoot to N.Y. and take time to lunch leisurely with me and tell me how

"1. Democracy can be defended which is so easily fooled by selfish, insincere mediocrity like Whitman [who had been elected Governor the week before].

"2. One can be a lawyer and learn any law at all while practicing? What is the connection between chasing larcenous bankrupts around the corner and principles of jurisprudence? What has the XIV Amendment to do with lying in wait for adulterous husbands, smoothing out irritations between cotton brokers, saving men from prison, intimidating crafty automobile agents, etc., etc. I almost believe the law is only to pass bar exams—at least until you get famous and get real 'briefs.' It seems to be 50 percent personality, 40 percent sense, and 10 percent law. Why not have at H.L.S. a laboratory course in common sense? I had a conference yesterday with a Harvard A

[19] The letter began: "Now if I were you, I could start off with some strikingly apposite quotation from Sanskrit or Gaelic or Aramaic! The nearest I can come to it with my linguistic limitations is: 'Don't drop dead—here's the hundred I borrowed of you several generations ago!' " (Buckner to Pound, 10/29/14).

man, a real scholar, who is an ass in three languges besides English.

"3. How to pry loose business from the 'established' firms, many of whom are really not much good.

"I wish you the best of success—but why wish it? You have it and the Harvard men are already vying with each other to tell great tales of your intellectual thaumaturgy."[20]

4

If it was dubious policy to go hunting criminal business, it was of course perfectly respectable to accept assignments by the court or referrals from other lawyers, and during the 1910s Buckner defended a number of people accused of serious crimes. In the last year of his life, he wrote up two of these cases as cautionary tales for the young men in his office. Both were striking examples of his belief in facts rather than law, and his ability to accept the realities of a situation—even a most unfair hard-luck situation—rather than try to force unreality through the legal process. Indeed, the hard-luck case, involving a cabbie who had unwittingly provided transportation for a pair of bank robbers, he presented as "an illustration of an extremely satisfactory way of practicing criminal law":

One of the very first "daylight holdups" in a crowded section with escape by automobile occurred in Brooklyn in December, 1918, when two men walked into the East Brooklyn Savings Bank, held everybody inside the bank cowed with pointed pistols, shot the teller and another employee, filled a black bag full of currency and escaped in a taxi. This was a front-page story in every paper in New York. A tremendous hue and cry went up for immediate solution of the crime and the punishment of the criminals. The shooting in the bank had attracted police officers who immediately ran to the rescue just as the two bandits were fleeing to their taxi in open daylight. There was a pistol duel on the street, but the men got into the taxi which was standing on the curb one block from the bank with *its engine running*. The bandits pushed their pistols into the chaffeur's back and told him to drive on. The policemen shouted for him to stop, but he drove on as directed. At a certain elevated station they directed the driver to stop, took the elevated and escaped. They handed the taxi driver $10 and told him in their flight that they had left something in the cab for him for his trouble.

[20] Buckner to Pound, 11/12/14.

The frightened and bewildered chauffeur drove around a few blocks, hunting for a policeman or a station house (Brooklyn was as strange to him, like most Manhattan taxi drivers, as Buenos Aires). He came to a drug store and telephoned his manager, telling him the whole story from start to finish. The manager told him to go to the nearest police station. He drove on until he found a mounted policeman, who directed him to the nearest station. . . . A policeman immediately went out to the cab and brought in . . . $170 in cash. They told him he had come to the right place, and the first thing they did was to escort him to a cell and lock him up, telephoning headquarters at the same time that they had the taxi driver who was wanted in the bank robbery.

The publicity continued in a big way and went all over the country. Detectives at once examined him in the station and then he was taken to the Brooklyn District Attorney's office, where he was submitted to further examination. After such examination he was permitted to get an attorney, and there were "follow-up" stories in the papers every day. The attorney gave out statements of his intention to apply immediately for a writ of *habeas corpus,* as the chauffeur was being held without basis, and the District Attorney retaliated by saying that indictments would immediately be found.

At this posture of affairs Shearman & Sterling telephoned me, saying that they represented the Black & White Taxi Company; that the president was very indignant at the arrest and forthcoming indictment of the chauffeur, who had the best record of all his drivers, having been with them since they moved from Chicago to New York, and being with them in Chicago, a total of five or six years; that he wanted the chauffeur to have an experienced lawyer and was prepared to pay for his defense, not only to clear the chauffeur, but the publicity was not good for the company.

The occasion called for very quick action. To me the program was obvious and directly contrary to the policy being pursued by the driver's attorney. I immediately got in touch with this attorney, who came to see me, told him of my being called into the case, which I would accept if agreeable to the defendant, and I would want him to be associated with me, and told him that I would see that the company paid him more than a chauffeur (a personal friend) would possibly be able to pay him. He went right along with me, thus making it unnecessary to utilize the services of any one of our staff of six lawyers.

I went immediately to the Assistant District Attorney in charge of the case in Brooklyn. I told him I realized the pressure he was under because the whole city was inflamed; that I had come into the case as senior counsel, and that I had no objection whatever to his going ahead and getting an indictment; that there would be no application for bail, no *habeas corpus* and nothing to interfere with him in any way, but I had seen the young man and had heard his story, which he had told from the beginning to all the officials who had examined him, and that I believed thoroughly in his innocence.

The strongest point against the chauffeur was the fact that his engine was running as if in wait for the bandits. His explanation of this was the fact that he had been stopped for the second time on the trip directly in front of a saloon and was told to wait for about fifteen minutes. The previous stop at another saloon had taken only five minutes. When they got out the second time, he stopped his engine for three or four minutes but, expecting them back at any moment, he had gotten out and cranked up his car so as to be ready when they returned. The big point here is to remember that in those days the self-starter had not been invented and all taxis and all cars had to be cranked up. The great point in his favor was that he was in a regular taxi stand at the Hotel Navarre and was the first car in line when the two bandits walked up to the hotel and beckoned for a taxi.

I explained to the District Attorney that the chauffeur would be a necessary and valuable witness for him if the bandits were ever caught; that we wished to cooperate with him and would keep the chauffeur at his disposal to identify any suspects as they were picked up from time to time; that probably after six months, when things had quieted down, he would be willing to admit the chauffeur to bail and no application would be made before then; that it was his duty to protect a man from electrocution by the mob via official machinery as much as it was to send to the chair the bandits, if ever caught.

I saw the prisoner in jail, a fine, upstanding, honest-looking man with a perfect record, and told him my program, which he most reluctantly consented to because of his sense of injustice. His young wife and four-year-old boy were in jail to see him, and he had counted heavily on getting out in time to take Christmas dinner with them outside of jail. I told him he would eat his Christmas dinner in jail but that his family could join him; that he must sit right there until I got him out, which might be several months away. He took this hard. Months went by; he was repeatedly called upon to identify various suspects, none of whom was the right man, the agitation disappeared while the whole country was combed in search of the bandits. In a few months, according to my original program, the District Attorney admitted him to bail, which was provided by the company, and by that time other things had happened to fill the first pages of the newspapers.

About a year later the scene shifts to California. There, in either San Fransicso or Los Angeles, lived a young woman whose husband had brought home a boarder. She did not like the boarder and felt that he had a very bad influence on her husband. She had read in California long stories concerning this Brooklyn holdup and a description of the pair of bandits. One evening when the crook was a little tight he boasted that he had once pulled off the biggest coup in the country, which, because of the description published in the paper, excited the suspicion of the wife, already highly suspicious and fearful of him, and she wrote the New York Police Department the facts. The man was picked up on suspicion, brought east and was immediately and positively identified by the taxi driver as "the tall man" and leader of the pair, who gave his name as Hamby. He was put to trial, the chauffeur being the main witness, was very tough and defiant throughout and was convicted and electrocuted. Some reporter even wrote a series of articles which were published in one of the sensational papers over Hamby's signature, giving the story of his life of crime. This series was full of exhibitionism but a trifle shy of concrete episodes for which he might be prosecuted. Nothing could induce him to tell anything of his confederate, "the short man," who has never been caught. He went to the chair as he had lived, a tough guy, upright and defiant. . . .

The driver is still around, has a good job, and I hope that both he and his friends have long since forgotten the dark days of twenty-two years ago.[21]

The other story Buckner told from those years had a less happy ending. It concerned a twenty-one-year-old Swedish immigrant houseboy named Arthur Waldenen who had got into bad company around pool halls, and together with another of the house boys had admitted one of their new friends to the home of his elderly widowed employer so he could rob the place. During the course of the robbery, the lady was killed; the gag the robber had tied over the lady's mouth slipped, and he choked her to death. Because the law required charges of first-degree murder for any association with a killing committed in the course of a felony the court felt that it could not accept the boys' plea of guilty to murder in the second degree. In 1917 conviction on first-degree murder carried a mandatory sentence of death.

[21] 21 *Bull* 121-126; 3/30/40.

Buckner handled Waldenen's trial on appointment from the court; his associate counsel, also appointed by the court, was Congressman William S. Bennett. In such cases, appeal is required by law, and Buckner carried the case to the Court of Appeals, where he submitted a brief which began with the words: "The nature of this appeal is unusual. It is a hopeless formality."

The brief cited the relevant statutes and briefly told the story of the crime. "The defendant," Buckner wrote,

did not dispute the evidence offered by the People upon any material point. On the contrary, by repeated confessions to police officers, to a private citizen, and to the District Attorney, as well as by his own frank testimony upon the trial, he corroborated the People's case in every detail. . . . Counsel gave careful consideration to the question as to whether the defendant's frank confessions before the trial and upon the trial were sufficiently corroborated within the requirements of law. The corroboration seems so ample, coming from several witnesses, that counsel cannot, under the authorities, say to this court that the defendant was improperly convicted. . . . It is therefore in a sense true, as stated by the District Attorney in his summation to the jury at folio 1287, "This case is absolutely undefended." . . .

It is humiliating to file a brief in this court without urging the validity of any exceptions taken during the course of the trial, but counsel do not deem it their duty, for the sake of appearance, to press exceptions which are clearly without merit.

We trust the court will not think it improper for us to say that the jury submitted to the court a signed recommendation for the commutation of defendant's sentence. Application for such commutation has been made to the Governor of the State, but, under the consistent practice of the Governor, applications for commutation in this kind of case are not entertained until after an appeal has been prosecuted to this court.[22]

Both the boys' records prior to this case had been completely clean; indeed, the brief could be written as it was because everything about the case breathed the spirit of commutation. The Governor was Whitman; and Buckner, fearful of the influence of bad personal relations, had Bennett present the application. Sentence was commuted for Waldenen's associate, who had been separately represented, but not for Buckner's client. Waldenen died in the electric chair in July,

[22] 21 *Bull* 46-49, 2/3/40.

1917. Buckner at the time believed Whitman had sent the boy to his death as a gesture of personal revenge at his former assistant; and there is reason to believe he never spoke to Whitman again.

5

Elihu Root's term in the Senate ended in 1915. He had been elected by the New York State legislature; if he chose to run for re-election, he would have to undergo the rigors of a campaign and the hazards of popular election—and a three-cornered election, at that, because the Progressives were unlikely to support a man who had been so good a friend and then so hated a foe of Theodore Roosevelt's. He chose to return to private life and, he thought, to semiretirement, though in fact he was at the beginning of what would be perhaps his most active decade of public service. Needing a place to hang his hat, he became "Counsel" to his son's firm of Root, Clark, Buckner & Howland. Almost immediately, he went off to be chairman of the state's Constitutional Convention.

Senator Root's name on the letterhead changed the environment of the firm. "The truth is," Grenville Clark wrote in 1945, "that the Senator pretty much set us up in business."[23] After 1915 the smaller size of the firm's stationery, rather than waste space listing partners and associates, would mention only "Elihu Root, Counsel"; after 1937 it would offer only "Elihu Root, 1915-1937." With the Senator presently came work for the Guggenheims and for Marshall Field, much of it handled by Howland, with whom Root became quite close. In the fall of 1915 the firm hired another associate, Robert P. Patterson, fresh from Harvard Law School and on his way to a most distinguished career as federal district judge and appellate judge, and ultimately as Secretary of War. In the fall of 1916 another associate was hired from law school, Vanderbilt Webb, later to be Patterson's law partner.

Buckner's part of the practice, however, was less markedly advanced by the occasional presence of the Senator. In October, 1915, he wrote Roscoe Pound, "The law practice in New York, especially for the young men in independent practice, is very much in the doldrums."[24] Judge Jonah Goldstein, who had testified about the evils

[23] 26 *Bull* No. 4, 1/27/45, p. 4.
[24] Buckner to Pound, 10/22/15.

of Lower East Side pool halls in the Aldermanic Investigation and had come to know Buckner in its aftermath, remembered running into Buckner on the street downtown and asking him how business was since the Senator's arrival. "Not so good, Johnny," Buckner replied. "We're too small to handle the things he might bring in, and with him in the office we look too big for the kind of things we ought to be getting."

A letter to Frankfurter in 1916 indicates that Buckner had been asked to contribute legal services to a war relief organization, and had replied that he would have to be paid something: "[I]t may appear to put me in a mercenary light. Only those who know the situation intimately can appreciate that it is not at all mercenary and that if I contribute part of my services I am making a sufficient subscription. . . . However, I am willing to see the whole thing through in its present status if you think it is for the best."[25] In 1917 Buckner was compelled to undergo the embarrassment of asking Henry Stimson and Learned Hand, who had proposed and seconded him for membership in the University Club, to move his application back on the waiting list by some 250 names, to insure that he would not be accepted that year: he could not afford the $290 the membership would cost.[26]

Through those years, the office was interested in much more than business: it was united in a passionate insistence that the United States must intervene in the World War. Clark became one of the founders of what was called the Plattsburg Movement, because the young men who joined it went to get their military training in Plattsburg, New York. In the summer of 1916 Elihu Root, Jr. of Company C won the gold medal on the target range at Plattsburg with 232 hits in 250 shots. Senator Root was reunited with Roosevelt in the national campaign for military preparedness and in excoriation of the Hun. Henry Mayer remembers a fist fight between the pacifist Shelton Hale and Patterson, who would not acquire the nickname "Fighting Bob" until the war but was already on his way to earning it.

In 1916, largely at the insistence of Roosevelt and Senator Root, the Republicans ran on a military preparedness platform which clearly looked toward American entry into the war against Germany—

[25] Buckner to Frankfurter, 12/4/16.
[26] Buckner to Hand, 4/24/17, 4/25/17.

though their candidate, Charles Evans Hughes, who had resigned from the Supreme Court to accept the nomination, was not quite so enthusiastic as some of his sponsors. Frankfurter was unhappy, and wished it were Roosevelt again. He apparently wrote Buckner a parody of a Hughes speech and a diatribe against Root. Buckner replied calmly: "I think your hypothetical speech of Hughes is very good, although I think you minimize his intelligence by stressing his self-deception and Puritan conscience. I think he accepted the nomination for President because he wanted the job; that his talk heretofore about the sanctity of the Supreme Court was due to the fact that the opportunity for unanimous support was nothing like so great as at present and furthermore he had not been so long upon the Bench.

"The rest of your speech is just about what I think is in his mind, and I respect him the more in that his campaign is a 'failure.' He is very much of a lawyer, a document lawyer, a fact lawyer, with judgment and emotions well in leash until the facts of a situation indicate their appropriate character and direction. The real statesman, I suppose, is the man with the hunch, who has his conclusion well in mind subject only to the veto power of inconsistent facts. With Hughes, facts are a condition precedent; with you and [Herbert] Croly[27] and Walter[28] and probably with Brandeis and Root, they are a condition subsequent; with T. R., I suppose, they are well-nigh functionless both fore and aft. Hughes is very likely a better Judge than President, but he will do well enough in the latter capacity. I think on the whole I would rather see him President than Wilson, though I think it probable that Senator Root would make a better President than either, even from your and my point of view. I have not sufficient data to have any judgment on the issue joined between you and Morris on E.R., but I am certain that his offhand disposition of the matter is entirely erroneous. When it comes to distrust of the capacity of the electorate at large, is there anyone really more of an autocrat than T.R.? I suspect that T.R.'s belief in the ability of the people at large to know exactly and precisely what is best for them in the long run is limited to the one issue of vesting in *him* complete power and responsibility in the premises."[29]

[27] Editor of *The New Republic*.
[28] Probably Walter Weyl, author and social philosopher.
[29] Buckner to Frankfurter, 10/5/16.

Frankfurter in 1916 was a professor at the Harvard Law School and on the side an active lawyer arguing before the Supreme Court the validity of the Oregon minimum-wage laws. The case had been in Brandeis' hands before his elevation to the bench; and among the reasons for Frankfurter's continuing antagonism to Root, undoubtedly, was the Senator's appalling performance as one of a cabal of conservative lawyers who had sought to block the Senate's confirmation of the great Boston lawyer. When war came to the United States in 1917, Frankfurter returned to Washington as executive secretary and counsel to the War Labor Policies Board, and called on Buckner often for help in recommending people for jobs and soothing the egos of people who had been passed over. In one of the many letters they exchanged, Buckner must have expressed a feeling that Frankfurter was performing admirably in an important job but perhaps taking himself (indeed, both of them) too seriously—which prompted Frankfurter to release the diapason stops in reply:

"You are one of the joys of my heart. The implication of a community will at once appease your democratic desires and save you from the inundation of my emotions. In which one of the novels, which is the joint inspiration and work of you and James, do we get the qualities, the chiaroscuro of a character, revealed through the reflex of the personality upon others? Even so, you encourage and render genial my egotistic tendencies—by giving me the satisfaction and delight at the pleasure and pride I arouse in you. Acting upon sound Stevensonian principles—that one does not want his admirer to be a fool—you are, of course, compelled to give significance to my praise. You assure yourself [of] that significance, and at the same time bathe in the luxury of your own discrimination by discounting mine. James himself would like that stunt of a versatile personality—you eat the cake of vanity and have it too.

"I follow you completely, even if not in practice, in your exclusive reverence of *thinking*. I know, of course, the rational slave you have always been to Pure Reason. Your feelings have never betrayed your thinking—but why should your feelings subordinate your humor? I had a scientific and ill-concealed pleasure in phrasing the very sentence which to you shows merely my occasional undue allegiance to words. (Be respectful of words, for you know what a bond they are between us!). . . .

"Anyhow, I never suspected you liked surf bathing. I am glad to know it and life is the cheerier because of your letter."[30]

6

Four of the seven young men who had been practicing law at 31 Nassau Street in March, 1917, were in the Army by the end of April. Root, Clark, Patterson and Webb all volunteered with the declaration of war; and, as Plattsburg veterans, all were instantly commissioned. Buckner and Howland, thirty-nine and thirty-seven respectively, fathers with no source of income other than their work, stayed behind to maintain the office. Senator Root, when not in Russia for Wilson, became an active practitioner in the office, and soon Buckner's normal admiration of the older lawyer's "think box" became a deeper affection for the man. It was partly at Root's urging that Buckner returned that fall to politics, to manage John Purroy Mitchel's campaign for re-election as Mayor.

Mitchel's outstanding quality, for both Root and Buckner, was his vigorous support of the war effort. Judge John F. Hylan, his Democratic opponent, had of course supported the Wilson slogan, "He Kept Us Out of War," in 1916; Tammany boss Charles F. Murphy had full control over Hylan, and Murphy was not prepared to sacrifice the German and Irish antiwar vote. Mitchel's other formidable antagonist, Morris Hillquit, was a Socialist and openly opposed to the war. During that summer, moreover, Mitchel's luck had run out. A conservative Republican group had refused to accept the renegade Democrat as their nominee, and had run Congressman Bennett, Buckner's recent colleague in the Waldenen case. On the first count in the Republican primary, Mitchel was declared the winner by a few hundred votes; but the Bennett forces claimed fraud, and Mitchel to disprove their claims demanded a recount. The recount did not show anything that could really be labeled fraud, but it did switch enough votes to give the nomination to Bennett. The day after this result was apparent, Fusion opened a separate office for the re-election of Mitchel, and installed Buckner as its director.

He ran a modern campaign, complete with fleets of trucks equipped with motion pictures, steady attack on precisely two issues, and a game try at creating a bandwagon psychology. One of the issues, in-

[30] Frankfurter to Buckner, 8/26/18.

evitably, was Tammany; and at the beginning Buckner in his public statements refused to take seriously either Hillquit or Bennett. Mitchel would be willing to debate Hylan, he announced, but he would not appear on a platform with the others. (Hylan was not debating anybody; indeed, he made few public appearances.) The real choice for the voters, Buckner insisted, was between Mitchel and Charles F. Murphy. Even more prominent than the Tammany issue, however, was what Buckner called "Americanism." He told reporters on taking over the office, "Patriotism must be the paramount issue in the greatest city in the U.S. at a time when we are engaged in the greatest war in history." Such loyal Republicans as Root, Stimson and Whitman accepted this position, and probably for the only time in their lives cut their own ticket to endorse an outsider. Meanwhile, a flock of prominent Democrats headed by Buckner's courtroom antagonist, the former Congressman Martin W. Littleton, formed a party called City Democracy to fight for the re-election of the anti-Tammany Mayor. Buckner in addition organized a "Mitchel League" to give a home to the nonpartisan element which wished to organize and contribute money. A great deal of money was contributed—more than even Buckner knew, as he had to admit unhappily to a grand jury which investigated the election at the end of the year.

As election day neared, Buckner switched tactics to try to convince the large group of Democrats who supported what was now Wilson's war that the real danger lay in the election of Hillquit. Hylan, he declared, in statements given front-page treatment by the *Times* and the *World,* was now out of it; a vote for Hylan meant a danger of electing the radical pacifist Hillquit. On October 28 he declared that the Mitchel forces were "no longer alarmed at the possibility of Tammany winning the election."[31] The next day he declared himself really "alarmed at the report of growing Hillquit strength."[32] But by November 2 he was no longer alarmed at all: "Nothing can stop the swing that is now going to Mitchel."[33]

On Wall Street, which was where the election betting odds were made before the days of Las Vegas, Hylan was a 1-3 favorite the

[31] *New York Times,* 10/29/17.
[32] *New York Times,* 10/30/17.
[33] *New York Times,* 11/3/17.

week before election day (up from 2-5 the week before). And on November 6 New York cast almost 300,000 votes for Hylan, little more than 150,000 for Mitchel (and 140,000 for Hillquit; Bennett polled less than 60,000). Buckner "candidly" told reporters he was not surprised.

Mitchel became an aviator and was killed at an Army training camp when he fell out of an airplane. In a city remarkably light on monuments to its public servants, there is a stone bust of Mitchel at Ninetieth Street and Fifth Avenue, just inside the park.

7

Nineteen-nineteen was the *annus mirabilis* of RCB&H. Root and Clark, Patterson and Webb returned from the wars; Senator Root was retained by the railroads to argue their case for instant restoration of their property from the wartime government seizure, and by the brewers and distillers to argue the unconstitutionality of the Volstead Act—and, indeed, of the Prohibition Amendment itself. Both Marshall Field and Andrew Carnegie died, elevating the young law firm from a status as counsel to two very rich old men who had little work for lawyers to the status of counsel for two very large estates. The Guggenheims got into serious trouble with their stockhholders over the administration of American Smelting & Refining. A large and continually troubled new client—All-America Cables, later ITT —simply walked in the door, drawn by a combination of the Senator's prestige, one director's gratitude for a collecting job the firm had done for him personally some years before and another director's memory of serving on the jury of a case Buckner had tried while Assistant District Attorney.

Buckner himself was retained for what was by some margin the largest commercial matter he had ever attempted: the defense of the National Association of Automobile Accessory Jobbers against a Sherman Anti-Trust prosecution which came to trial on January 13, 1919. There were seventeen corporate and twenty-one individual defendants, and to run the team of outside counsel Buckner organized for the trial Frankfurter had recommended Thurlow Gordon, an associate in the firm of Cotton & Franklin, whom Frankfurter had come to know as an able assistant in the Justice Department. "The case," Gordon recalled in 1967, "was full of opening drawers and discovering documents. The government thought it was a simple price-fixing case, but there were so many different people who had written letters and were ready to give testimony, it became quite complicated."

Buckner in theory was the solicitor rather than the barrister in the case. "Our chief counsel is James H. Wilkerson from Chicago," he wrote Frankfurter, "and our chief annoyance is your old friend Claude H. Thompson. He thinks he is chief counsel and is constantly attempting to 'express his personality.' As you can well imagine, Gordon is organizing the case magnificently, although it would be a little better if we had another month. However, one of a lawyer's jobs is to take things as he finds them."[34]

Even complicated antitrust cases were tried expeditiously in the 1910s, and by February 7 the defendants had been acquitted. It was the last time Buckner would be asked to work in a courtroom as supporting player to another "leading counsel." Gordon remembered that "Wilkerson had none of Emory's magnetism. Everybody turned to Buck for leadership all through the case—realized what a brilliant man he was. His plea to the jury was one of the finest legal arguments I ever heard—we all felt that was what got the defendants off." Most of the defendants were from out of town, and during the course of the trial they all stayed at one hotel, most of them with their wives. When the verdict was in, at Buckner's suggestion, a dance was organized for all the defendants and all their lawyers. "Most enjoyable case I ever worked on," Thurlow Gordon said in 1967.

Of all the developments of 1919, however, the most important for the future of the firm was the addition of a fifth partner— Arthur Ballantine, who had been Solicitor to the Collector of Internal Revenue and was not eager to return to Boston, where he had practiced since his graduation from law school. Buckner seems to have made the arrangements himself. At the end of 1918 he wrote Frankfurter: "I shall spend next Sunday in Washington, as I wish to talk with Arthur Ballantine a few minutes, by which I do not mean that I do not intend to talk to him more than a few minutes, but wish to indicate that the occasion of my going to Washington is to see him."[35] With Ballantine would come a weight of tax law

[34] Buckner to Frankfurter, 1/13/19.
[35] Buckner to Frankfurter, 12/13/18.

work, and a growing collection of clients drawn by the new partner's brilliance and aggressiveness.

Throughout 1919 the firm expanded at an unbelievable pace. At the beginning of the year, there were six lawyers at 31 Nassau Street—the Senator, Buckner, Howland, and associates Alfred C. Intemann, Henry Mayer and Reed B. Dawson, a recent Harvard Law graduate hired in 1918. By the end of the year, there were twenty-four lawyers in the office—those six, the four veterans returned from the war, the new partner, and no fewer than thirteen newly employed young lawyers.

CHAPTER SIX

Buckner's Young Men—I

"The office," Grenville Clark recalled, "was Buck's whole life, to an extraordinary degree." By the end of 1920 there were more than thirty lawyers in the firm, and RCB & H had added the ninth floor at 31 Nassau Street and built an inside stairway so people could flow down from the tenth floor without leaving the office. The logistics of the operation intrigued Buckner and occupied the forefront of his mind. When Henry Mayer announced at the end of 1920 that he wished to leave the office and go into practice for himself, Buckner told him he would be making a big mistake—if he stayed another year or two, he would get invaluable lessons in how to run a big law office. Mayer, who was planning to run a very small law office with his wife, found the argument peculiar; but in 1920 Buckner would have thought it strange that anyone would *not* be interested in how to run a large law office.

He "took a systematic over-all view of things," Elihu Root, Jr. wrote many years later, "and reformed our happy-go-lucky methods of procedure, made us keep our time accounts, and send our bills, and follow up our calendar, and systematize our work; and for thirty years he never ceased to be the presiding genius of the office as an office. He started with it at zero and trained it up in the way it ought to go. It was peculiarly his creation and he loved it. Of course he was fond of the people in the office, but he also loved the office as an institution."[1]

This love created a mystique. "We hear much about the spirit of the office," Buckner wrote in *The Bull,* the inner-office newspaper, in 1922.

We hear it from outsiders, We hear it among ourselves, What is it?

We have here an association of a large number of lawyers who are practicing law together in a great joint endeavor. . . . No client is a "personal" client of any of us. He is a client of us all. Frequently the man who introduces a client to the office is not the best equipped or the most economical man to do the work. I have frequently introduced corporation clients and faded away after effecting attornment. . . .

This feeling of solidarity removes corroding competition *inter se.* It would be destructive of our spirit if any one of us should consciously strive to forge ahead of someone else; if anyone should try to take on more work than he can do well simply in order to get it on his calendar; if anyone should manoeuvre in order to work only with seniors, or if we should chafe at chores, such as reading proof, because we are too old or too "important." Mr. Clark, last year, learned of a hurry-up mass of mechanical work in a matter not under his charge and stayed in the office all night to help a junior at it. . . .

The only way to be democratic and cooperative is to *feel* democratic and cooperative. . . . When I was a cub visiting daily junior witenagemot at the Exchange Buffet, I used to hear contemporaries openly state, referring to men in their offices, "There is the fellow I have got to beat." The spirit in this office is, "There's the fellow I want to help."[2]

Over the years, Buckner would be on terms of affection and respect with almost everybody who worked in the office—with one exception: the managing clerk. His standards for what the man in that job should know and do were impossibly high. Even when the firm grew to a size of fifty lawyers, Buckner tried to know everything that was going on. His own room was always right off the reception area, and he kept his door open, so he could see who was coming in and going out. In theory, his secretary, Mathilde Sandstede, was the receptionist for the office, and he would try to keep an eye on the quality of the girls being hired for the stenographic pool by asking for "somebody who's free" to take his dictation.

[1] 22 *Bull* 119, 3/15/41.
[2] 3 *Bull,* 10/21/22, pp. 1-2.

Buckner designed systems using what William P. Palmer (who arrived in 1920 and remained to become a partner) called "a snowstorm of blue slips, white slips, pink slips, green slips" to take care of new account reports, time sheets, progress reports, calendar reports, close-account memoranda and so forth. He hammered at the need to keep the files in the file room: "Last Monday, a holiday," he wrote in *The Bull,* "I noticed forty-one office files scattered throughout the office. If there is doubt as to the administrative advantage of having the files in the file room, let us argue that, and, if wise, change the rule. If there is no doubt about it, then I am bewildered."

When *The Bull* in 1920 casually assigned key phrases to a dozen members of the office for identification purposes, the one applied to Buckner was "Let's organize it." His own desk was a model of what he talked about: it was a table without drawers, always clear, everything disposed of in the early morning, all letters answered, papers properly routed, filed or thrown out, all diary entries made in correct form the same day. "The man who can lay his finger on his shirt studs," he wrote, "is the man who will know whether the case his opponent cites has been overruled."[3] For one of the office parties he wrote a parody to the song "Everybody Works But Father":

> Everybody works but Buckner,
> He sits around all day,
> Shoving his work upon us,
> Tells us that's his way;
> While we all are slaving,
> He is gay and free;
> Everybody works at our shop,
> But E.R.B.

Perhaps the greatest tribute to the warmth and stability of Buckner's personality was the fact that his incessant systematization was never resented. (People did occasionally have some fun with "Sheik Even Em Ory, the Great Organ Izer."[4] The August 26, 1922, issue of *The Bull* suggests that "the following diary entries be made: Sept. 30th: Return to file room all folders kept out all summer. Oct. 2nd: ERB returns.") When Buckner spoke of the interest of the

---

[3] 2 *Bull,* 4/30/21, p. 5.
[4] 3 *Bull,* 6/17/22, p. 1.

office, he clearly meant just that, not his own interest. He was one of four—then five—equal partners at the top of the firm, and even when his trial talents were a major source of profitable new business it never occurred to him that any one of the seniors should take more than any of the others.

Once when a man left, Buckner said to some of the other associates, "He's going to make twice as much in that other firm as you're making here—but he deserves it, working for *them*." Anyone could see that while Buckner thought about fees for the office he never thought about wealth for himself. "We all knew," Palmer recalled, "that he would have run this firm on bread-and-water for himself." Root-Clark was the first large law office to distribute to associates as an annual bonus (paid in January, soon after the books were closed) a share of the profits that would otherwise have gone to the partners. What appealed to Buckner about organization was not the budgetary savings but the economy of effort—the elegance, almost the aesthetics—of running a law office properly.

Buckner knew more about every man than just his work; Buckner's own time, his affections and his intellectual resources were always available to anyone in the office. "He was," Root wrote in the memorial essay,

the most satisfactory friend to go to when you had a piece of good fortune. If you got a client, or won the argument of a motion, or even invented what seemed to you a bright idea, it seemed natural to go first-off around to his room to tell him about it. . . . And, per contra, if anything went wrong—if you got so put upon by the press of work that you felt you couldn't carry on, or if you got so angry that you felt your judgment was being warped, or if you just had a piece of plumb misfortune—you could go to Emory and get at once the feeling that you get sometimes from a very good doctor—your temper was calmed down by the application of a longer point of view, your excessive burdens were lifted from your shoulders and redistributed, your ill-luck was cursed and sympathized with, and if necessary you were bundled off on a vacation if that seemed to be the thing.

Such services, and more, were available to the youngest man in the office as well as the senior partners. One associate long remembered a time of family tragedy which had left him financially embarrassed. The blow fell on a Friday; the following Monday when he came in he found a check for a thousand dollars on his desk, with a note to see Mr. Buckner. "I know you're in trouble," Buckner said. "You take that and don't mention it—it's not part of your salary."

In return Buckner expected everyone to accept his full responsibilities toward the office and toward the work that had to be done. People were responsible for work, not for hours; one of Buckner's first reforms when he became U.S. Attorney was to end the practice of noting lawyers' hours of arrival and departure. "I will know," he said, "who's working around here."[5] Vanderbilt Webb, an ardent Yale man, came into Buckner's office the morning of the 1919 Yale-Princeton game and asked if he could take the afternoon (lawyers worked Saturdays in those days) and go off to Palmer Stadium. "*I* don't know," Buckner said. "Can you?" The answer was yes, and Webb went off.[6] If possible, Buckner also wanted from his young employees some of his mystique, the feeling that what went on in the office and among the men who worked in the office was more important than anything else in life. Until he permitted the spell to be broken by his two-year term as U.S. Attorney in 1925-27, he increased every year the number of lunches, coffee hours, cocktail sessions, dinners, evenings to which the men of his firm were invited. There was a "Nisi Prius Golf Club,"[7] and an "office Brook Farm in University Heights."[8] "Truly," said a note in *The Bull,* "life at RCB & H is just one dinner after another."[9] To an associate who begged off from one of those social occasions on the grounds that he wanted to be with his family, Buckner once said, "If you let your life be bound by your wife, your baby and your home, you'll be just as narrow as that."

Buckner's older daughter remembered that her father would sit at the breakfast table for an hour or so on Sunday and be "madly amusing"—and then he would get up and stretch and say, "I think I'll walk down to the office and catch up on the mail." (This was not a matter of bringing in a secretary; Buckner never felt any shame about typing his own correspondence.) For nine years, though he sent his family to the country every summer, Buckner took no vaca-

[5] George S. Leisure to author, 1965.
[6] Reed B. Dawson to author, 1965.
[7] 1 *Bull,* 6/17/20.
[8] 1 *Bull,* 4/10/20.
[9] 2 *Bull,* 1/29/21.

tion; and when he went with his family to the Rockies in 1922 and to Europe in 1923, he was forever writing letters back to the office as other men might write their children.

Before leaving in 1922 he wrote a little grumpily: "How do I feel about the sabbatical summer? Mixed. Ever since I was a boy I have planned someday to go to the Rocky Mountains. . . . However, I cannot say my enthusiasm is unalloyed. I am sure there is no scenery comparable to the ninth and tenth floors. . . . Emphatically I am not going for a rest. Nothing can make one tired that is as much fun as practicing law."[10] Later he cheered up substantially, and wrote lyrically about pack trips:

All the way up we followed, left, returned to, crossed and followed again a torrential mountain stream cascading over rocks, breaking into rainbow sprays and tiny white ribbon falls, catching and laughingly throwing back bright splotches of sunshine, clear as crystal and as cold as the snows which melting gave it birth. It was beautiful beyond description and we marched to its matchless orchestration. Spirits were released, responsibilities forgotten, youth renewed where youth was past.[11]

Ultimately, Buckner bought his wife a summer house at Siasconset, on Nantucket, and added to it year by year until it become one of the showplaces of the island (its next owner was Roy Larsen of Time, Inc.). Sofy would spend six to seven months of the year at Siasconset, gardening and enjoying her house; and when her husband came out for (usually brief) vacations, the high point would be weekend parties for a gang from the office.

If "the office was Buck's whole life to an extraordinary degree," much of the burden would have to fall on Sofy Buckner and her daughters. When he thought about them, he doted on them. In the spring of 1926, he sent Ruth a letter to her school in Cannes:

Dear Offspring
Dear Absent One
Dear Seeker after Truth and Beauty
Dear Mermaid of the wine dark sea
Dear Eater of Caviar and Cheese by stealth in the quiet night, unrevealed save by Diana's chaste and silvered gaze
Dear Budding Cosmopolite

[10] 3 *Bull*, 6/3/22, p. 3.
[11] 3 *Bull*, 8/26/22, pp. 3-4.

Dear Restless One

Dear Fickle One (Thank all the gods for that, who have been worshiped
  since the first ray of light silently signaled the first morn of Time.)

Dear Kid

Time, time, time! Oh, that I could retrieve some of the wasted hours
at this moment when the days and nights are not long enough to serve
the things desired and compelled, most important of all in the desiderata
being this radioing to you, but of necessity yielding to the compellata
(Italian) . . .

  Frinstance . . .[12]

At home and not working, Buckner would read aloud to his
daughters, long stretches of Victorian novels, especially Thackeray.
He would do their homework with them, admiring the Brearley
School for its demands on them, priming them for exams in a half-
serious way. If he caught a piece of conversation about something
his wife or children might want, he would instantly supply it. Once
his older daughter spoke in praise of the sweaters in the window at
Brooks Brothers, and the next afternoon fourteen sweaters arrived
from Brooks. But in the absence of feast there was famine. One
spring when Sofy was already at Siasconset and Ruth, then twenty-
one, was proudly keeping house for him, Buckner forgot to call
home to say he wasn't returning for dinner and might not be back
at all. Finally, at three in the morning, frantic, his daughter called
Max Steuer, opposing counsel in the case Buckner was trying; and
Steuer kindly informed her that her father was sleeping on a couch
in the courthouse.[13] Buckner's impress on his older daughter was
so great that she named her first child "Emory Buckner"—even
though the baby was a girl. The sporadic extravagance of his atten-
tions was so obviously related to their sex that all the ladies of the
family would joke about it, and speculate about whether he would
have been any different at home if one of the children had been a
boy, who might have grown up to be a lawyer and part of his
firm.

2

"The thing that must be stressed about Emory Buckner," said Leo
Gottlieb, who came to RCB & H in the fall of 1920, "is his kindness to

---

[12] Buckner to Ruth, 3/7/26.
[13] Mrs. Gouverneur to author, 1964.

young men." It was an aspect of Buckner's work with which Gottlieb was particularly closely connected. After becoming a partner in the firm in 1925, only five years out of Harvard Law School, Gottlieb served as Buckner's chief assistant and confidant in the annual decision about which of each year's law school crop the firm should hire. The correspondence between the two men, during the years when Gottlieb was heading Root-Clark operations in Santiago de Chile and Boston and the years of Buckner's illnesses, is overwhelmingly devoted to discussions of the applicants, their backgrounds and their apparent qualities. In effect, Buckner did all the hiring for the firm, though he always consulted the other senior partners. ("They of course will do anything I want for personal aides," he wrote Gottlieb in 1927, "but I shall not press it as I want their judgment—not merely consent. That's the way we operate."[14]) Gottlieb interviewed many of the candidates. But Buckner interviewed all of them; his door was always open to any law school senior who had come to New York looking for a job. On New Year's Day, 1931, when Buckner came into his office "to clear my desk which is in very bad shape," he wrote Gottlieb that "I have interviewed extensively at least seventy-five men in two weeks."[15] If Buckner didn't think there was a job for the man at Root-Clark, he would advise him about where there might be jobs, and often he would get on the telephone with his colleagues at other offices to make appointments for the young stranger. Judge Henry J. Friendly of the Court of Appeals for the Second Circuit, an associate and then a partner at Root-Clark, said, "There's never been a lawyer before or since who made such an effort to help younger lawyers." And it was not only the men who worked for him who, a quarter of a century after his death, carried the memory of Emory Buckner's extraordinary kindnesses.

One such case of which there is a written record concerns Arnold Levy, a protégé of Frankfurter who came to New York in 1934 looking for a summer job between his second and third years at Harvard Law School—"a thing," Buckner wrote Frankfurter, "which is getting more and more common. My explanation is the depression, both in its effect upon sons of the former well-to-do or moderately well-to-do

---

14 Buckner to Gottlieb, 1/19/27.
15 Buckner to Gottlieb, 1/1/31.

parents and its effect upon the tutoring racket which so frequently gave a good man a summer's job in Europe or in Maine nursing lame ducks. I was greatly impressed with [Levy]. . . . He did not get a position from us . . . and I wanted him to make some headway in these summer months, both in securing an offer for his regular job and in exploring without commitment some office for the purpose of forming his own conclusions. I took so much interest in him that I finally located Horace Hitchcock, a Yale man and a protégé of mine in the DA office, who is a junior partner of Chadbourne, Stanchfield & Levy in charge of personnel, and told him he must absolutely talk to Levy on Monday morning before he went other places, because the office that got him for the summer, an unimportant thing in itself, would get him upon his graduation if he found the office congenial as well as professionally opportune. Hitchcock did this, and took him on. I had a letter from Levy at the close of his summer term, giving me far more than appropriate thanks for a thing I like to do, but also telling me about his ambition to become a secretary [to a judge] for one year although he had received the offer for next year which I had hoped he would receive from Hitchcock."[16]

Buckner agreed that a year with a judge would be a good idea for Levy. "I am sure," he wrote the law school senior, "you will greatly enjoy the experience and I shall be glad to see you after you come to New York. I think the thing for you to do is to go with C.S. & L. after you finish your secretaryship, and my advice is to conclude that arrangement, if possible, at this time so that you can put it completely out of your mind. If you agree with this and if you would like to have me do so, I shall undertake to see if I cannot arrange the matter for you with my two intimate friends, Mr. Whiteside and Mr. Hitchcock, members of that firm, both of whom I had the pleasure of recommending to the firm at the time they went into the office."[17]

But Levy had had yet a third thought—after his year as clerk to Judge Julian Mack in New York he might have a chance to serve a similar function for Justice Brandeis in Washington. He turned down Buckner's offer with great embarrassment: "As I look back upon the events of the last six months, I am moved to comment

---

[16] Buckner to Frankfurter, 1/21/35.
[17] Buckner to Levy, 1/9/35.

upon what I shall ever consider one of the richest experiences of my youth. At a time when I am ready to leave the realm of the cap and gown for a world which so often is painted as selfish and unkind, it is indeed an inspiration to meet you, whose every action has given the lie to the myth of universal self-seeking."[18]

Buckner was unperturbed: "I think you will find after two years of being secretary to two such distinguished judges that your chances of securing a satisfactory position will be enhanced rather than diminished."[19]

Once a man had worked for Buckner—at Root-Clark, in the U.S. Attorney's office, or in one of the outside teams of "minutemen" he was always putting together for the preparation of large litigations —a private career-development service was always available. "He kept people in mind," said Bethuel Webster, who started his legal career under Buckner in the U.S. Attorney's office. "I remember once he just called up and asked me if I'd like to be a professor of criminal law at Harvard."

Another who in effect started in the law as an assistant to Buckner in the U.S. Attorney's office was David Peck of Sullivan & Cromwell, at one time presiding Justice of New York's First Appellate Department. "He was," Peck recalled, "a one-man employment agency. That's how I got to Sullivan & Cromwell. They needed somebody of my vintage in the litigating department—I was five years out of law school. Dulles called up Buckner: 'Got anybody to meet these specifications?' I was working for IT & T. Buckner called me there, said, 'Call John Higgins at S & C, he wants to talk to you!' " (Buckner was paid back rather cheerlessly for this service the next year: "A *Harvard Law Review* man who wants to be a litigator and was very anxious to get in here," he wrote Gottlieb, "was persuaded at the last moment by Mr. Higgins of Sullivan & Cromwell . . . to go there because of their determination to organize a litigating department in which task 'Mr. Buckner had recently rendered assistance by getting Mr. David Peck.' "[20])

Buckner once explained in a letter to Frankfurter "the great interest that Root-Clark took in placing their own graduates who had se-

[18] Levy to Buckner, 1/18/35.
[19] Buckner to Levy, 1/21/35.
[20] Buckner to Gottlieb, 1/7/31.

cured a Ph.D. degree, finding in that function not only a discharge
of what we conceive to be our responsibility, but also a great personal pleasure in doing so; not only to open up greater opportunities
for our graduates than we could afford to extend in such large numbers and indefinitely, but also to put the corporation or the law
firm lucky enough to secure our best senior associates under deep
obligation to us."[21] Alexander Royce of Chadbourne, Parke, Whiteside & Wolff, who had been at Root-Clark from 1920 to 1924 and
then had headed Buckner's Anti-Trust Division at the U.S. Attorney's
office, remembered that "One of the things that made him loved was
that if people were successful he would always say, 'One of our
graduates, one of our alumni.' I was in parnership with [Bernard]
Knollenberg and [George S.] Leisure, and he sent for me, asked me
if I was happy. I told him the way I'd been trained, in heavy corporate
work, I missed working for a big firm. I was restless for the financial
work. He had sensed this. Chadbourne had come to him and told
him they were looking for a man, and he thought of me. He said,
'Let me handle this.' He handled the negotiating for me. And when
they asked me to come over they made me an offer beyond my
imaginings."

Lowell Wadmond of White & Case gratefully remembered Buckner's original and continuing interest in him: "I came to the bar in
Illinois in March, 1924, with the firm of Tolman, Sexton & Chandler.
Small, fine firm, but specialized in corporate work and examination
of special assessment bonds—a youngster could only carry a brief.
The dean of the Chicago Law School arranged a possible job for
me in Washington. On my way back, I passed through New York
and saw an editorial in the *Herald-Trib,* about 'Emory Buckner's
Law School' at the U.S. Attorney's office. This was July, '25. The
editorial said Buckner was assembling a young staff from all over
the country. On the spur of the moment I walked in, went to the
second floor, saw his secretary: 'Well, Mr. Buckner is trying to get
away for vacation, but . . .'

"When he was working hard, Buckner looked like a lion—big
head, fangs, long hair, leaning forward—short sleeves, button-down
collegiate collar. The first thing he said was, 'You a Republican?'

21 Buckner to Frankfurter, 1/21/35.

"I said, 'Yes—are you?'

"After a while he relaxed. He said, 'Why don't you write me a letter?'

"I said, 'That's no use—if you want a job you have to see people. . . .'

" 'Well,' he said, 'I guess that's right.'

"I went home and wrote. When I came back from my vacation in northern Michigan I found a letter from him offering me a job in Prohibition at three thousand dollars a year. Then it turned out Senator Wadsworth wouldn't approve. The Senator said, 'You can find enough young lawyers in your district without bringing in carpet-baggers.' I wrote Buckner a letter thanking him, and got a telegram back, telling me to come to New York, all expenses paid—'My firm Root, Clark, Howland & Ballantine has a job for you.' But I didn't want that—I wanted to learn to try lawsuits.

"Now along about October 1 he wrote me a letter: 'My wife and daughter and I are going to Lincoln. We'll arrive at LaSalle Street station Thanksgiving morning, and we can have a talk.' He told his wife and daughter to vamoose, and we talked about my situation. He said, 'I understand your problem—you're an English solicitor's clerk.' When he got back to New York he went to talk to Sam Koenig [Republican leader for New York], and Koenig said, 'If you really want him that much, I'll settle it with Wadsworth.'

"I came April 1, 1926, and talked with Buckner about fifteen minutes. He said, 'Let's call John [Harlan] in here—he's got a file of cases for you, something he wants you to argue tomorrow.' The next day I was arguing a contested motion before Judge [William] Bondy, who was a tough guy.

"I stayed at the U.S. Attorney's office until June of 1930—moved over from prohibition to criminal under Tuttle. Around June 1 that year, Judge Knox told me, 'You ought to get out.' I went to see Buckner, who said, 'Yes, Lowell, it's time you got out.'

"I told him I had a chance to go to White & Case. He said, 'It's a great thing, a couple of years with a great New York law firm—it will give you training. But just forget you ever were at the U.S. Attorney's office. Up there, you could say, if somebody didn't do something you wanted him to do, you could press a button and a U.S. Marshal would come take him away. You can't do that any more—you won't have the power of the U.S. Government behind you. Just remember that.'

"We'd have reunion dinners once a year, those of us who'd been in the U.S. Attorney's office under Buckner. As the years went by there was a bond that grew, an affection. I came to feel sort of I was part of his family. I'd get word back that he'd talked about 'Lowell.' He felt we were his sons. We called ourselves 'the Buckner boys.' "[22]

As soon as a decision was made (by the man or by the firm) that a young lawyer should leave Root-Clark, Buckner went to work to find something else for him. One of the last letters he wrote to Frankfurter, a month before he died, was a request to the Supreme Court Justice to check with his friends in Washington and see if he could find "some position appropriate to his age (which is 33), to his abilities (which are highly substantial), and to his great desire to get into administrative work," for John C. Pirie, a Root-Clark associate later to be general counsel for Pan American Airways, a Root-Clark client.[23] Such services were performed even when Buckner badly wanted the man to stay with the firm. In 1929, for example, he wrote a letter to Robert M. Hutchins, then the new dean of the Yale Law School:

"We have upon our staff a man named Wilber G. Katz. He is a graduate from the University of Wisconsin where he received Phi Beta Kappa honors. He graduated from the Harvard Law School in 1926. He was second in his class at Law School and was Note Editor of the *Harvard Law Review*. He is fifty per cent Jew, by which I mean that his father is a Jew and his mother a Gentile. He is one of the smartest fellows and one of the nicest men we have ever taken into our office. It is difficult for me to express our enthusiasm concerning him both on the personal and on the professional side. In the two and a half years that he has been with us he has worked on general matters, has been the principal junior in one of the largest litigations we have ever had, has spent a year doing real estate and Surrogate work, and has spent the last six or eight months in corporate financial work. Everything he touches he does extremely well—difficulties become soluble and disorder becomes ar-

[22] Wadmond to author, 1965.
[23] Buckner to Frankfurter, 2/7/41.

rangement. He has a modesty one does not always find in a young man of his power, which shows that he has a sense of proportion—an intellectual quality not always recognized as such by the *Review* men. . . . Like many very bright men, he has been considering teaching law as a profession ever since he graduated from Harvard. . . . He plans to go to Cambridge next October and take a fourth year, securing a doctor's degree, and work out a job from there. I have told him that that seems to be the wisest course as a general proposition, but I would like to have you see him as I think you may become interested in him. Felix Frankfurter has written him that of course he can secure a fellowship. I am writing you not with the idea that he will take a fourth year at Yale but with the idea that you may be interested in him as a possible addition to your faculty, either next fall, or, if you like him as well as we do, and have no place for him next fall, you may wish to make some arrangement with him for a year from next fall and direct his study at Cambridge accordingly. . . .

"The idea of writing you is wholly my own. His leaving us will be a serious loss because he has a brilliant future ahead of him here."[24]

Hutchins had nothing for Katz, who went on to Harvard and during the next year was in due course considered for an appointment there. President A. Lawrence Lowell was undergoing one of his recurrent fits of anti-Semitism, and Roscoe Pound, always one to roll with the punch, was concerned about recommending Katz for a Harvard faculty. A rumor was spread around the law school that Root-Clark had been pleased to see Katz go because he was pushy and Jewish; Professor E. M. Morgan, head of the faculty committee on appointments, wrote a letter of inquiry on the question to Elihu Root, Jr. Buckner was furious that such accusations could be made about "a young man who has captured the admiration and affection of this entire organization."[25] He wrote to Professor Zechariah Chafee and at length to Morgan, enclosing a copy of his previous letter to Hutchins. He never forgave all concerned for the fact that Katz did not get an appointment at Harvard; and more than a decade later, when Katz was dean of the law school at the University of Chicago, he was still writing about the incident to Frankfurter. His feeling that

24 Buckner to Hutchins, 4/12/29.
25 Buckner to Frankfurter, 1/31/30.

Frankfurter had failed to fight as hard as he should have fought for Katz's appointment was for some years an irritant in their friendship.

3

Though Buckner in an idle moment once counted twenty-two law schools which had produced associates for Root-Clark, Harvard— meaning Frankfurter—was by far the largest single source of his young men. "Buck would call," Frankfurter remembered, "and say, 'Send me six of the good men.' He always bought wholesale. I used to send him all the boys who wanted to go to New York, because he would explore the New York market and find jobs for them." As he wrote Buckner in 1925, "I shunt them, by telling the facts, in your direction."[26]

What Buckner was looking for was brains, and about the only bias he had was a favorable one toward Nebraskans. ("We used to joke," said the Nebraskan Hugh Cox, a Root-Clark associate who became a partner and the leading antitrust litigator in Washington's Covington & Burling, "that if you were from Nebraska and you could read and write, you could get a job with Buckner.") Leo Gottlieb recalled that "he put a great deal more weight on law school grades than even I, who had good grades, thought was reasonable. A man might be out of law school fifteen years, Buckner would still remember his grades: 'He isn't a very good man—he was only a C man.' "

In addition to grades and faculty recommendations, Buckner placed considerable weight on a recommendation from a man's class-mates. "What counts," he once said to Aron Steuer, who was second-ing his father at a trial, "is what the men in your own generation think of you." There survives from 1920 a charming letter signed by three *Harvard Law Review* men who had already been hired by Buckner for the next fall, and had been asked, in effect, if there were any more at home like them. The three editors listed three of their fellows on the *Law Review* "not yet placed, who may go down to New York," and then added as an afterthought: "There is one other member of our board—Jewish—who is going to New York, but he has already taken a trip to New York and will probably soon close up with one of the firms which he called on. This is Leo Gottlieb,

26 Frankfurter to Buckner, 1/15/25.

our Case Editor, an extremely able man, and an agreeable personality."[27]

Buckner replied: "I thank you for your joint letter. It was right to the point. The man in West Virginia and the man in Washington should go home to practice if they come from cities of 50,000 or more and if they have definite connections which will assist them to a good start. . . . If you think it would help these men for me to talk their personal affairs over with them, I should be glad to take the time to do so.

"I should not wish you to speak to Gottlieb about coming into our office, but not at all for the reason of his religion. Our roster demonstrates what we think of that proposition. The reason I do not wish you to speak to him is because he told Mr. Frankfurter who urged him to come and see me that he preferred to go elsewhere. . . . If he should approach you, you may tell him that you know that I should be glad to see him and that opportunities in the office are not entirely foreclosed."[28]

Laporte, however, had already broached the subject to Gottlieb, who wrote Buckner a formal letter of application. On Buckner's immediate and enthusiastic reply (Gottlieb was first in his class), he drew off a little: "Since I have been considering somewhat the possibility of coming back here next year to take an S.J.D. [Doctor of Juridical Science], I am, at this time, a little uncertain whether or not I shall go to New York next fall. Therefore I should like to postpone for a while the interview that you so kindly offered to give me."[29]

Buckner by return mail suggested "that instead of postponing your trip to New York until you decide whether to take another year at Cambridge, it would be better for you to postpone deciding the latter question until after you talk to me. I should think that you could not wisely decide the question of another year of training until after you get more completely in touch with actual practice by going over the situation carefully with me as well as others."[30]

Nevertheless, Gottlieb decided (tentatively, as it turned out) to

[27] Laporte, Royce and Palmer to Buckner, 2/18/20.
[28] Buckner to Laporte, 2/20/20.
[29] Gottlieb to Buckner, 2/23/20.
[30] Buckner to Gottlieb, 2/25/20.

remain at Harvard: "Your very interesting and considerate suggestion in your letter to me made vivid the reason behind the enthusiastic
mention of the name Buckner by all the men in my class who have
been down to N.Y., talking with the various firms, and I thank you
sincerely for your letter." In explanation of his decision to stay,
Gottlieb wrote: "I had been expecting to go to Washington this fall,
as secretary to Mr. Justice Brandeis, but it developed that the present
secretary, Mr. [Dean] Acheson, would stay another year. However,
I have been advised by Prof. Frankfurter, who virtually selects the
men for that place, that if I stay for a fourth year, the very strong
probability is that the position will be available for me at the end
of that year.

"In the second place, my previous education has been largely
scientific.[31] It has not been the broad and liberal training that I am
now convinced should be part of the background of every lawyer."[32]

Presently, however, Gottlieb came to New York for a visit, and
Buckner entertained him at his home on a Sunday. No pressure was
applied ("I thoroughly appreciate your attitude in not wishing to
press me to give up the fourth year," Gottlieb wrote[33]), but in May,
rather suddenly, Gottlieb reversed field and asked if there was still a
place for him. There definitely was.

Another major source of young lawyers for Root-Clark was the
group of Rhodes Scholars at Oxford. The first to arrive in the office
via this route was John M. Harlan, who had gone directly from
Princeton to three years at Balliol, where he studied jurisprudence.
"He worked very hard at Oxford for three years on everything except
law, as we understand it, and is an extremely valuable man," Buckner
wrote Frankfurter in 1925, when Harlan had been in the office about
eighteen months. "How much is due to innate ability and how much
more or less capacity he would have if he had taken the Harvard
Law course, instead of the Oxford course, it is impossible to know."[34]

"I went to Root, Clark, Buckner & Howland," Justice Harlan recalled recently, "because of my brother-in-law, Roger Derby, who

[31] Gottlieb had graduated from the Sheffield School of Yale in 1915 and
worked two years for construction firms before entering law school. In the war
he had served as an officer of Engineers.
[32] Gottlieb to Buckner, 2/29/20.
[33] Gottlieb to Buckner, 5/14/20.
[34] Buckner to Frankfurter, 1/22/25.

was a classmate of Clark's. When Buckner saw me, his comment was, 'Well, you'd better go to law school.' I said, 'Well, if I've got to do that, I'll go into business. I've had enough of studying.' The upshot was that I got a job, time off in the afternoon for the New York Law School thing, where I was given two years' credit for one year's work."

Harlan was to become Buckner's chief assistant in nearly all his major trials, and the one man Buckner took with him from Root-Clark to the U.S. Attorney's office. Toward the end of his life, Buckner wrote to Frankfurter about the "really precocious maturity of a man like John."[35] From early on, while Harlan was still a very junior associate, his recommendation carried considerable weight. It was Harlan who brought into the office Buckner's second Rhodes Scholar, Roy M. D. Richardson. "I am trying to get into the office," Buckner wrote Frankfurter, "another Oxford man who took a double first and then worked two years in the legal department of W. R. Grace & Co. along lines which are not 'helpful' to a law office, and Grennie [Clark] and I propose to rate him as if he had been with us from the beginning."[36] Harlan and Richardson both became partners, and offered daily recommendations for their sort of training. "We are taking on eight new men," Buckner wrote Gottlieb in 1931, "with the idea that we might well add one or two more if Oxford men drift along."[37] With the single exception of George Cleary, every man who became a Root-Clark partner while Buckner lived was a product of either Harvard or Oxford. Most of the Oxford men who left went on to distinguished careers; among them was Judge George T. Washington of the Court of Appeals for the District of Columbia.

Buckner wanted only the best, and when for one reason or another he couldn't get it, he was willing to do without entirely. The distinction, he once wrote Frankfurter, had to be made "between a man who is a good average earnest student and a man who is a real honest to God Laporte or Gottlieb."[38] In 1924, though Root-Clark's volume of business was continuing to increase, he allowed the staff roster to drop back from previous years and explained his reasons in *The Bull:*

[35] Buckner to Frankfurter, 2/7/41.
[36] Buckner to Frankfurter, 1/22/25.
[37] Buckner to Gottlieb, 1/7/31.
[38] Buckner to Frankfurter, undated, 1923.

We shall probably be short-handed for a year, and it may be necessary for us all to take some punishment. During the past twelve months fifty or sixty candidates for positions have been in the office, but, except for Mr. [Robert P.] Hamilton [later a professor at Columbia Law School], none seemed up to our standards. . . . It has seemed to us better for the whole organization to maintain our standard rather than find ourselves in a position where the work might suffer from a lowering of the standard or where we might find ourselves not free to accept candidates who may appear next year and who measure up to our requirements.[39]

Advising a new graduate he really wanted cost Buckner considerable self-restraint, but he felt a first obligation to the man. A letter to Gottlieb once described a candidate who "said he had had a very hard time in deciding between the Cravath office and our own. He has eliminated all other offices. I told him he would not regret it whichever one he took. . . . [A]fter all was said and done he must use his instinct."[40] Buckner wrote Frankfurter in 1925: "All of our invitees have not yet finally determined on New York, and I do not wish to push them or even argue New York to them."[41] The farthest he ever went in selling the job, probably, was with George Cleary, who was already six years out of law school in 1920, and working for the Bureau of Internal Revenue in Washington. Even here, his letter is suffused with the consciousness that a young man must be concerned first of all with his own situation:

"I can readily understand your perplexity, but it is impossible to forecast the future. You have two things to decide: (1) whether you want to come to New York; (2) whether if you do you want to come to our office. Answering the second question first, our office is, I believe, as good for you as any in town both from the standpoint of getting experience which you need outside of tax work, and from the standpoint of the possibility of a permanent association. So far as finances go, we are 'charged' by some and 'credited' by others with paying everyone more than the 'market price.' We have associates who are mature and have been in other offices before coming with us. They find themselves receiving more than they did before elsewhere and more than they think they would have received had

---

[39] 5 *Bull*, 10/18/24, pp. 1-2.
[40] Buckner to Gottlieb, 1/12/28.
[41] Buckner to Frankfurter, 1/13/25.

they remained with their former offices. Then we have a number of younger men who have never been anywhere else. They find themselves receiving a little more here than their classmates in other offices.

"You see it is impossible to predict how valuable you will prove in tax work or how much tax work we may get. We are not like a commercial house with fixed institutional 'salaries' or definite 'positions.' Had you been a single man, we should probably have felt that $3,600 with a $900 guaranteed dividend would have been adequate, perhaps a little more than 1914 men are getting in other offices, though with us much more depends on the man than the vintage. . . .

"If you come to New York, you will look back after two years or so when you get the New York situation 'sized up' and see how utterly impossible it is for me to do more than give you the general talk on New York which I did and the particular guarantee for yourself for one year. If I should say that you would be advanced in 1921, it might be unfair to us because things might work out in such a way as to make a continuance of your $6,000 guarantee the only fair thing. . . .

"You have this advantage: You will be coming as an associate of a firm which has hunted you up and invited you for a particular purpose: tax work for your major activity. You are not in the usual case of a man's applying for a job. You have the advantage of being asked to be the first assistant of Mr. Ballantine and Mr. Howland in that work. If the work develops and if you prove useful, you will be in the position of having a specialty in an organization where such a specialty is required. Since so far we have not had routine tax work, it is probable that for the most part your tax work will be important. In fact, for routine tax work you can rapidly train an assistant.

"I do not know whether I have helped you or not. As an expert on New York for Western men with no definite connection elsewhere I recommend this association. If you do not do as well as I think you will, it is because you are not as good a man as I think you are. If you do not do as well as you think you ought, it will be because New York is not as good as place as you think it is. What New York actually is and what you can actually do in a city practice can only be discovered by experience, and it may well be a good plan to come on here even if you think you may later go elsewhere. That was my plan. Others have stayed a while and gone, finding in their new field that their experience and connections here proved valuable."[42]

The one argument Buckner would never permit as a legitimate reason for choosing an office was the starting salary. "Nothing in your life will you later consider quite so immaterial," he wrote Arnold Levy, "as the precise amount of pennies which you draw from the first law office you enter. I mention this because during the past fifteen years I have found an astonishing lack of judgment upon this matter. Boys just out of law school looking for the best possible professional apprenticeship frequently think they are just entering business and swinging a real-estate deal."[43]

In early 1927 Root-Clark lost to Cotton & Franklin a *Harvard Law Review* editor named Edmund Burke, and Buckner wired Gottlieb: "Believe Burke as well as many young men influenced by trifle larger salary not being able to appreciate financial and spiritual advantages our system. . . . Time for us to join in standardizing rates."[44]

Presently Buckner started an institution on Wall Street. In a letter to Frankfurter, he called it "the big employers' trust. . . . For reasons which you would thoroughly approve—there being a factual background—I called twenty firms to lunch—knowing someone in each —and we made an effort to stabilize the situation for a probationary period of fifteen months. I do not expect anyone to believe it but it was at least fifty percent in the interest of the young men. You will be interested to learn that there was a hot discussion on the question of discriminating between A and B men, A men being those with either an A or a *Review* election and B men being all others. For three sessions of an hour and a half each this discussion waged, and I must say the arguments were about equally strong. I don't know which side you would be on. Without thinking it out very carefully, we have always been on the no-discrimination basis. We realized that the men would separate in time, but for the start, although we always asked men not to disclose their salaries, we treated

[42] Buckner to Cleary, 2/18/20.
[43] Buckner to Levy, 1/21/35.
[44] Buckner to Gottlieb, 2/2/27.

all alike. We thought it would help a good B man's morale. He would pull off his coat and say, 'Thank God Bull Warren does not belong to this firm,' if by any chance he blamed the Bull for his failure to get an A. Sullivan & Cromwell, with more thought, and much more feeling, had the same idea. Likewise Cotton & Franklin. On the other hand, Hughes and Cravath firms were equally strong contra. So we compromised by having an enforced discrimination last only for nine months out of the probationary fifteen.

"At the last session and for a period of five minutes were the rates discussed. They were proposed by a firm, not our own, paying among the highest, and adopted. The rates were a mistake, because too low. It came over me later. I can't hope that faculty members and candidates will . . . believe if told that the precise salary is immaterial, inasmuch as the saving would not pay a small fraction of the OFFICE BOYS' payroll in a large office. So I got the group together again this fall [1928], and all instantly agreed that the rates had been put too low—some of the leaders having had the same experience and feeling that I had—so they were immediately raised and made permissively retroactive as to the crop just in. Again the old flame over discrimination burst out and that again took an hour, but instead of the conference being evenly divided, this time some had changed their minds and the mandatory discrimination was abandoned. . . .

"Of course, Root-Clark (between ourselves) has always paid more than anyone else because of our dividend system, but that was secret and a man was pledged to keep it secret so the precise amount of it never became known to the other firms. It did not hurt them because during recruiting a young man never figured it. It has always put us way out in front in pay although we have always been and still are the poorest large firm—meaning by that the five or six big ones. This dividend we do not save. Under the combination we do not pay it to the boys the first fifteen months, but we simply turn it over to the men who are beyond the fifteen months."[45]

4

Buckner's counseling of the law school seniors brought him into growing conflict with Frankfurter over the question of the "fourth year" program at law school which lay close to Frankfurter's heart.

[45] Buckner to Frankfurter, 11/25/28.

At one point in the dialogue Frankfurter felt so strongly that he complained to Grenville Clark about Buckner's "voraciousness for juniors." The issue had been raised as early as Leo Gottlieb's indecisions in 1920, but it first came to a head in the matter of Henry J. Friendly in 1926-27.

Frankfurter had chosen Friendly to be law clerk to Justice Brandeis (a benefice which was in his gift) for the October, 1927, term of the Supreme Court, with the expectation that Friendly would return for his fourth year in Cambridge after completing his time with Brandeis. Then Frankfurter agreed to teach at Oxford in 1928-29, which would have meant that he would not be in Cambridge while Friendly was in attendance, and he suggested to Friendly that he take his fourth year first, going down to Brandeis thereafter. It was very much in his mind that Friendly would thereupon join the Harvard Law School faculty.

Friendly had worked for Buckner in the U.S. Attorney's office (on Frankfurter's recommendation) during the summer between his second and third years, and he now came to Buckner for advice. "I have advised Friendly," Buckner wrote Frankfurter, "not to take a fourth year at Cambridge but to go to directly to Brandeis. I suppose you may feel that he ought to take both a fourth year and a year at Washington. I asked you once why you were so often late at appointments and why you were unwilling to stop a conversation in order to keep an appointment and begin another promptly and you replied 'intellectual greed.' I think you were right. Now, when one goes to a buffet supper and finds everything under the sun spread out for selection, he simply has to choose. If he takes a little turkey and a little ham, he should kiss the lobster salad goodbye without regret. I told Friendly you and I were in agreement [about] a substantial experience [of] practice before teaching even if he should finally decide to teach, as to which he is by no means certain and as to which a man of 23 ought not to be certain. I think, in his particular case, he has had enough of school for a while and that going to Brandeis next year is just exactly right. Then, of course, for the year after, he will want to come to 31 Nassau."[46]

Frankfurter reacted almost violently. "Inasmuch as you are advising men and your views are properly influential," he wrote, "and

46 Buckner to Frankfurter, 11/24/26.

since you are acting yourself on assumptions in regard to the fourth year, I suggest that you better 'take a look,' inform yourself more about the fourth year than you are at present informed. In essence, you regard the fourth year as a kind of pleasant gentlemanly indulgence of the same order as having a year in Europe. Let me come to a square issue with you on that by putting it this way: knowing all I know about practice and having regard to the importance that I attach to the requirement that lawyers have also capacity for forecasting the direction that law and legislation will take, say for the next twenty years, and knowing what I do about the content of fourth-year work, I say without hestitation that if I had your responsibility toward recruiting for offices, I should aim for fourth-year men. So far as possible, I would prefer men who had a fourth year and encourage men to take a fourth-year preliminary to getting into my office. This on the most practical of grounds!

"To be a little specific, I assume you would not want to have any men in your office who did not have corporations, conflicts and constitutional law. I am wholly confident that the courses in jurisprudence, comparative law (usually called Roman law) and administrative law are more valuable as bread-and-butter courses, have more 'cash-value' than corporations, conflicts or constitutional law. . . . For grasp of operating ideas, for stimulation in legal resourcefulness, for adaptation of old methods to new situations, for preparedness in meeting new and changing conditions, the fourth year is more than worth its weight in gold. . . . It gives these men not only more data for practice, greater mastery in technique, great legal inventiveness, but compels them, by being thrown on their own mentality, by being compelled to think out things in a way they are not compelled either in the undergraduate years or even in an office, to become maturer minds and more solid men than they otherwise would be . . .

"What surprises me about all the lawyers with whom Friendly talked in New York, and even about your comments to him, is that you did not treat Friendly as a very special case—a man of truly extraordinary talents, under no pressure of immediacies, still very young and potential of very great things in all sorts of ways. . . . [D]on't you think it is terribly important that there be deposited in an unusually talented person like Friendly thoughts and reflections, not merely with reference to his success in New York during the next five or ten years, but that he should keep in mind what would equip him for the rest of his life as a civilized, reflective mind, with a deep inner life, instead of becoming as narrow-minded and as sterile as are all but a negligible few of the leading members of the present day bar? . . .

"And this brings me to one more matter. Nothing saddens me more than that during all these years I have not known of a single New York lawyer of importance encouraging anybody to pursue the profession of a law teacher. In fact, quite the contrary! All their weight has been thrown in discouragement of men who might be tempted by the allurements of life at the law school. I am not now saying that at twenty-three a man should choose to be a law teacher, although frankly I don't know why not, any more than choosing any other profession at twenty-three. Nor am I saying that men should be vigorously pushed in the direction to whom the career doesn't present itself as a choice. What does astound me is that insofar as the influence of the bar is concerned, insofar as it helps to shape the ambitions and ideals of young men, no influence whatever emanates from it towards the kind of a life that Ames and Gray and Thayer led. Unless men of absolutely first-rate quality pursue the life of a teacher, you might as well close your law schools. . . . And I think lawyers ought to stop long enough in their preoccupation with their daily chores to reflect on why significant men in the law, after the pressure of daily practice is removed, men like Taft and Root and Brandeis and Cardozo and Learned Hand, are all in agreement that when it comes to a life full of joy for the individual and of greatest possible service to law and therefore to society, the life of a law teacher ought to be made as inviting to young men of talents as possible. Certainly I expect no disagreement from you on that score."[47]

Buckner replied somewhat abashed: "Of course, I cannot pass intelligently on a fourth year without detail[ed] knowledge of just what a fourth year is. I am a little surprised that you appear to attach so much importance to it as against other alternatives. A brilliant man like Friendly gets to the point where he feels he has 'gone to school' about enough for one stretch, and I should attach less importance in his case to doing a fourth year. . . . I never attempt to

[47] Frankfurter to Buckner, 11/30/26.

dissuade anyone from the career of a teacher if he has any inclination in that direction. It may be that I have at times suggested the economic factor in the situation, the raising and education of children, etc., but that I think is a kindness. But it is most essential to get the right men into teaching, and you have frequently asserted that you do not want them prematurely committed but prefer to get them a few years later and not only will they be more valuable as teachers but more certain of their decision. If Friendly finally wants to teach, he can easily do the fourth-year work as, of course, law professors do much more studying when they begin teaching than they ever did as students. I hope Friendly will come with us after he finishes with L.D.B. and he can make up his mind in three or four years what he wants to do and still be young enough to be a beginner."[48]

But five years later the issue rose again, with Buckner questioning not only the value of the fourth year at law school, but even the significance of a term as a judge's law clerk. (Indeed, Buckner had stolen personnel from judges before, though never one of Frankfurter's boys. In 1926 he had talked Arthur Schwartz into working at the U.S. Attorney's office rather than working for Justice Harlan Stone at the Supreme Court. "He said," Schwartz recalled, " 'Why go to the Supreme Court? I'll hire you to argue a case before the Supreme Court.' ") Now the subject of the dispute was Telford Taylor, later an American prosecutor at Nuremberg and a professor at Columbia Law School, whom Frankfurter had destined to be law clerk to one of the Hands or to Julian Mack. "During the last twelve years," Buckner wrote Taylor, "I have been asked over and over again to advise upon this question. . . . My position has always been as follows:

"I do not regard such a position as a better opportunity than a good law office. It is, in a general way, a projection of law review work for another year. A man will deal intensively with records, which is an excellent training, but he will also deal with records in a law office and with facts before they have become crystallized into a record. He still deals with facts, whatever his department in whatever office, even though removed from actual or potential litigation. I always wind up my advice with the statement, however, that a man should not take the decision too seriously or worry about his age for fear

48 Buckner to Frankfurter, 12/21/26.

of losing a vital year in the practice of his profession. If you were a year older you would not think of retiring from the Law School on the ground that you were too old to begin to practice law. . . .

"In my advice as to taking a fourth year, as to a secretaryship, as to teaching a year, I always say that a young man should look at the matter from the point of view of his own personal pleasure, and not from a utilitarian angle. . . . Professor Frankfurter and I differ sharply on this (except as to teaching). He feels that ten years later a man with a fourth-year training or a secretaryship will have a sense of strength he would otherwise miss. I do not believe that this is true.

"You remember I told you that all seems to be grist at the mill of maturity. I remember having a talk with _____ several years ago, a brilliant member of the Review Board, who sought my advice as to a fourth year and as to a secretaryship. His father wished him to enter a certain New York firm, for personal reasons, if he should come to New York. It is a good firm. He had put his problem to them, and they had told him that he would not be worth any more to them after a fourth year or a secretaryship than he was at the moment. I told him we took a different position ourselves, and although he did not desire to enter our own firm, we would, as a matter of fact, be willing to give him second-year rating whether he took a fourth year at Cambridge, became a secretary in Washington, went around the world, tutored a lame duck, or drove a taxicab in New York City for a year. I told him that in his particular case I had added the last possibility because it was apparent that that form of activity would do him far more good and be a better legal education than any of the other possibilities. . . .

"In your own case, you are mature for your years, you have had one year of teaching, and I advise you to enter an office next fall."[49]

Buckner did not send a copy of this letter to Frankfurter, but young Taylor shared it with his professor. Frankfurter wrote to Buckner:

" 'That's an awfully slick letter,' said Marian after reading your Telford Taylor document, and added, 'It's almost fairer than you have a right to expect from Emory, considering that he probably disapproves altogether of fourth year or a secretarial year.'

"If I were arguing the case against you before an appropriate tri-

[49] Buckner to Taylor, 1/9/32.

bunal, I should stand on your *facts,* reinforced by my own. . . . [A] half dozen of the juniors in your own service have had a secretarial year and were glad of it. . . . They get something they would not get any other way, certainly not so well, namely, a concrete and personal participation in an authoritative way of how the fellows who brew 'the law' really brew it. And that you learn neither in the law school nor in a law office in the way in which men who are behind the scenes actually get an insight into things that, of course, you and I know about, but know about as a result of long years of experience and intimate familiarity with judges—experiences that come, on the whole, to very few people at the bar. . . .

"While you make a concession to the secretarial experience as a 'happy form of indulgence,' it's an obviously argumentative concession without any conviction behind it. This is where I find myself most in disagreement with you. I think your attitude derives from your own unique qualities and your own unique fullness of life at the New York Bar. I think you are not adequately aware of the discontent that rumbles in the hearts of many of your own contemporaries and of younger men, and therefore undervalue the importance of stocking up their intellectual and spiritual larder with resources to draw upon when times of doubt and questioning and discontent arise—resources that will be secure against all the corrosions or attacks of outward circumstances. . . . I venture to believe I know more about those things than you do, because from time to time former students come and talk to me as men talk in the confessional. And a year with men like Julian [Mack] and B [Learned Hand] and Gus [Augustus Hand] —whom you and I take for granted as to be had for the asking because we have been lucky enough to have had them as friends since we were kids—taps veins of wisdom and leaves memories that are distinctly important sources of strength and illumination when in later life strength and illumination are needed."[50]

Buckner defended himself in reply to Frankfurter, closing with the statement that "your guess is as good as mine and it will never be settled because we can not have the same guinea pig who both is and is not a secretary."[51] But in his next letter to Taylor, he withdrew the one negative example he had originally given, that of "the Editor-in-

[50] Frankfurter to Buckner, 1/13/32.
[51] Buckner to Frankfurter, 1/18/32.

Chief of the *Yale Law Journal,* a man of thirty, [who] asked my advice as to becoming secretary of the Chief Justice. I advised against it rather strongly in his particular case. He took the job and regretted it."[52] Now Buckner added that this young lawyer "later went into a good office for two years and regretted that and then went into business for two years and regretted that, so you can see his situation is quite special."[53] In the end, Buckner seems to have lost the argument: Taylor not only took a clerkship; he turned down the job offer from Root-Clark.

[52] Buckner to Taylor, 1/9/32.
[53] Buckner to Taylor, 1/18/32.

CHAPTER SEVEN

Buckner's Young Men—II

1919-1925

"[T]his is a splendid place," Buckner wrote Roscoe Pound, soliciting candidates for the firm, "on account of the necessity of our very young men taking a great deal more responsibility than ordinarily falls to their lot. This is because we are so young and have grown so abnormally fast. There are fifty of us lawyers altogether and I am the oldest man in the shop. So you see it is the most outstanding young man's club in town."[1]

In 1922, when the office reached the size of thirty-nine lawyers and became one of the half-dozen biggest in town, Buckner was only forty-four. Apart from the potent name of Root, the appeal of Root-Clark to the new graduates was its youth and vigor, and the drive and sparkle of its most publicized partner. But delivering on the promise of the interview was no easier for Buckner than it was for the applicants. What made it possible for him to keep up with so many men in the office was the fact that his professional career became exclusively trial work—which is exhausting but sporadic. Other men in the office had clients who needed constant attention in one way or another; Buckner had cases to be handled in individual bursts of work. Between the bursts he could enjoy himself, organizing the office and cultivating the young men.

"He kept the contact," said Herbert Brownell, who spent two years

[1] Buckner to Pound, 1/2/28.

at Root-Clark en route from Nebraska to a partnership in Lord, Day & Lord and a position as Attorney General of the United States. "His purpose was to keep you from feeling you were just a cog in the wheel. We all felt the sky was the limit—we were with a young, growing outfit."

From 1920 to 1925 Gottlieb was one of Buckner's assistants in litigations. (When Buckner went to the U.S. Attorney's office, Gottlieb got out of the courtroom. "I hated litigation," he said. "I just liked Buckner.") He remembered that "at a trial, Buckner would be sure to give you some role to make you feel you were participating —even if it was only questioning to identify documents. He thought about that sort of thing, gave it consideration. He'd usually let assistants argue procedural motions, and even appeals on them." At the U.S. Attorney's office, Buckner told the newspapermen that the proper form for reporting his actual courtroom appearances was to say that he was assisting his assistants in the trial; and except in the Daugherty-Miller case, where issues of great public importance were involved, he gave his assistants the invaluable professional publicity of making the opening statement to the jury.

He was forever pushing the young men ahead by talking about them. "If anybody asked him about a young man here," William P. Palmer recalled, "he'd never say, 'He's doing fine.' He'd talk ten minutes about the man." Melvin Steen, who came to Root-Clark from Minnesota in 1929, as a result of Buckner's letters to the deans of Midwestern law schools asking for recommendations of the top men in the graduating class, remembered a visit from "some important businessmen in Minneapolis whom I did not know. They had a substantial lawsuit against an Eastern firm, and they wanted it handled on a contingent basis. They asked around Minneapolis, and somebody gave them my name. I took their letter to Buckner, and he said, 'Well, we rarely take contingency cases, but if these people will come to New York, we'll talk to them.'

"We spent four hours with these businessmen when they came. Buckner was in the middle of preparing the Bank of the United States case, but he took the time. Whenever they'd ask a question, he'd say, 'Well, my tentative opinion on that is as follows—but I wouldn't want to express a final opinion until I consult with Mel Steen here.' He was coony. He always expressed his opinion first so he'd never be in a position of disagreeing with me—it was a deliberate build-up job."

Buckner also had the gift of ennobling lesser chores by doing them himself when necessary—even to the point of taking dictation from juniors. Palmer remembered a trip to Montreal on a case for a client of Silas Howland. At the last minute, Howland couldn't go, and asked Buckner to take over. The conference was on a Sunday, and Buckner and Palmer arrived at the deserted offices of local counsel late on the Saturday. Buckner said to Palmer, "You know how to draw this contract and I know how to type—so you dictate it and I'll type." Palmer later recalled, "There he was in this vacant office in Montreal, rattling away at the keyboard. Once he read the contract, of course, believe me, he had some suggestions."

When possible, Buckner kept up personally with how the young men were doing on their assignments. "When I arrived," Henry J. Friendly recalled. "they apprenticed me to G. Clark. He'd had a nervous breakdown and came back after a year, and they thought he ought to have competent help. The problem was, he didn't know how to use help. Mr. Buckner came into my room and found me doing crossword puzzles. He said, 'You don't seem to have much to do.' I said, 'Mr. Clark doesn't give me anything to do. I like *him,* but I don't like not having anything to do.' Buckner smiled and said, 'Well, we thought it might work out that way. Now I guess we'd better find you something to do.' "

But if the office was to be held together as a unit over a long growing process, Buckner could not rely on his own browsing; he needed institutions. He exalted the managing attorney, an associate who was expected to be, as *The Bull* once put it, "a general manager, comptroller, office manager, purchasing agent, personnel director and welfare director all rolled into one";[2] and he built up the office of managing clerk into a separate entity manned by two associates and four or five law school students, to keep track of litigations and do procedural research for the men who were trying the cases. Until the fall of 1918 the few associates met every Saturday morning in Buckner's office to talk over all pending matters; then for a year the growing group of young lawyers were fed a weekly lunch at the Bankers Club grill room; then for two years the large staff dined

[2] 5 *Bull,* 10/11/24, p. 2.

together at the University Club every six weeks. Finally Buckner turned over the routine job of keeping in touch with everything to the managing attorney, and instituted written "progress reports" (on pink paper), which everyone was to file every other week.

Despairing briefly of getting the whole organization into his dinners, Buckner established in the fall of 1920 a fortnightly dinner of "the Wranglers" for the men working in his own litigation department; at these seminars (invariably broken for a "recess" of "music and song"), half a dozen men would present for the edification of their comrades the legal issues in pending litigation. Presently the other lawyers in the office were also invited, and the Wranglers dinners were cut down to one a month. To occupy the now dropped Wranglers dates between the monthly sessions, Buckner tried to institute a "Round Table" dinner at which attendance would not be compulsory, but the new affair would not take. Instead, a monthly lunch at the Bankers Club, to which each of the firm's six departments sent delegates, kept the seniors in touch with what the juniors were thinking.

Social events in and out of the office helped Buckner impress his personality on the associates. Several late afternoons a week, he would trot up the corridors poking his head into the juniors' offices to announce "a committee meeting in fifteen minutes"; and then everybody would gather in Buckner's large room to drink whiskey out of paper cups—good whiskey, too, through the depths of prohibition.

The Buckners were always convivial. Through the 1910s they had entertained a great deal at their apartment on Park Avenue. Having hugely enjoyed the conversation at the "House of Truth" where Frankfurter and his bachelor friends lived in Washington, Buckner invited for the evenings writers and editors, architects, sculptors and artists, city officials and business men with Fusion political interests—as well as his fellow lawyers. Frankfurter would stay overnight almost every time he passed through New York (indeed, the Frankfurters lived with the Buckners most of the summer of 1926, when Frankfurter was a visiting professor at Columbia). Frankfurter remembered particularly the visits in the 1910s, when Ruth Buckner was a little girl. "How I loved that child!" he said shortly before his death. For her part, she remembered her father's coming home just before dinner one evening and finding Frankfurter with her while she ate in the kitchen; and saying, "Frankfurter stands by the kitchen sink,/Eating himself up, link by link."[3]

Toward the end of the 1910s, the Buckners' entertaining grew increasingly social. Goldthwaite Dorr, Buckner's former chief in the Stimson office and host to the Buckner family of 1908 and 1909, had been in Washington during the war, and remembered picking up with the Buckners again at the beginning of 1919. "They were high, wide and handsome," he recalled. "We felt they were losing the cutting edge —they thought it was a grand thing to live on Park Avenue and spend all that money." It was fiercely expensive—the apartment, the rented summer houses in Rye, the two in help, private school for Ruth and then for Betty, and medical care for a third daughter. "One day," Dorr remembered, "Emory called me aside and told me he thought he'd been stupid—'Spending everything I make and a little more'— and he said he was cutting it out and going to live on University Heights. That was a hard thing to do, and I admired him for it."[4]

With the move to University Heights Buckner gained early morning and evening as well as daytime access to many of his young men. Around the four-story wood-frame house which he bought there were a number of rather inexpensive apartments, where the young men could live conveniently. "He'd have a drink or two with the young lawyers at the office," said Leo Gottlieb. "Then at night a number of us would come over and we'd sit over a highball and talk about the office." In the mornings, the RCB & H University Heights contingent (which at one time included more than a third of the associates) would walk together three miles to the El station at the Polo Grounds and ride down together to Cortlandt Street. (Every so often they would be joined by Judge John C. Knox, who also lived in the neighborhood, and whose daughter every morning shared Ruth and Betty Buckner's taxi to their school in Manhattan.) The men who held Buckner's memory most green and fragrant a quarter of a century after his death were those who had first come to work for him during the six years he lived on University Heights.

In 1921 the University Heights residents in the office formed a "Buckwick Club," a play-reading group which met at the Buckner house and launched itself with Wilde's *Lady Windemere's Fan*. Later

[3] Ruth Gouverneur to author, 1964.
[4] Dorr to author, 1965.

that spring the members of this organization gave a dance for the office; and the next fall the nonmembers reciprocated the favor. The next dance was paid for by the office itself; and though there were several hiatuses, an office dance became an annual affair.

Most memorable to all the participants was the institution of the annual dinner, held the evening after what Buckner called "dough day," when Elihu Root, Jr. summoned the associates into his office one by one and awarded them their annual "dividend." These affairs were stag and (to say the least) informal. The seniors told stories, some of them scatological, football-playing members of the office tackled each other, on one occasion a piano was tipped out of one of the big windows of the University Club, on another a lawyer suffered injuries when the table on which he had risen to make a speech was removed from under him. Grievances were lightly disposed of, as when Howland offered "a carefully prepared statement directed against the doctrine of mutual obligation and cooperation which, so he continued, under the nefarious and sinister administration of E. Rabelais Buckner was undermining the independence and initiative of each and all of us."[5] The centerpiece of the entertainment, however, was always a group of parodies written by Buckner himself with some of the associates, relating to recent events in the office or its practice—for example, "Dick Nicks the Divvy" (sung to the tune of "Upidee"):

> The Trainer Manville case is in,
> Rotten luck, rotten luck,
> The cost is mounting up like sin,
> What was wrong with Buck?
> We took it on contingent fee,
> We did, alas, the more fools we!

Not every associate was equally delighted with the antics of the annual dinner. "Some of the partners who were difficult when sober," one of them said many years later, "become impossible when drunk." Roy Richardson, who did like the parties, remembered that he had been hired to report for work the Monday following one of them: "It was debated whether I should be invited, but decided that it would give a new young man a decidedly wrong impression." Buck-

[5] 5 *Bull,* 2/2/24.

ner worked hard on the parties personally, night after night at home with the song writers, and valued them almost superstitiously. "The first year I was with Root-Clark," James A. Farmer remembered in his later office as solicitor of AT & T, "I missed the annual dinner— had to be in the South on a real-estate problem. When I came back he gave a party at his house and had the people who had written the songs to re-enact the annual dinner for me—for a person who had been with the firm only a year! To do that for a neophyte—to me he was a great man."

2

The most original of Buckner's organizational ideas was an intra-office newspaper, published originally on January 24, 1920, as *Weekly Bulletin*, a name presently shortened to *The Bull*. This journal, edited by one of the associates and narrowly restricted in its circulation, announced new matters that had come into the office, activities and theories in litigation or prospective litigation, developments (real and fictional) in the personal lives of the staff. It had its lighter moments —for example, an amended "Section 23" to the

Office Code of Practice and Procedure: Whenever any lawyer in this office shall be absent during regular business hours and while so absent is known to be playing golf, in answer to the inquiries as to the where-abouts of said lawyer, the following form should be used:
Mr. _____ is out in Westchester County (or other county, if known), going over a piece of property.[6]

In its early years, however, the first purpose of *The Bull* was to provide a forum in which Buckner could preach to the young lawyers his philosophy of practice. "A man's training will be broadened," he wrote in one issue, explaining one of the reasons behind the publication,

his fun increased, his sympathies enriched, if he takes a lively interest in what is going on. Get in the habit of lunching and talking with men with whom you are not constantly working. In this way one frequently discovers an opportunity to jump in and lend a hand where in normal events he might never be called upon. It may be proof-reading, it may

[6] 4 *Bull*, 11/11/23, p. 6.

be looking up law, it may be the giving or the criticism of an idea. Whatever it is, it helps the office, and without the office, where are we?[7]

Some years later, enclosing one of these homilies by "my favorite author," Buckner would write deprecatingly to Learned Hand about "a little Pollyanna piece of pabulum which I handed out to the young fellows in the office in our little office paper. This sort of thing is designed to anesthetize them so they will continue to work as poorly paid law clerks and like it!"[8] In fact, he took these essays seriously, and in his last years he reprinted many of them.

Two subjects predominated: loyalty to the office as an office and the necessity for maximum care in the interests of both the office and its clients. "My definition of an enthusiast," Buckner wrote in one of the earliest issues, "is a man who says at every opportunity 'I rise to make a few remarks on R.C.B. & H.' "[9] A month later he wrote: "Suppose each of us were alone in practice. With what serious concern we would exhaust every job, realizing that if we fell down it would cause irreparable harm. And yet precisely that situation exists here. One's work cannot be checked in detail. Each of us should do every job as if no one else is ever to see it. Let us be tremendously serious about it. It is the price of responsibility delegated. . . . Let us develop not *alibis* but clients."[10]

Prompt work [Buckner suggested a year later], letters answered, clients pursued when in default, no mistakes, no personal engagements, clients' troubles carried on the train, on a walk, to bed—above all care pricked with speed, and speed checked with care—these will not get all the business in the world, but are guaranteed to get some business with unfailing regularity. Such work will not get a trust company owned by a man whose son-in-law is a lawyer; or a trust company one of the controlling officers of which is a brother-in-law of a lawyer; or a bank the president of which is a brother-in-law of an attorney (names and addresses of these actual cases will not be furnished on request accompanied by stamped envelope) but there is quite a little business which, as Mr. Buckwick would say, is without the curtilage of consanguinity.[11]

[7] 5 *Bull,* 3/22/24, p. 6.
[8] Buckner to Hand, 6/1/33.
[9] 1 *Bull,* 3/6/20, p. 2.
[10] 1 *Bull,* 4/10/20, pp. 1-2.
[11] 2 *Bull,* 4/30/21, pp. 2-3.

He was a hard man to satisfy. Throughout the early 1920s the firm's reputation soared; but in early 1921 Buckner wrote that "A look back over 1920 does not reveal a satisfactory quality of work taken as a whole."[12] At the end of that year, though he saw "decided improvement all along the line," he also felt that "there have been many mistakes made—a few of them embarrassing, and some of them harmful—and much needs to be done."[13] In late 1923 he was still complaining that "We have made professional mistakes during the past year. There are instances where, although no concrete mistakes have been made, clients have not received that last 10% of effort and sustained concern which produces far-reaching results."[14]

Month after month in the pages of *The Bull,* Buckner hammered on the need for care. "You so often hear people speak with horror," he wrote, "of the time in England when two hundred offenses, some of them trivial, were capital crimes. They speak as if slight offenses are no longer followed by such cruel consequences. As a matter of fact clients hang lawyers constantly for trivial infractions of the statutes of capacity and care."[15]

Buckner's phrase for what happened when standards of care were violated was "paying the freight." In 1924 under that title he made a full statement of the problem and the office policy:

For several years one of the best law offices in town in the line of work to which most of its attention is devoted had represented an active corporation. During this time one man in the office had done all of its work and given satisfaction. Recently his task was a bit out of line of his experience. Any one of a dozen distinguished members of that organization could have given him a tow up the first hill but he chose to operate on his own power. The client was much dissatisfied and is through with the office.

A substantial client recently went to a lawyer for the first time. This lawyer is practicing alone with one or two assistants. The client had much present work and large possibilities. The lawyer turned the job over to an assistant who worked on it for four weeks and the corporation papers were sent to the client. A few days later the lawyer called and said that his assistant had done everything wrong. He asked for the papers and

---

[12] 2 *Bull,* 1/29/21, p. 2.
[13] 2 *Bull,* 12/24/21, p. 3.
[14] 4 *Bull,* 12/29/23, p. 1.
[15] 4 *Bull,* 5/26/23, pp. 2-3.

said he would do the work over. The client declined with thanks and looked elsewhere.

Certainly in the first case, and probably in the second, serious injustice was inflicted upon the office. Nevertheless, an office is always judged by a client in accordance with the particular job in hand. While the loss of substantial clients is serious, the damage inflicted does not stop there; but for years to come the experience will be narrated whenever either office is brought up for consideration and thus the office keeps on paying the freight.

Both clients are now in our office. *Hinc illae lacrimae!*

For many years the basic principle of our organization has been to have more men on a piece of work than is usual or than may be absolutely necessary. The objective is to reduce the chance of costly mistakes. With collaboration, with less hectic rush, with as much poise as the situation permits, clients are bound to be better served. . . . Every argument but one is in favor of our scheme of organization. The only argument against it is cost of overhead. But when we pay overhead it is paid in full. When we pay the freight, we pay, and pay and pay.[16]

A good man, however, was not hung for a single error. "We have moved _____ on to corporate experience now," Buckner wrote Frankfurter about a recent Harvard alumnus, "in which, by the way, he started with a serious careless mistake. It will do him a lot of good. He wrote 1928 instead of 1929 in an important contract and it went clear through to a final printed form and was circulated among a group of bankers, and who in hell do you suppose was the first to discover it? Charles Hayden himself! Our client. And we only get an occasional job from them, so we were especially anxious to use the lipstick j-u-s-t r-i-g-h-t! As _____ is the cockiest young gentleman we have ever taken on, so serious a jolt is bound to be beneficial to him, however damaging to the firm."[17]

This comradeship, personal attention and cheerful exhortation entailed one inevitable hardship: it could not stay just as it was as the men grew older. Eventually most of the associates would have to leave, and some would have to become partners, which might drive out others whom Buckner personally and professionally wished to keep. "He had a great line we used to josh about among ourselves," said William Palmer. "He'd talk about somebody as a 'functional

16 *Bull*, 2/23/24, pp. 1-3.
17 Buckner to Frankfurter, 11/25/28.

junior partner.' " The first new partners were chosen in November, 1925 at Buckner's urging, although he was temporarily out of the office serving as U.S. Attorney; Cleary and three of the *Harvard Law Review* men of 1920 (Gottlieb, Laporte and Palmer) were taken into the firm.

Four other men left—"as the inevitable result," Buckner wrote Frankfurter unhappily, "of our taking into the firm younger men than themselves. I think the other older men will stay. This whole business of partnership does not square with the actual facts in New York, and I spent two years trying to invent a status which would fit the facts but gave it up because it became apparent that I could not recruit the office. The feeling that one must join a firm of some kind (any old kind of a firm) or be a failure is purely traditional and goes back to the time of the articled clerk. The next generation may invent new bottles for new wine."[18]

3

Throughout the period 1919-25 Buckner had an immensely active trial practice, and probably negotiated to a settlement half a dozen cases for every one he tried. He was also engaged in organizing cases for Senator Root, who was actively "Counsel" through much of this time. (The firm also listed as "Counsel" Willard Bartlett, the retired Chief Judge of the Court of Appeals, but Bartlett was virtually inactive.) Buckner helped Root put together the independent team that prepared the hopeless challenge to the Volstead Act and the Prohibition Amendment, and very likely recruited much of the special group that worked on the multiple problems of the Marshall Field estate. Buckner undoubtedly helped, too, with the matter which must have been the most fun of all the work in this period, and was known around the office as "the drunken Ford case."

The drunken Ford was New York State Supreme Court Justice John Ford,[19] whose performances on the bench had disgusted the Appellate Division. The last straw came when he called some lawyers up for a discussion, and in open court leaned over and hooked the cigars out of one lawyer's inside breast pocket. There was in those days absolutely no way of disciplining a judge other than by impeachment, but the Appellate Division did have certain powers of

[18] Buckner to Frankfurter, 11/4/25.
[19] See Chapter 2, note 25.

assignment. They arranged that Ford should hear nothing but negligence cases before a jury, where he wouldn't write any opinions. He thereupon sued the Appellate Division to force them to assign him an equity part, where he would hear and decide cases by himself.

"We went to dinner with the judges of the Appellate Division," Grenville Clark recalled. "They wanted to defend on the merits, tell all the stories. Senator Root and I said, 'No'—undignified. I served as Root's law clerk—read everything the judge who was going to hear the case had ever written, opinions and articles. Root's peroration was word for word from an article the judge had written on the administration of justice. We went up to the Court of Appeals. Root was eighty, but he gave the best argument I ever heard in the Court of Appeals. He began, 'May it please the court, it was just fifty-four and one-half years ago that I argued my first case before this court, in the little stone courthouse that stands across the square.' Of course, he had drafted the clause in the 1894 Constitution which defined the powers of the Appellate Division." The power of the Appellate Division to keep Ford under wraps was duly confirmed.

Buckner handled all kinds of litigation, for plaintiffs and defendants, and gave the office a motto: "When we are for the plaintiff, nothing can stop us; when we are for the defendant, nothing can start us."[20] The cases ranged from *Ricordi* v. *Columbia* ("contracts between bureaus engaged in scattering music of the highest class, and highest price, among the provinces of the country. The work was interesting emotionally, perplexing legally, and disastrous financially"[21]) to *Goldstein* v. *D. Goff & Sons* (an "action brought to recover $1167 for improperly dyeing goods of the plaintiff. The defendant paid $700 and retained the goods which can be sold. Our clients may have dyed poorly but they died game"[22]). Buckner handled bankruptcies and will cases, cases for textile companies, sugar companies, coal companies, metals companies, life insurance companies, tobacco companies, automobile dealers, Wall Street brokers, even couturiers.

The clients in the ladies' fashion field were the Boué sisters—Jeanne Boué Baroness d'Etreillis and Mme. Sylvie Boué Monteguit—and their troubles were with customs. The Buckner ladies bought their clothes from the Boué sisters, and Buckner for their sakes swallowed his usual distaste for defending clients whom he thought to be guilty, and got them off. "He said all women smuggle," his daughter Ruth recalled. (She may have misplaced the occasion for this remark, which is at least equally suitable to the day when Buckner was U.S. Attorney and the lady escorting his daughter home from her finishing-school year in France was caught at customs smuggling in two dresses and compelled to pay a combined duty and fine of $1,550.)

Buckner in 1920, quite unusually for a Wall Street lawyer, undertook the defense of the Amalgamated Clothing Workers Union against a suit for a labor injunction in Rochester, New York. The union had organized most of the Rochester men's clothing business (which included Hart, Schaffner & Marx), but the firm of Michaels Stern had refused to sign a contract. The strike was for recognition of the union, and Michaels Stern went to court and got a temporary injunction against picketing. "Sidney Hillman," said Robert Szold, whose firm represented the Amalgamated, "set out to show this powerful company that they couldn't just go into court and walk all over his union." As Frankfurter recalled the case in his memoirs, the bill of complaint also charged that the Amalgamated was an "illegal organization" which should be disbanded. In any event, Hillman used the threat of this part of the action to secure Frankfurter as his attorney, which meant the case had to be tried during the Harvard Law School Easter vacation.

Among Frankfurter's conditions for taking the case, he wrote later, "was that I couldn't do it all, that one needed legal assistants, that I'd been out of the business of actually trying cases for some years and that I should want somebody more skilled in cross examination than I deemed myself to do that active part of the trial of the case, and therefore I wanted to be free to choose as my associates professional lawyers who ought to be paid."[23] Frankfurter also wanted an economic adviser to build a factual case for unionism, in the manner of the Brandeis appellate brief. For his economist, he chose Leo Wolman; for his trial counsel, Buckner.

As Frankfurter was in Cambridge, teaching law, it was incumbent upon Szold and his partner Max Lowenthal to prepare Buckner for the trial. "We would meet at his office and at his home," Szold re-

[23] *Felix Frankfurter Reminisces*, p. 172.

called. "It was preparation morning, noon and night, and at meal-times, before Rochester and at Rochester. He was a tremendous worker but an easy worker; he didn't get excited. It was a new sort of problem to him, but he was a trial lawyer and it was a trial."

The case took five weeks to try, much of the third week occupied by Frankfurter's efforts to introduce the economic and social material Wolman had developed. Justice Adolf J. Rodenbeck refused to admit the evidence. Frankfurter, after conducting the direct examination of Hillman, returned to Cambridge; and the case became a courtroom battle royal between Buckner and Michaels Stern's lawyer, Arthur E. Sutherland, who had formerly sat in Rodenbeck's chair. Outside the courtroom, Buckner and Sutherland got on famously—"It shows you," Frankfurter said, "how little laymen understand: my wife was shocked that Buckner and Sutherland were great friends."[24]

At issue, once Frankfurter's attempt to justify the strike had been ruled irrelevant, was the question whether the picketing had been peaceful. Rodenbeck ruled finally that the strike had been coercive and intended as coercive, that the temporary injunction should be made permanent and that the union was liable for any damages the company suffered because its efforts to prevent the company from hiring workers to replace the strikers were inherently illegal. Frankfurter in his "reminiscences" described Rodenbeck as "an incredibly wooden judge"; in conversation shortly before his death he spoke of "the very stupid judge."

In fact, as Sutherland's son Arthur E. Sutherland, Jr. (a professor at the Harvard Law School) pointed out, Rodenbeck had chaired the committee which redrafted the Consolidated Laws of New York in 1908 and 1909, and had written the labor code. He was not stupid at all, but he was strongly biased against the Amalgamated Clothing Workers. The employees of Michaels Stern, he wrote in his opinion,

although they had secretly joined the union, knowing of the wishes of the plaintiffs to keep their factories free from the influence of the Amalgamated Clothing Workers, had the legal right to quit work, as they had the legal right to join the union, however their conduct might be viewed from an ethical standpoint under the circumstances. . . . The plaintiffs were required to win their way in the world of business by hard and honest competition, and by the quality and character of their goods;

[24] Frankfurter to author, 1964.

but the Amalgamated Clothing Workers, instead of endeavoring to secure recognition by an example of an enlightened and reasonable administration in other factories, chose to force their way into plaintiffs' factories by secrecy, and by a strike backed by its powerful influence and supported by acts that the law condemns.[25]

Buckner liked his colleague Robert Szold, who became one of the group of a dozen younger lawyers (among the others were Embree, Thurlow Gordon, and Henry Nordlinger of the then new firm of Nordlinger & Riegelman) who were frequently on call as "minutemen" at five dollars an hour ("Good money in those days," Szold said) to help staff the outside offices Buckner would establish to handle a large litigation. Buckner also liked his client. The description of the case in *The Bull* ended with a note that "The sole comment of Sidney H. Hillman . . . when informed of the opinion of the trial court, was: 'Are the papers being prepared for the appeal?' "[26] The papers were prepared, but before the appeal could be heard the parties settled, Hillman dropping the strike in return for Michaels Stern's dropping the damage suit.

One amusing result of *Michaels* v. *Hillman* was a comment in the *Times* when toward the end of 1920 Buckner was retained by Samuel Untermyer to prosecute some of the men who had perjured themselves in the investigation of building-trades graft that Untermyer was running for the Lockwood Committee of the state Senate. "Mr. Buckner," the *Times* noted in a front-page story, "is known to be sympathetic to trade unionism, and his most recent labor case was that of counsel to [the Amalgamated] in their fight in the Rochester courts."[27]

Among the matters that got into the newspapers in this period were Buckner's representation of a committee of citizens protesting the behavior of the police at a birth-control rally in Town Hall, and his successful defense of a Mount Vernon unlawful-assembly statute against an attack by the Socialist Party. He also defended the publisher Thomas Seltzer, indicted for obscene libel for the publication of two books by Arthur Schnitzler, and *The New Republic* against a plagiarism suit by the author of a pamphlet on Calvin Coolidge from

[25] *Michaels* v. *Hillman*, 183 NYS 197 at 198.
[26] 1 *Bull*, 6/25/20, p. 5.
[27] *New York Times*, 11/1/20, p. 1.

which a writer in the magazine had cribbed quite extensively. In 1921, arguing a procedural matter with substantive overtones (to determine whether the government would have to return seized private assets and sue for them or the owners would have to claim from the government), Buckner made his first appearance at the Supreme Court. *The Bull's* "Washington Correspondent" noted the event:

Mr. Buckner proved Sunday that the one-man office is a possibility. He opened and closed the office, cleaned his desk, looked up the law, wrote a memorandum, typewrote a brief, and argued the case in the Supreme Court the next day. Incidentally, both Mr. Buckner and his tailor made a fine showing before the Supreme Court.[28]

Buckner's most heavily publicized case in the first half of the 1920s, however, was odder than any of these. His client was Prince Felix Youssoupoff, the litigious assassin of Rasputin (who some years later would win from a British jury an award of £25,000 for the alleged libel of his wife in an M.G.M. film about this episode). Youssoupoff retained Buckner to recover from Joseph E. Widener of Philadelphia two Rembrandt paintings which the Russian had either sold or pledged as security for a loan of £100,000 in 1921. Exchange rates in 1921 were such that the loan had amounted to about $350,000; by 1923, when Youssoupoff came to America to retrieve his paintings, the pound had risen to the point where repayment, at 8 percent interest, would cost him $520,334. But the paintings were worth a million dollars, and Youssoupoff had a buyer: Gulbenkian, who was financing his case.

The contract between Widener and Youssoupoff had been in form a contract of sale, but it provided that the Prince could buy back the paintings at any time up to January 1, 1924. The two men had made a handshake deal on it in London, but before signing the contract, after his return to America, Widener had added the condition that for Youssoupoff to redeem the paintings he had to be in a position to keep and personally enjoy them. Youssoupoff had already begun spending the money, and went along with the condition. His legal position in trying to regain the paintings for purposes of resale depended on

[28] *2 Bull,* 1/15/21.

whether the contract was essentially a sale with a condition or essentially a loan.

The high point in Buckner's work on this case came on October 20, 1924, in the examination before trial of Mr. Widener, held at the Root-Clark offices with Theodore Kiendl in attendance as counsel for Widener and the room full of press and Root-Clark juniors enjoying the show. Widener used the occasion to express strong views of the Prince; in the words of the *New York Times,* he "characterized Youssoupoff as an assassin, a degenerate, a buffoon and a joke."[29] He denied that he would ever have written social letters to the Prince or expressed sympathy with his condition or warned him not to trust dealers; and was only moderately abashed when Buckner produced a sympathetic "My dear Prince" letter in which he had cautioned Youssoupoff about the London dealers. For some of the men in the office, the best story to come out of the examination was one which ran in the first edition of the New York *Sun,* announcing that the Prince himself was in the audience. Later, *The Bull* announced, "the Sun reporter, a Harvard catcher of a few years ago . . . seemed to have some doubt as to his scoop and came over and asked Mr. Bushby if the man sitting over in the corner was not the Prince. He was then introduced to Mr. Harlan."[30] Youssoupoff's suit was still pending in March, 1925, when Buckner left Root-Clark to be U.S. Attorney for the Southern District of New York. The client was not ready to have anyone else at the firm appear in court for him, and outside trial counsel was hired—and that November the case was lost. The paintings are now in the National Gallery in Washington.

A few of the cases Buckner handled in the early 1920s cast unseen shadows before them. One group of suits involved the Alien Property Custodian and large clients, with large sums of money at stake. Buckner represented both kinds of parties at interest in these matters— for one client (Munich Reinsurance), he unsuccessfully worked to recover assets which the federal government had seized during the war on the grounds that they were enemy property; and for another client (American Bosch Magneto) he successfully defended against both criminal charges and private lawsuits new owners who had purchased seized German property at a government auction. In both cases he

[29] *New York Times,* 10/21/24, p. 1.
[30] 5 *Bull,* 10/25/24, p. 8.

learned the ins and outs of the operation of the Alien Property
Custodian's office; and he grew suspicious of President Warren Harding's appointment of war hero Thomas W. Miller as head of that
office. A few years later Buckner as U.S. Attorney would send Miller
to jail.

Another such group of cases grew out of persecution of the Nichols
Copper Company by the office of the Borough President of Queens,
Maurice E. Connolly. The question involved the right of the com-
pany to close off what the borough said was a public street which ran
between parts of its plant; and there can be no doubt, reading through
The Bull for 1920, that Connolly was holding up Nichols for a bribe.
One result of Nichols' resistance to these demands was Connolly's
encouragement of a series of suits in equity to drive Nichols out of
Queens for creating smoke nuisances at its factory. In 1927, when
Governor Alfred E. Smith retained Buckner as the state's special
counsel in an investigation of Connolly's conduct of his office, Buckner
did not have to rely on newspaper stories for his belief that the
Borough President was a crook: he already knew.

An office comment on one minor matter from this period makes
interesting reading in the light of history. The case involved an effort
by the directors of a company to use the machinery of the bankruptcy
court to prevent their ouster by their stockholders, and Root-Clark,
representing the stockholders, had moved to discharge the company
from the proceedings. "Mr. Henderson," *The Bull* reported, "thinks
our motion will be granted. Mr. Buckner thinks otherwise. Mr. Henderson knows the law and Mr. Buckner knows the judge."[31] The judge
was Martin T. Manton, who later became Chief Judge of the Court of
Appeals for the Second Circuit, and was sent to jail for selling the
judgments of his court.

[31] 1 *Bull*, 9/11/20.

CHAPTER EIGHT

U.S. Attorney
1925-1927

The year 1924 was hard on Republicans, as Senate investigating committees drew from both eager and reluctant witnesses quite unbelievable but often true stories of how the United States Government had been conducted in the administration of the recently deceased Warren G. Harding. On the cabinet level (three Harding cabinet officers were to be indicted for crime) one of the worst offenders had been Attorney General Harry M. Daugherty, the architect of Harding's nomination in 1920; and early in 1924 Calvin Coolidge requested (indeed, demanded) Daugherty's resignation. As his new Attorney General he chose Harlan F. Stone, until recently dean of the Columbia Law School and briefly a partner in Sullivan & Cromwell, with whom Buckner had a nodding acquaintance.

Stone turned out not to be the man to clean up what Daugherty had left (his prior knowledge of what he was to find is well indicated by his question to a police sergeant outside the White House directly after Coolidge appointed him: "Where," he inquired, "is the Justice Department?"[1]) The dean was too easygoing, insufficiently thorough, and overly committed to the proposition that Senator Burton K. Wheeler in his attacks on the department had been motivated solely by political malice—indeed, Stone continued to press the charges against Wheeler which Daugherty had trumped up in an attempt to

[1] Mason, *Harlan Fiske Stone: Pillar of the Law*, p. 147.

forestall the Wheeler investigation. Stone did, however, replace the unsavory William J. Burns with J. Edgar Hoover at the head of the Bureau of Investigation, and he installed Paul Shipman Andrews and Jerome Michael to scour the administration of the War Transactions Division, which under the statute of limitations had six months more to dig up evidence of frauds against the government in the recent unpleasantness. Looking around the country, Stone also saw a number of places where the public reputation of the government absolutely required a change in the local U.S. Attorney's office. One of them was New York.

Colonel William Hayward, Harding's appointment as U.S. Attorney for the Southern District of New York, had been content for three years to serve the national and local Republican organizations without too much care for any other considerations. Hayward was a Nebraskan, and had been a colleague of Buckner's at the Whitman office; and Buckner was immensely reluctant to criticize him in public. Once, however, under high provocation at a meeting of the Association of the Bar of the City of New York, Buckner said that when he arrived at the office he found that its corridors "reeked with the stench of bondrunners, lawyer-runners, fixers and chiselers, as those parasites are called who purport to be able to bribe officers of the law."[2]

Stone had known Buckner well enough to appreciate his reverence for Stimson, and in the late fall of 1924 he began talking with Buckner about whether he might be interested in taking the job Stimson had held. It still paid $10,000, but in early 1925 Buckner was completely free of money worries. His law firm and the stock market had generated more income than even he and his wife could spend, to the point where University Heights had become unsuitable and the family was about to move to one of the most elegant apartment houses in New York, at Sixty-seventh Street and Lexington Avenue. (Reporters noted that the rent on the apartment just about equaled Buckner's salary as U.S. Attorney.[3]) And he wanted the job. Two weeks before his resignation as U.S. Attorney, he told a jury, "What little success I have attained is all due to this old, dirty, repulsive, non-elevator building. I was proud that somebody thought that after seventeen years I should come back at the head where I had come in as an assistant fresh from law

[2] New York Times, 10/9/25, p. 25.
[3] New York Times, 3/15/25, II, p. 2.

school, a stenographer from Nebraska, knowing nobody in the City of New York."[4]

What made Buckner hesitate, Justice Harlan recalled, was his "distaste for the prohibition law. He recognized that if he took the job he would have to do something about it. He didn't want the office as a political steppingstone. He wanted his U.S. attorneyship to redound to his stature, to the firm's stature in the private practice of law. Now, the question was, was the sacrifice involved in upholding the prohibition law too great for that?"

To the extent that Buckner's decision to accept the post was influenced by any desire to work with Harlan Stone, he was to be disappointed, because shortly after submitting Buckner's name Stone was elevated to the Supreme Court. Charles B. Warren, whom Coolidge nominated to be Stone's successor as Attorney General, failed of confirmation by the Senate in a tie vote (the opposition to him relied, interestingly, on his former connections with the American Sugar Refining Company at the time when Buckner was helping to prosecute it). The man finally chosen for the job was John Garibaldi Sargent, from whom Buckner could expect no support. "The Attorney General," he wrote his daughter, "is a fine old Yankee lawyer from a small country town, more or less bewildered by the executive vastness of his job, and I have no doubt that he is annoyed by the militant frankness of my conduct here and my outspoken exposure of conditions, but I cannot consider such matters and when he cannot stand it any more he can ask me to get out. My job is not like a subordinate in an army. He is my superior, but the relationship is anomalous and it has never been determined just what the hegemony is. It differs with different men."[5]

In February, when the news was out, Buckner dropped a note to Learned Hand, thanking him for kind words on the impending appointment; in a postscript he added: "Honestly, I am getting very keen to do the job. No fireworks, but a 3 or 4 year steady crescendo."[6] On March 2, 1925, Buckner's office sent out messages announcing the change in the firm's name to Root, Clark, Howland & Ballantine; and Buckner arrived like a tornado in the U.S. Attorney's large, circular office on the

---

[4] *New York Times*, 2/26/27, p. 17.
[5] Buckner to Ruth, 3/7/26.
[6] Buckner to Hand, 2/7/25.

second floor of the old Post Office Building, at the point of what is now City Hall Park. In the month between his letter to Hand and his assumption of office, he had looked at the job, and he had discovered he needed fireworks.

2

Buckner seems to have laid down two conditions for accepting the post of U.S. Attorney—that he would have complete discretion in deciding what his office would and would not prosecute, and that he would be able to recruit his own staff. The latter promise was not one even Stone could have stood behind, and in the event Buckner had to work out his own solutions.

The staff he found was "terrible. . . . During the Hayward administration," he wrote Frankfurter some years later, "appointments were made almost one hundred percent political. And when I say political, I mean political. . . . [N]ot only were all appointees required to be Republicans, but 'organization' Republicans—quite a different matter. I found that not only was this true, but that different district leaders were entitled to allocated quotas, including some of the upstate counties, and of course the Bronx. I found the Negroes had, and therefore were entitled to have in perpetuity, a representative. The same was true of the Italians, with their large voting strength. It had gotten worse and worse as Hayward's ambition to be governor grew. You and I are very familiar with the argument for organization appointments. It is plausible. I have never been able to answer it more than partially. 'You want us to work and get out the vote, and then give the jobs to people'—they could say like Frankfurter and Buckner—'who never worked for the party.' . . .

"I talked with Sam Koenig [Republican leader in Manhattan], and later with Dick Lawrence [Republican leader of the Bronx] when he tendered a man I would not and did not appoint, and told them I realized their problem, and WHAT a problem it is for the Rep Party in New York, but that I had my problem and I HAD to succeed, not fail, and the thing was to consider the office a less tangible asset, but still a real asset, if administered in an efficient way. . . .

"I had a most happy inspiration, and conditions were so bad in the DA's office for one thing, and, well, I am sure I do not know what the considerations were which made Sam accept my formula, only asking for four or five exceptions out of over forty appointments I made. This was the inspiration—one of my best in my whole life—I said: 'Sam, I have looked over many applicants, and it becomes apparent that the party cannot help me in my extremity. But I think I can help the party in its extremity. The party apparently cannot recruit for me, but I can recruit for the party. Most boys have no politics anyhow. I can find enough men of the kind that I want to appoint—generally speaking the kind that would go into Root-Clark (with some exceptions) who either are Republicans or, being wholly politically epicene, can become Republicans. Probably none of them will be organization Republicans. They will have to join the regular organization. It will be fine for them to do it anyhow.' (I never did in the beginning, but such men as Sec[7] and Charlie Hughes and Tommy Thacher, and a host of our other friends did as soon as they came to NY without thought of fleshpots.)

"Then Sam and I revived the long defunct Young Men's Republican Club as a more congenial political home for many of my boys than would be their local district organizations, and that was accepted as an alternative. . . . Once in a long while (not often because most kids nowadays are eunuchs) I ran into an out-and-out Democrat or Socialist that I would have appointed otherwise, but that was no great loss, when you consider how I was solving a very practical problem and was saving the office. Had I nominated these men, they would not have been appointed by Washington."[8]

This problem of getting the right people for public legal jobs disturbed Buckner all his life, as it still disturbs many thoughtful observers of the American scene. Amidst all the talk about the courts and the police, the role of the public prosecutor tends to be ignored— but if law is to control the largely administrative process of criminal justice, its major point of influence must be in the district attorney's office. The overwhelming majority of district attorneys are elected, and the appointments to their staffs are usually dictated by the political leaders responsible for their election. Even the U.S. Attorney's office is far from free of patronage: though the U.S. Attorneys are appointed by the President, Presidents too want all the political friends they can get. Able and incorruptible people—even puritans—make careers in these offices, but so do a lot of others.

[7] Elihu Root, Jr.
[8] Buckner to Frankfurter, 2/1/32.

Buckner puzzled unhappily over possible answers to the question long after he had ceased to be publicly active or influential. On the one hand, he wrote in 1939, he had "a strong conviction that political considerations should have no place in appointment of public servants whose function is either legal or judicial. My observation has been that it is very rare that the head of a legal staff in public service, by some hook or crook, some device or formula, has been able in some way to meet the pressing and difficult-to-answer argument of those who 'get out the vote.' When the appointing power falls into the trap of *ceteris paribus,* it seems to turn out that every political candidate falls within the category of c.p." On the other hand, he wrote in the same letter, "It does not seem to me that I could have done any of my jobs with the type of men who . . . seek security and a career through the Civil Service route."[9]

Buckner recognized the force of Frankfurter's arguments that there should be a "public career" for men in government service, and that some kind of guaranteed tenure was essential if men were to be asked to make a public career. At Frankfurter's request in 1939, he solicited suggestions from Thomas E. Dewey, then District Attorney in New York County, who proposed as "a useful compromise . . . some plan for free selection by the appointing officer with tenure depending on good behavior, *in the opinion* of the appointing officer. This is, in reality, about what the Federal Civil Service amounts to now. When the officer in charge of a public office deems the services of any Civil Service government employee incompetent, he may file charges and dismiss him. The fact that charges have to be filed is a great deterrent and yet enables freedom of action where the employee is genuinely incompetent."[10]

Buckner was not wholly convinced. "[I]t is a constructive suggestion," he replied to Dewey, "and personally I think it a better solution than to go over completely bag and baggage to Civil Service. I was in your office two and a half years . . . and I know in a general way how the office has been run until your election. You would have been helpless had you found frozen into the staff sixty men selected by district leaders. I found much the same situation on March 1, 1925, when I became United States District Attorney under a Republican President. The subject will stand much thought and experimentation.

[9] Buckner to Frankfurter, 3/23/39.
[10] Dewey to Buckner, 4/11/39.

"I congratulate you," Buckner added, "upon the efficiency and morale of your own staff, which of course is due to your personal leadership. These things do not happen by accident."[11]

In his first year as U.S. Attorney, Buckner appointed nearly fifty new assistants. In choosing them, he first considered recommendations from the law schools; and like Stimson, he looked for recommendations of men who had been out a year or two (there was a limit to the number of absolute neophytes he could take), though in 1926 he added to the staff seven new graduates, all Phi Beta Kappa in college and editors of their schools' law reviews. Sometimes he asked them if they were Republicans, but sometimes he did not; and Washington did appoint several Democrats for him, most spectacularly Edward S. Silver, later Brooklyn District Attorney and Surrogate, who was an active member of a Democratic club. Silver had been class of '24 at the Harvard Law School, and a year before Buckner had seen him on Frankfurter's suggestion at the Root-Clark offices. Now Frankfurter recommended Silver again, and Buckner called him at Hays, Hirschfield & Wolff, where he was working. "He asked me my salary," Silver recalled, "and I told him it was three thousand dollars. He said, 'Well, we only pay two. I've got to get three men who will work for what one political appointee receives. But I think it's worthwhile for you. I'd like you to start tomorrow—you won't be paid for a month, but that's the situation.' I told him I was working on some things in the Hays office, and he said, 'You can finish those in the evening.' I remember saying to him, 'Well, I'm impoverished anyway.' When I walked out of the Post Office Building, I didn't know where I was. I had a talk with Kenny Sutherland, later Kings County leader, then the leader in the Sixteenth Precinct. He said, 'If they're willing to give you a Republican job, you take it. But now you owe something to this guy; you make yourself scarce around here.' "

Over the course of 1925 and 1926, Buckner put together an astonishing staff. Among the future judges he appointed were Justice Harlan (who came with him), Chief Judge J. Edward Lumbard of the Court of Appeals for the Second Circuit; David Peck, presiding Justice of the First Appellate Department of the New York Supreme Court; Judge Samuel C. Coleman of the New York Civil Court; Surrogate Silver; and Magistrate Raphael P. Koenig. The group included Bethuel

11 Buckner to Dewey, 4/12/39.

M. Webster, future president of the Association of the Bar of the City of New York, and Arthur H. Schwartz, later president of the New York County Lawyers Association; and among the other future leaders of the New York Bar were Porter R. Chandler, Frederic R. Coudert, James A. Farmer, Ben Herzberg, Horace G. Hitchcock, W. Houston Kenyon, Jr., George S. Leisure, Nathan Margold, Carl E. Newton, Israel B. Oseas, Guido Pantaleoni, C. Frank Reavis, Alexander Royce, William E. Stevenson, Herman T. Stichman, Lowell Wadmond, William C. Whitney and C. Dickerman Williams. Two law school students who worked for Buckner as U.S. Attorney one summer also became notables —Judge Henry J. Friendly of the Court of Appeals for the Second Circuit, and Thomas Corcoran, later Roosevelt's Tommy the Cork, definitely not a Republican.

These young men (nearly all of them under thirty) had to be added gradually, and the Hayward appointments phased out. In the meantime, Buckner needed an executive assistant—an "Associate United States Attorney," as he put it—to hold the organizational strings. After something of a search, he appointed to this post Robert E. Manley, whom he later had occasion to recommend as a possible professor of criminal law at Harvard: "He was Assistant District Attorney of New York for ten years. . . . I think he was the most studious man in the office at all times during his tenure. He is a bachelor and a man of very exact and rather fussy habits and, having for ten years digested every criminal case in all the courts of New York State (and I think the United States Supreme Court), has kept it up for the succeeding 12 years because it was easier for him to maintain it than to drop it. . . . Though he appears frail he is in most excellent health, being a very assiduous golf player, which he plays with the precision, regularity, excellence and lack of emotion that he does everything else."[12]

Manley was in his mid-forties and could serve as a stabilizing influence, though he turned out not to be very useful as a senior prosecutor. (He did not try a case during his two years with Buckner.) With Manley as his aide-de-camp, Buckner now undertook to reorganize the office, break in increasing numbers of young men, and create in the Post Office Building the *élan* of Root-Clark. There was a monthly dinner and an annual outing, a pair of tables reserved for the office at Child's Restaurant every day at lunchtime (with the Chief

[12] Buckner to Jeremiah Smith, 3/29/28.

himself in frequent attendance), an official weekly lunch first at the Bankers and then at the Lawyers Club ("He would throw something on the table," Israel B. Oseas recalled, "and say, 'What do you think is the law on this?' "), a "Coffee Club," a "Soda Club" and an office magazine, *Scraps,* which would eventually acquire some of the quality of *The Bull,* though its humor tended toward the childish.

Most important of all, Buckner extended to his very young Assistant U.S. Attorneys the same responsibilities he had accorded to the young men at Root-Clark. He sent young Herman Stichman against Max Steuer, George Leisure against Hayward, Silver against the combined forces of George Z. Medalie, William J. Fallon and Leonard Snitkin. Bethuel Webster remembered that after delivering his maiden summation in a courtroom he turned away from the jury to find that Buckner had slipped unannounced into a chair behind the prosecutor's table. Buckner clapped him on the back and congratulated him for a good job. "That's *leadership,*" Webster said forty years later.

All the judges were not equally delighted with "Buckner's boy scouts." Judge William Bondy, dismissing a prosecution for fraudulent bankruptcy, said sarcastically that if the government wanted to win criminal cases it would have to hire competent lawyers. Buckner's reply was that he thought the case had been competently handled, especially considering that the defendants had pulled all sorts of strings in Washington to stop the prosecution and had secured from the judges no fewer than twenty-two adjournments.[13]

The young men could be sure that they would not be second-guessed, even when severe pressure was placed against their decisions. Buckner had laid down a rule that his office would not prosecute Mann Act violations unless commercialism or a minor was involved, despite the unfortunate and then recent Supreme Court decision that the law covered any and all interstate fornication. Silver remembered a case where a young lady came in with her parents, her lawyer and her influential clergyman, with a case based on the fact that once her fella had taken her across the river to a hotel in Newark. Silver said the government wouldn't prosecute. "Who are *you?*" the clergyman said angrily. "Who's your boss?" Silver took them down the long corridor Buckner had labeled "Criminal Alley" to the Chief's office, and Buckner wouldn't hear them. "You can go to the Attorney General," he said. "If he wants to appoint a Special Assistant to prosecute your

[13] *New York Times,* 10/28/25, p. 3.

case, that's fine. I won't." Silver said, "You can't know what it means to a young man to have a Chief like that."

Similarly, Raphael Koenig, dealing with immigration matters, had a case where a young Italian had bought a false passport and tried to smuggle himself into the country. Koenig had told the immigration authorities, "Poor fellow—all he wanted was to get into the United States. He's not a criminal; let him go home." The next he heard of the matter was a call from Buckner, who said, "Ray, I've got a complaint against you from the Department of Labor." Koenig told the story, and Buckner swung around at his desk and called Washington. "Do you have a quota system?" he asked an Assistant Secretary of Labor in charge of immigration matters. On receiving the answer he said, "Well, so do we. You'd keep the courts busy for fifty years with that sort of case." Koenig, looking back on the incident, commented, "He wasn't a government menial. He was a big man."

What Buckner wanted in return was enthusiasm, great quantities of work, a quest for professional improvement, and that sense of an office mystique which he carried with him wherever he went. "The week's brightest moment," he wrote in *Scraps*, "is when we sit around the Coffee Club and admire each other. Boosting is the best tonic in the world."[14] There were homilies on care and on "the extra ten percent," instructions to get the letters answered the day they arrive, suggestions about how to organize life so the secretaries knew at all times where the men were.

Buckner's sense of organization did not extend to saving money. Rather than go through the usual formalities, he paid for a number of expenses (including the travel of his young lawyers, then officially recompensed by a disgraceful four-dollar per diem), and had all the office telegrams charged to his own personal account. More experienced hands tried to save him from the worst of his self-imposed telegraph expenses, and *Scraps* carried an alleged example:

The Honorable John Garibaldi Sargent
Attorney General
Washington, D.C.

Dear Mr. Sargent,
Some time ago I wrote you that I would like very much to have certain photostats for use at the trial of the case of the United States

14 *Scraps,* 4/3/26.

of America, plaintiff, against Charles W. Endel *et al.,* defendants. No doubt, in the hustle of things my request has been overlooked, so I am taking the liberty of bringing the matter to your attention again. The calendar has been rather weak of late, and the case will probably be reached for trial before either Judge Hand or Judge Thacher in a few days.

I regret that I haven't your file number handy just now but if you have any difficulty in locating these papers I shall be only too glad to forward it to you by another telegram.

With kindest personal regards,

> Very respectfully yours,
> EMORY R. BUCKNER
> United States Attorney for the
> Southern District of New York.
> Office and Post Office Address:
> U.S. Courts and Post Office
> Building, Borough of Manhattan, City of New York.

MR. MERRITT REVISES

Attorney General, Wash.
Fifty thousand three. Send photostats Endel case immediately.

> BUCKNER
> New York[15]

Buckner made one final, extraordinary demand on the young men he hired into the U.S. Attorney's office: they had to swear off liquor, whatever their opinion of the prohibition laws. ("I was married during that time," said Israel B. Oseas, who worked in Buckner's Anti-Trust Division. "And there was no liquor served at my wedding, to the amazement of my friends.") Shortly after Coolidge sent his nomination to the Senate, on January 26, 1925, Buckner held a party at his home on University Heights, at which his own considerable cellar of bootleg wine and whiskey (Justice Harlan remembered it as an investment of more than a thousand dollars) was broken bottle by bottle and poured down the sink. Leo Gottlieb remembered that "it hurt my feelings—I would have taken them all and stocked them gladly"; another member of the "office Brook Farm" recalled suggesting to Buckner that instead of dumping the stuff he should leave his cellar unlocked by prearrangement one evening and let his friends

[15] *Scraps,* 3/20/26.

steal it. (Buckner was rather shocked at the idea.) Both summers he
was in office, Buckner took a fishing trip to the Harlan summer home
at Murray Bay, Quebec, where the younger men were released from
their vows but the Chief himself stayed dry. Even more sinister, for
those who thought about it, was Buckner's resignation from all his
clubs (even the Harvard Club) on the grounds that as U.S. Attorney
he might have to raid one of them.

If the government in its wisdom had given to its U.S. Attorney the
impossible job of enforcing prohibition in the Southern District of
New York, then this particular U.S. Attorney was going to attempt
the impossible.

3

At a distance of more than forty years, nobody could imagine the
condition to which the federal courts had been reduced by the prohibition law. Under the Constitution, people can be convicted of
offenses against federal law only by their own plea of guilty or after
indictment by a grand jury and verdict by a petit jury. By the middle
1920s, when Representative Emanuel Celler was inserting in the *Congressional Record* and distributing to his constituents George Washington's recipe for the home brewing of beer, and Representative
Fiorello H. LaGuardia was holding public demonstrations of methods
for the bathtub fermentation of malt, the number of offenses against
the Volstead Enforcement Act ran to literally millions every week.
The possibility of convicting any noticeable fraction of these violators
was especially remote in states like New York, where possession and
sale of liquor were not state crimes and the entire burden of enforcing
the law had fallen upon the federal system. There had been a state
prohibition law in New York, but it had failed—because, Buckner
once said, "It was drawn by its friends."[16] Violation of the law had
been made a felony, which meant that state defendants, too, were
entitled to jury trials; and the resulting jam-up of the state courts had
given a covertly wet legislature and an overtly wet Governor—Al
Smith—the excuse to repeal it.

Buckner described what he found at the courts in a speech to the
annual convention of the Georgia Bar in June, 1925, when the experience was still fresh:

"I went up to the Federal Building to look around for a few weeks

[16] XI *The Consensus,* No. 1, June 1926, p. 39.

before I was sworn in after my appointment, and I found the great United States Court in the Southern District of New York had degenerated not into a police court (oh, no, not at all) but into whatever is in the subcellar under a police court; because the United States Court was attempting to run a police court without the necessary background, without the railing, without the traditions, without the attendants, without the clerks, without the stenographers, without anything at all that gives some semblance of order and some dignity, and makes these people in New York City or the nether world crouch under the pressure of the city laws they have violated. All that was gone. I found that the Police Department and the prohibition agents were bringing into that Federal Building every year 75,000 people under arrest for violation of the liquor law—not 7,500, but 75,000 people—in fifty-two weeks. I found one United States Commissioner, who acts as a police magistrate, sitting there without a stenographer because one is not provided under the federal system, and I found perjury was so rotten that it stank.

"Of the 75,000 cases the Commissioner told me himself that 95 or 98 percent were thrown out by him when the police officers or the prohibition agents testified, because, although the arrests were made the night before, it seemed they had been somewhat mistaken, or they didn't exactly recall the circumstances. Bondsmen told me, judges told me, lawyers told me, that in this vast swarming crowd of 1,500 to 2,000 and 2,500 men and women the place was full of fixers and bond-runners and bond-crooks, and lawyer crooks; that money was passed freely; and there sat the Commissioner without any stenographer to verify the perjury of witnesses. He was throwing them out like this and that, and holding others, and there he was without any power to punish the perjurers. . . .

"Finally I followed some of these cases. They were sent up to the fifth floor of the Federal Building. The United States Commissioner would say, 'I hold you for trial.' When that is done all he has to do is to have an assistant of mine to sign the United States Attorney's name on a printed form with two lines of handwriting. That is sent down to the third floor of the same building to the district clerk's office. That is all he has to do. I found that he was six months behind. I found that it was taking six months for a piece of paper scarcely larger than that [indicating a little slip on the table] to go from the fifth to the third floor of the same building. I said to myself, 'Call that law enforcement? That's a farce. I will have none of it.' "[17]

Of the cases that actually got on the docket, the overwhelming majority were settled on payment of a fine, which was handed over cheerfully by the boss. (Indeed, if a man was needed on the job, it was common practice to hire a substitute to go down and wait in court and take the plea and pay the fine.) "Such a fine," Buckner told reporters his second day as U.S. Attorney, "is nothing but a license, a trifling addition to the overhead expense, and the Federal bench has suffered the indignity of being turned in reality into an excise commission for what amounts to the issuance of licenses, but without any regulation or inspection. To call such proceedings 'law enforcement' is a farce. To call such fines 'convictions' is grotesque."[18] A year later he would tell a committee of the U.S. Senate that the record in such cases should be changed to show not "convicted" but "escaped on payment of money."[19]

Large-scale prosecution to jail sentences was virtually impossible. Judges cannot average much more than two jury trials a week, and do not work much more than forty weeks a year. There were six federal judges in the Southern District; quite apart from any question of the size of the U.S. Attorney's staff, if all the judges did nothing but hear jury trials in prohibition cases, the government could dispose of about five hundred a year, at the outside. The police were delivering 75,000 a year. And these judges had other work to do, much of it more important than presiding over the trials of waiters and bartenders. Buckner firmly decided that in the existing state of the law he could not possibly enforce prohibition through criminal prosecutions.

But there might be another way. Included in the Volstead Act was a provision which made any place that was selling alcoholic beverages a nuisance in the common-law sense of the word. Using their equity powers, judges can suppress nuisances. On the testimony of a single credible witness that he had bought liquor in a restaurant or speakeasy, or at a drugstore or a garage or a brewery, a judge could seal off the premises—"padlock" it—for a considerable length of time. Padlocking

---

[17] Annual Address Delivered Before the Forty-Second Annual Session of the Georgia Bar Association, June 5, 1925, pp. 13-15.

[18] *New York Times*, 3/4/25, p. 1.

[19] *New York Times*, 4/9/26, p. 1.

was in every way attractive. It got at the owners and their profits. Moreover, it would bring home the realities of prohibition to the rich and well-fed of the city, most of whom had been living (like Buckner himself) as though no such law had ever been put on the books.

But nobody who hoped to padlock the city's most fashionable restaurants could rely on the normal prohibition agent to find him the evidence. Even if the agent were honest (and the betting odds were about four-to-one against it), at $1,300 to $2,100 a year in an alleged career service he had acquired neither the wardrobe nor the manners to make a waiter trust him. In the weeks before he became U.S. Attorney, Buckner asked some of the young lawyers in his office to get him the evidence he could use in padlock proceedings. Four of them accepted the assignment. Buckner wrote a personal check for $1,500 and gave it to John Harlan to cover their expenses.

His second day in office, Buckner announced padlock proceedings against fourteen places, some of them among the city's finest and longest established restaurants—Beaux Arts, Club Morite, Club Borgo, Club Mirado, Club Deauville, Colony, El Fey Club, Lido Venice, Meadowbrook, Monte Carlo, Mouquin's, Piping Rock, Crillon and L'Aiglon. "The policy of my administration," Buckner told reporters, "will be prohibition by padlock so far as the open selling of liquor is concerned."[20] Headlines screamed. At the weekend, the New York *American* ran a banner front-page headline: "BUCKNER TO 'DRY UP' CITY IN SIXTY DAYS."[21] James C. Young in the Sunday *Times* feature section announced, "One week the metropolis, admittedly moist, is derided at Albany as 'the bottleggers' paradise.' The next week it discovers itself to be the spearhead of a new thrust that may grow into a general nation-wide offensive against the rum legions."[22]

Not everyone was impressed. A new magazine called *The New Yorker,* in only its second month of publication, carried a sour leading article in which "our Prohibition Authority" argued that

If I was a promising young attorney, and I could have my name plastered on every first page in the country for the nominal personal expenditure of $1,500, I would dash right out and grab the advertising. . . . [M]ost of the prominent places against which Mr. Buckner and his Four Volunteer

20 *New York Times,* 3/4/25, p. 1.
21 New York *American,* 3/7/25.
22 *New York Times,* 3/15/25, IX, p. 8.

Horsemen procured evidence had had evidence procured against them before he took office, by the Prohibition Enforcement Unit. The legal machinery began working on them months ago. . . . And you might remember that Mr. Buckner served his apprenticeship as an Assistant District Attorney under Charlie Whitman, who also knew a good story, for him when he saw it. He knew a good story so well that he became governor, and Mr. Buckner could not help observing how it all happened. And every newspaper still has a front page, surmised our Prohibition Authority.[23]

Darling in the New York *Tribune* drew a cartoon showing Manhattan Island in a rainstorm, with bottles and cases floating all around it, and in the corner a man labeled "Law Enforcement" keeping the rain off a fishbowl labeled "Fashionable Cabarets." The line under the cartoon was "HOLDING AN UMBRELLA OVER THE GOLDFISH."[24] *The Bull* itself carried a letter signed "Nux Vomica" saying that "Some people can't understand what is going on at the Post Office Building. One fellow told me he knew what a padlock was but what in sam hill was this prohibition the D.A. was always talking about. You would think these crossword puzzles would have educated people a little."[25] *Scraps* itself had moments of being unconvinced: "Mr. Buckner in clamping the padlocks has unwittingly increased measurably the amount of the city budget. The Board of Aldermen can no longer present the key of the city to distinguished guests. The Board must in the future present a bunch of keys."[26]

And in fact there was a limit to how far the padlocking could go. Buckner went to Judge John C. Knox once and talked over with him the question of liquor served at banquets at the big hotels: what would Knox think of padlocking the Astor? The answer was: not much; and Buckner never attempted it.[27] Those who were hit, however, were hurt. Their restaurants were literally sealed—the newspapers made a fuss about a couple of cats allegedly imprisoned in Mouquin's—and the premises could not be used for anything else during the time of the injunction, which meant that the landlords would have to take the loss for any establishment that went out of business. With champagne at

[23] 1 *The New Yorker,* 3/21/25, p. 1.
[24] 85 *Literary Digest,* 4/11/25, p. 52.
[25] 6 *Bull,* 3/21/25, p. 8.
[26] *Scraps,* 3/28/25.
[27] Knox to author, 1964.

$25 a quart and drinks at $2 and up, profits had been enormous. Herman Forster, who had come from the managing clerk's job at the Cravath firm to work for Buckner, remembered Larry Fey saying wistfully, "I wish I could do business with you. I'd bring up a wagonload of money every day and just dump it at the door." The initial rash of proceedings, however, turned out to be less painful to the owners than they or Buckner anticipated.

"The thing Buckner had missed," John Harlan said many years later, "was the position he was putting these young men in. When the newspapers came, he realized that these young men at the thresholds of their careers would have to get up on the witness stand and testify to abusing the hospitality of places which many people thought were performing a public service by serving good liquor. Finally, he had to negotiate—*personally*—every one of those padlock cases, settle them with thirty-day consent decrees, to save the men from the embarrassment." Despite considerable pressure from reporters, Buckner never did reveal the names of the young men who had gone on the town to help enforce prohibition.

One name did get out, however, to Buckner's acute embarrassment —Gottlieb's. Elihu Root, Jr. and Grenville Clark had proposed Gottlieb for membership in the Association of the Bar of the City of New York, and half a dozen lawyers let the membership committee know that they would oppose Gottlieb on the grounds that what he had done for Buckner was unprofessional. Buckner, greatly upset, wrote Judge Augustus Hand: "I feel very badly that Gottlieb's great personal devotion to me and my desire to render what I conceived a notable public service to the bench and bar and litigants in this district should result in the personal humiliation incident merely to this criticism, let alone its possible consequences. . . . I feel that the entire Bar Association ought to present Gottlieb with a medal instead of subjecting him to chagrin."[28] Five federal judges—the two Hands, Hough, Thacher and Knox—wrote letters to the Association at Buckner's urging. If the members of the Bar Association wished to attack anyone, Judge Augustus Hand wrote, "they ought to bring Buckner before the Appellate Division and not badger a young man who performed a public service at his request."[29]

[28] Buckner to Augustus Hand, 6/11/25.
[29] *New York Times*, 10/9/25.

Unfortunately, the matter did not end there. Led by Selden Bacon, a violent antiprohibitionist, a group of lawyers announced their intention to oppose Gottlieb at the annual meeting. (The New York *Evening Post* editorialized that "The objectors might serve the Bar Association better if they devoted their energies to supervising lawyers who are less zealous for law enforcement."[30]) Under the rules of the Association, a candidate required 80 percent of the members present and voting to be accepted, so the danger of Gottlieb's public humiliation was real. Buckner rallied his forces and procured an attendance of more than 350—the greatest in the history of the Association. He spoke for an hour and separately answered the four men who spoke against Gottlieb's candidacy. The motion to postpone consideration of Gottlieb's name failed, and he was elected, apparently with an easy margin even under the four-fifths rule.

Once these initial fourteen cases were finished, Buckner upped the ante on padlocking, and the normal injunction ran six months on a "guilty plea," a year if the proprietors insisted on a trial. By January 1, 1926, Buckner had padlocked more than four hundred restaurants and drugstores.

The Drys, a masochistic lot anyway, liked the padlocking. But there was another side to Buckner's coin which the Anti-Saloon League found less admirable—his insistence that federal criminal process not be invoked against the minor retailers and consumers. "I have no sympathy," Buckner told the Park Slope Masonic Club in one of the speeches he gave twice a week throughout his first six months as U.S. Attorney, "with that kind of prohibition enforcement which clogs my calendars with a criminal charge against a man arrested on New Year's Eve for having in his automobile a single bottle of champagne when hundreds of bootleggers and rum-runners go unarrested and unconvicted."[31] In his first announcements, he said he was going to dismiss eight thousand pending cases, but this medicine was too strong for Washington (where the Justice Department, as John Harlan put it, "liked to show ten thousand convictions a year in the Southern District of New York"). He would process all the little cases, Buckner said, if the government would provide federal police courts without jury trials. When constitutional objec-

[30] New York *Evening Post*, 10/8/25.
[31] *New York Times*, 5/28/25, p. 1.

tions were urged to this course, he commented that "apparently it has become easy to amend the Constitution for other purposes."[32] In the meantime, he invented a kind of police court, "Bargain Days" at the old Post Office Building, which he hoped would clear out two thousand cases a week by publicly promising light fines in return for guilty pleas.

The bargain court opened July 26, 1925, before Judge Edwin L. Garvin, imported from Brooklyn for the purpose. Buckner wanted the chairs and tables out of the courtroom to make room for the crowd, and when the custodians refused to do the moving without specific authorization from Washington, he and the young assistants carried out the furniture themselves. "We want to clear ourselves of all stock of this character," Buckner said, looking over the five hundred defendants who jammed the court, "and we hope to open in the Fall with an entirely new line of prohibition goods."[33] A week in the bargain court did clear out fifteen hundred cases, with Judge Augustus Hand spelling Garvin on the bench; but both the judges and the staff found the proceedings exhausting and disgusting.

What bothered the prohibitionists more than anything else was Buckner's refusal to say nice things about the law. "I can find nothing in my oath of office," he told reporters his first week on the job, "which compels me to give my personal opinion of any of the laws which I have sworn to enforce."[34] The matter came to a head six months after his appointment, as the result of an interview with *New Yorker* reporter Morris Markey, presented in that magazine's most supercilious fledgling style. According to Markey, Buckner said he never would tell what he thought of the prohibition law, but also pointed out that he had often said he got on the wagon for the first time when he was appointed U.S. Attorney. "The inference," Buckner added, "should be clear."

The quote that infuriated the Anti-Saloon League came in response to Markey's question, "What, then, do you think of the man who accepts a drink, or buys a drink when the mood strikes him?"

Markey reported that Buckner "took out his pencil and made a small mark on the pad that lay before him. He probably would have

32 *New York Times,* 1/3/26, VIII, p. 9.
33 *New York Times,* 7/27/25, p. 1.
34 *New York Times,* 3/9/25, p. 1.

frowned, except that he never frowns, or smiles, or discloses any of his mental processes in his immobile face. He took out his pencil, which is his closest approach to a gesture of any sort." And in part of his reply, according to Markey, Buckner said, "As long as he is frank about it, and professes his dissatisfaction in words and votes as well as deed, I have no particular quarrel with him."[35] This was direct condonation of crime as the law was written, and Buckner the next day was compelled to tell the press that *The New Yorker* had misquoted him. Frankfurter was concerned, and Buckner wrote him: "I think you would approve everything I have done, even to giving an interview to the reporter for *The New Yorker*—smart, smug and hostile as it is—upon his assurance that he would send me a copy of the interview. He simply lied, but this is the first time I have ever known a newspaperman to break his word. He now says he made no such promise and his boss very pertly backs him up. Walter [Lippmann] says he could have warned me because on a previous occasion they behaved badly in printing some confidential matters concerning the New York *World*."[36]

More important than the careless quote in riling the Anti-Saloon League, however, was Markey's conclusion to the article. He wrote that he and his readers had been

chuckling at the ardent clown imagination makes of Mr. Buckner when stories of his further empty and futile raids among the ephemeral cabarets of Broadway are printed; chuckling at the sonorous and peppy speeches which he casts into the air over radio; at his self-confessed vanity, and at his amazing want of a ticklish spot anywhere on his active figure.

But I am not so sure that the Buckner who sits in his office, articulating with certain grace and undeniable honesty a wise and knowing philosophy upon the dubious phenomenon of prohibition, is to be laughed at. . . . He is approaching nearer and nearer to that bright morning when he will announce that prohibition cannot be enforced and ought to be repealed. He is a clear-sighted and thoughtful citizen with a faint and ineradicable streak of Rotary and Babbitt in him, it is true, but curiously wise and penetrating. In gentlemen of his sort lies the hope, at last, of those to whom prohibition is obnoxious.[37]

[35] *The New Yorker*, 11/14/25, p. 7.
[36] Buckner to Frankfurter, 11/25/25; Lippmann was then in charge of the editorial page for the *World*.
[37] *The New Yorker*, 11/14/25, p. 8.

This was insufferable, but was about right; and the Anti-Saloon League sensed it. In reply to its counsel, Wayne B. Wheeler, Buckner could write (in a letter which was spread over the front and editorial pages of the newspapers) that in seven months he had expanded the Prohibition Division of his office "from a group of two lawyers and three clerks to a group of fourteen lawyers and thirty clerks."[38] (This had been done, incidentally, by special arrangement with the Treasury Department, which hired Buckner's young men for him and assigned them to his office. By a quirk of the government salary schedule, these prohibition lawyers were paid $3,000 while the young lawyers on the Justice Department payroll got $2,000. "I remember I was driving back from a funeral and I was stopped by a cop," said Arthur H. Schwartz, one of the new men in Buckner's prohibition Division. "I showed him who I was and he said, 'Oh, you're one of them prohibition agents.' That's why Buckner paid you more, I think—to pay for the ignominy.")

Within this division, Buckner and Harlan (who became its chief in the fall of 1925) had by sleight of hand created the air of a holy cause. One of the few men Buckner hired who left the office before he did, C. Dickerman Williams, recalled that "I rather liked the crusading atmosphere. But I discovered I was crusading for a law I didn't like." The few Drys in New York could not help sensing that for all Buckner's drive toward law enforcement, and his insistence that all his men take the pledge, nobody in his office approved of prohibition. Eventually the prestige these men were gathering in public office would be turned to the cause of repeal.

In 1926 Buckner did move in that direction, urging the Congress to let each state define for itself the percentage of alcohol in a beverage that would make it "intoxicating" for prohibition purposes. A number of people were shocked, among them Buckner's father; the Reverend J. D. M. Buckner gave an interview in which he said, "Emory is wrong."[39] In fact, though he grimly continued to padlock and prosecute, Buckner was becoming convinced that the law could not be enforced in New York. His first nine months' efforts, he told the Women's Forum at the Hotel Biltmore, had made New York only 10 percent dry. And meanwhile, in the course of trying to catch and prosecute the rum-runners and the big operators who redistilled

[38] *New York Times*, 11/17/25, p. 1.
[39] *New York Times*, 4/16/25, p. 17.

denatured alcohol to make it potable (maybe—deaths from poisoning by bad liquor in New York City ran at a rate of six hundred a year through Buckner's incumbency), he had found something that frightened him much more than simple public disregard for this law.

"I had no idea until several months ago what prohibition lawlessness meant," he told the Economic Club of New York on the first anniversary of his swearing in as U.S. Attorney. "The majority of you have no idea of what prohibition lawlessness means. You don't know it. You cannot know it unless you get in a position where you get a little peep at it, unless you get in a position where you see this open sewer from which the noxious vapors are at present emerging and which threaten our safety and threaten our existence. Many people think that prohibition lawlessness is buying a case or two of liquor from some nicely laundered, nicely dressed steward of his club whom he has known for many years and who, in all probability, is himself a teetotaler. They think that this is prohibition lawlessness, and he is the law-breaker. That is not the kind of lawlessness I am talking about.

"A short time ago I talked to a man who had been arrested and who, for many years, had been violating the law in a very substantial way. I knew, of course, that he could not have operated for so long a time in such an obvious and substantial way unless, for some reason or other, his operations were not seen by those charged with the supervision of his operations and their prevention. He told me that he had paid gangsters thousands of dollars for his protection. He did not know of his own knowledge where the money went. He knew that he was unmolested. I said, 'If you will testify before the Grand Jury and give the names of those gangsters that you are talking about, I will do nothing whatever to you. We will turn you free, and I will do nothing to your place of business if you stop breaking the law.' He said, 'I would rather take any jail sentence that I am likely to receive than be killed within 24 hours.' I am quoting him. Maybe he was mistaken. I am telling you what he thought, and he took a jail sentence to make good his word. . . .

"Four or five months ago we made our first direct challenge to an organized bootlegging ring. . . . One of the most important witnesses in that case was a subordinate who, in the parlance of the underworld, had squealed, and who was our most important witness because of the disclosures he had made. Some three weeks ago he committed suicide in a hotel in which he had locked himself. Why? Had somebody run away with his wife? Not that I ever heard of. Was he caught short in the market? We have not heard that he was in Wall Street. We did not know of any of the usual conventional reasons for suicide. I don't know why. I cannot tell you. I just state the facts. There was the most important witness in our first direct challenge to a big, wealthy, powerful and hitherto unmolested gang of bootleggers, and our most important witness committed suicide within three weeks. Is that prohibition lawlessness, the kind I am talking about? Nothing controversial about that; nothing debatable about that; no question there of personal liberty. I am telling you what is happening. . . .

"Now, I will take up the other half, the second half of what I call prohibition lawlessness. Millions and millions and millions of dollars made by bootlegging in this vicinity in the importing business and, of course, the real business is the bootlegging of industrial alcohol from which liquor is made. For the most part the millions and millions of dollars made cannot be made without a perfect carnival of corruption and bribery and perjury and violation of somebody's oath. That is the thing that gives you sort of a jolt when you get into these things, and you see it. It cannot be done without corruption, and again, if you think for a moment that you can have wholesale gigantic corruption of the National, State or City employees, going along very nicely and doing no harm whatever because the law happens to be one as to which there is a difference of opinion, I think you are greatly mistaken. You . . . have blood poison on your great toe from a dye in the sock. You say, 'That is all right, I don't mind losing a toe, I think I will just keep it down there. I believe in it. That is the way I feel about it.' You cannot control the spread of poisonous pus in that way; and think of the effect on our entire civil service, National, City and State, to whom we look for the operation of our government, to whom we look for the operation of our city, to whom we look for the protection of our property, to whom we look for our very lives. . . . I say that prohibition lawlessness, the consequence of the passage of a law without any machinery for enforcing it, or without any effort to modify or repeal it, has been a very serious contribution to the present condition of crime."[40]

[40] 11 *The Consensus,* June, 1926, pp. 24-30.

It is a measure of the hopelessness of reasonable men in 1926 that Buckner at the time of this speech still felt it more likely that New York State would add its laws and courts and jails to the struggle against liquor than that the insane Amendment would be repealed. When, instead, the state legislature authorized a popular referendum on the question of prohibition (which the voters thereupon opposed by a four-to-one margin), the cause of enforcement was clearly lost. For more than a year, Buckner had been completely absorbed in the task of reorganizing his office, hunting for ways to enforce prohibition, and speaking to groups which might do something about the catastrophe the law had made. He was far too experienced and sophisticated a man not to recognize his own failure. After April, 1926, he stopped making speeches about prohibition. For the remaining year of his service as U.S. Attorney, he would work for the government mostly as a trial lawyer.

4

Actually, as Buckner kept trying to tell the groups to which he spoke, the prohibition law was only a small fraction of the work Congress had given the U.S. Attorney. Personally, Buckner was always particularly proud of the work of his staff in prosecuting fraudulent bankrupts (the office secured more than a hundred convictions on criminal charges in bankruptcy cases during his first year), and he made speeches to businessmen's groups to urge creditors to press their complaints. "Commercial fraud," he told the National Association of Credit Men, "is a rather genteel term applied to this class of crimes. I call them business burglaries."[41] In a speech to the members of the Associated Dress Industries, he asked, "What would you think of a man who had his pocket picked on the subway, then offered to settle on a fifty-fifty basis and not prosecute?"[42]

Regardless of prohibition, the office had to carry the traditional burden of prosecuting customs, narcotics, mail-theft, counterfeiting, white-slave, tax-evasion and other criminal cases; and there were mountains of work, mostly dull, in a civil division. Buckner fought to win control over antitrust prosecutions in the New York federal courts, and this battle was formally successful, in terms of newspaper announce-

41 *New York Times,* 3/23/25, p. 23.
42 *New York Times,* 10/8/25, p. 54.

ments; but Alexander Royce, who headed the division, said many years later that "the real decisions about which cases to prosecute were, are and always will be in the hands of the Attorney General." Buckner was, however, proud of the conspiracies (particularly those in the food trades) uncovered and prosecuted to consent decrees by Royce and his staff.

Most of the young men wanted to work in the Criminal Division, where the trial load was heaviest; and as they won their first cases, Buckner would celebrate their accomplishments in *Scraps*. "Carl Newton," one such note read, "tried the first case of his career this week and secured a conviction. This is the first time in American jurisprudence that a colored man has been convicted of selling narcotics where the case was prosecuted by a member of the English Bar. The defendant stated afterwards that had he known he was being prosecuted by an English barrister, he would have pleaded guilty for fear the case might result in an acquittal."[43]

David Peck was less fortunate; he had a counterfeiting case where the defendant had been assigned as his lawyer Congressman Martin Ansorge. His story was that he had got the bogus fifty while selling cases of bootleg whiskey on a dimly lit wharf in Weehawken; and Ansorge went out to the Irving Trust Company, got a fifty-dollar bill, and showed the jury how difficult it would be to tell the real from the fake even in decent light. Peck took the loss philosophically: "He was lucky he was assigned a lawyer who could get a fifty-dollar bill."

Perhaps the oddest case that came into the office was an unwanted gift from Buckner's old friend Henry H. Curran, moved from the Board of Aldermen some years before to be Commissioner of Immigration to the Port of New York. An elegant English lady named Vera, Countess Cathcart arrived one day en route to Washington for the tryouts of a play she had written, called *Ashes*; and where her statement on entering the country called for marital status, she penciled a "D" for divorced. A few questions were asked, and it developed that her divorce had been a spectacular one, with her husband as complainant and the Earl of Craven named as corespondent. The immigration laws forbade the admission even as a visitor of anyone who had committed a crime involving moral turpitude; and so far as the Immigration Department was concerned an admission of adultery was just that.

[43] *Scraps*, 5/22/26.

It was announced that Countess Cathcart would be sent to Ellis Island and thence home, and hell broke loose.

Buckner put Samuel C. Coleman to work on definitions of moral turpitude in other countries, and sent over a request to Root-Clark for anybody who was free to look up some law for him. Gottlieb was in London working on Guggenheim problems, and Buckner sent him a wire: "Cable me immediately whether adultery is crime in England and in Capetown South Africa and by what statute."[44] The reply the next day showed why Gottlieb had become one of Buckner's favorite young men: "Adultery not crime in England. This is opinion our own solicitors Slaughter & May and of solicitors for London police Wontner & Sons and has been confirmed by Sir Travers Humphreys, leading criminal barrister. Neither is adultery crime in South Africa. This is opinion Bircham & Co., solicitors doing large South African business including divorce and of British High Commissioner for South Africa."[45] That disposed of that problem.

As the newspapers developed the story, it turned out that the Earl himself was in the United States; and women's groups waxed furious that in a case of this kind the man had been admitted while the woman was excluded. (The Earl, the immigration people explained lamely, had written "M" when asked marital status, so nobody had inquired.) Arthur Garfield Hays sued the government for the Countess' release and Buckner was in the middle. The adultery had occurred in France, where supposedly it was a crime (!), but the divorce suit had been brought in South Africa, where adultery was not a crime. Hays knew nothing about the South African law, but Buckner's people had found it. The Labor Department agreed to release the Countess for ten days, without explanation. Frankfurter wrote an article for *The New Republic* condemning the barbarity of American immigration; and Buckner tried to head him off with a telegram:

I think you ought to postpone writing on Cathcart case until the next development. I suspect Department released her because of what I told them would be my attitude on question of getting . . . South African law [before the court]. I told them I would not be a party to suppression of a material fact and would not rely on technical position of state of the

44 Buckner to Gottlieb, 2/19/26.
45 Gottlieb to Buckner, 4/20/26.

record and burden of proof being upon alien but I offered to abdicate my job as government lawyer for this case with public statement as to why I [had] done so. All this confidential and not for publication. The mysterious release followed without my knowledge. . . .[46]

Eventually Hays got the government to court on a writ of habeas corpus, and by prearrangement Buckner and the department did not oppose; and the matter passed into limbo.

It had a strange sequel, however. While the Countess was in New York, Earl Carroll held a party at his theater where the *pièce de résistance,* at about four in the morning, was a naked chorus girl bathing in a tub filled with some sparkling beverage widely believed to be champagne. The men in the audience were invited to come up to the stage and fill their glasses from the tub, and about twenty of them did so. In the *Daily Mirror* the next morning the story of the party was front-page news; and there were rumors around town that Countess Cathcart, who had been at the party, was the girl in the tub. This was not true—the display was of a seventeen-year-old chorine with the stage name of Joyce Hawley—but everything considered the incident seemed to call for investigation by the federal grand jury. Called to testify, Carroll not only denied that there was champagne in the tub or that liquor had been served, but refused to identify his guests or his bootlegger, and actually swore that there had never been any girl in any tub. He was summoned to the grand jury room again, and repeated all his denials, and Harlan and Horace Hitchcock, who were running the grand jury, secured his indictment for perjury.

The trial of Earl Carroll, in May, 1926, was the first case in which Buckner as U.S. Attorney played a major courtroom role. Harlan handled most of the direct examination himself, drawing out from various witnesses, some of them prominent, the story of a rather distasteful party, and building up Miss Hawley as a much-abused young lady. Under cross-examination, Miss Hawley (who had been posing nude as an artist's model from the age of fourteen) seemed far less wholesome, if no less toothsome; and, of course, the notoriety of the case had greatly advanced her stage career. Guido Pantaleoni of Buckner's office, who didn't much like the prosecution, commented to him, "What would this girl have been doing if she wasn't in the tub? She'd have been sweeping floors."

[46] Buckner to Frankfurter, 2/24/26.

Herbert C. Smyth, Carroll's attorney, rested his case on the proposition that the government hadn't proved there had been alcoholic beverages served at the party, and the questions about Miss Hawley had not been material to the purpose of the grand jury investigation. If Carroll had lied to protect Miss Hawley, after all, "he lied like a gentleman." Buckner in his summation treated Miss Hawley as once he had treated Stokes: "Miss Hawley's not mine. I didn't put her in a bathtub. She's Carroll's. I brought her here because she is the woman he put in the tub. Any time that Earl Carroll puts a better woman in one of his bathtubs on the stage of his theater, then I'll bring a better woman to this courtroom." What stayed in everybody's mind was Buckner's redefinition of the crime of perjury for the benefit of the jurors. Carroll, he said, had *"spat upon the Bible* and thrown it down four flights of stairs."[47]

The jury convicted, and the Court of Appeals affirmed. Buckner wrote rather bitterly in *Scraps*:

The idea seems to be that it would have been ungentlemanly for Carroll to have disclosed the name of his bootlegger or at least to disclose something, whatever it was Mr. Smyth had in mind. Whenever a man is before the Grand Jury and feels that telling the truth will not be gentlemanly, then it would seem that he should be willing to refuse to testify entirely and go to jail like a gentleman. This martyrdom would have raised the issue neatly and in a dignified way without polluting our courts. A gentleman ought not to want to get something for nothing.[48]

As Carroll was led out one door of Judge Henry W. Goddard's courtroom, another show business figure was led in the other, and Buckner remained. Charles H. Duell, Jr. had been a magnate of the silent screen, organizer of Inspiration Pictures and proprietor of a seven-year contract, running from 1922, with Lillian Gish. Indeed, at one point he and Miss Gish had been engaged to be married. This had fallen through, and so had much else, and in 1926 Miss Gish went to Louis S. Levy of Chadbourne, Stanchfield & Levy for advice on getting out of the contract. Levy duly provided a theory under which Duell had been guilty of a breach, and Duell brought suit in federal court to enjoin Miss Gish from working for anybody else for the duration of the contract. A lawyer himself, Duell drew his

[47] *New York Times*, 5/27/26, p. 1.
[48] *Scraps*, 1/15/27.

own affidavits, which were both complicated and—it developed—dishonest. Miss Gish's trial counsel, Max Steuer, tore Duell apart under cross-examination, and Duell owned up to such serious misstatements both in his documents and in his testimony that Judge Julian Mack held Duell in $10,000 bail for perjury and referred the transcript to the U.S. Attorney's office.

Buckner turned it over to George S. Leisure, who had come to the U.S. Attorney's office after three years in the Charles Evans Hughes firm because he wanted to try cases. After winning his first one, *Scraps* reported in its first issue, he "soared to the clouds on wings of elation. Upon his return to earth, he immediately appropriated the balance of the term for the trial of his cases."[49] Of all the young men, he had the most spectacular record of success before a jury: Buckner liked to say it was because he looked so honest, he had an "affidavit face." Leisure prepared the case. "I walked uptown with him to his house every day," Leisure recalled. "He'd say, 'Give me the facts.' When I wrote the trial brief, he knew everything that was in it. He told me to make the opening statement and put in the direct case, while he handled the cross-examination and the summation."

The Duell case took three weeks to try, before a courtroom crowded every morning by spectators hoping against hope that Miss Gish herself, who was known to be in town, might be called as a witness. She had appeared, munching carrots on the stand, during the trial of the injunction proceeding. Leisure and Buckner decided not to call her, largely, one suspects, for fear of what might come out on cross-examination about her relations with Duell and perhaps with other backers of the film company Duell had founded. Buckner, delighted to be practicing his profession again after so long a stretch as an administrator and public speaker, opened one issue of *Scraps* with a page occupied entirely by the words

ACTUALLY ENGAGED
United States vs. Duell
E.R.B.[50]

Nathan Burkan in his summation charged that the whole prosecution was a combination of a publicity stunt by Miss Gish and a search for revenge by W. Averell Harriman, one of the backers of Duell's

[49] *Scraps,* 3/21/25.
[50] *Scraps,* 6/12/25.

former company, who had reason to seek revenge. Buckner in summation complained, "We have tried to try one case, and Mr. Burkan has tried to try another. We are trying the case of the Government against Duell; he is trying Duell against Gish. He has tried to confuse the issues by trying the Gish case all over again. It is of the highest importance to the courts, to the profession of the law, and to all citizens that this man should not be allowed to come into the courts and perjure himself and get away with it."[51] But the best the government could get was a hung jury.

"As a matter of fact and as a matter of law," Buckner wrote in *Scraps,*

I believe the case was proved. From a jury standpoint, there were many considerations which operated strongly in defendant's favor. The most powerful of these considerations was the fact, brought out by defendant's counsel, that during the time Lillian Gish worked for Duell she received nearly $300,000 and during the same time Duell lost every cent he had put into the enterprise and the company itself operated at a heavy loss; that at the present time, Lillian Gish has a contract calling for many thousands of dollars a week and that Duell is penniless, ruined, friendless. . . . All perjury cases are extremely difficult and to be successful, the perjury must be dramatic, clearly proved, and the sort of perjury which shocks the moral sense of the jurors. We tried to persuade the jury that all questions of sympathy were for the judge on the sentence and not for the jury on the verdict and during most of the deliberations, five of the jurymen took this point of view. The best vote scored by the defendant was 8 to 4 for acquittal.[52]

Presently, with Judge Mack's consent, Buckner nol-prossed the case.

Next on the calendar (among Buckner's reforms had been an insistence on keeping the office active through the summer) was the largest of the bootlegging cases in the office, involving indictments against more than sixty persons, members of the ring in America and elsewhere, and in the Coast Guard. (This was the case Buckner mentioned to the members of the New York Economic Club, where a key witness had committed suicide in a locked hotel room.) The case had been prepared by Herman Stichman, William Stevenson and Harlan, with substantial help from A. Bruce Bielaski, the first

[51] *New York Times,* 6/15/26, p. 27.
[52] *Scraps,* 6/19/25.

head of the Bureau of Investigation in the Department of Justice, now under contract as an investigator for the Prohibition Administration (at a fee one-third larger than Buckner's salary). The chief defendant was William V. Dwyer, man about town and part owner of the Mount Royal Race Track in Montreal and the Coney Island Race Track in Cincinnati.

When the case came to trial July 7, Dwyer asked for an adjournment on the grounds that he had just had to fire his counsel, who had demanded an exorbitant fee, and needed time to prepare the new man. Buckner pointed out that the next day was opening day at Dwyer's Cincinnati race track, which was a more likely reason for his wishing a postponement, and the trial proceeded. Picking a jury was not easy, the normal problem of New York's preponderance of Wets being compounded by the reluctance of any citizen to sit three or four weeks in a hot courtroom in July. One venireman excused himself because "in the first place I am against Prohibition, and in the second place I am against its enforcement."[53]

Again, the announcement was that Buckner was "assisting" his assistants, and Stichman, who was all of twenty-four years old, put in the opening statement, crediting Dwyer and his friends with having bootlegged $40 million of booze between October, 1923, and June, 1926. (To relieve Stichman's nervousness, Buckner had him "rehearse" the opening before all the government's lawyers in the case.[54]) It was not an easy prosecution, partly because the most important witness, a "mariner" Bielaski had found and primed (and, with several other witnesses, put on the government's payroll for more money than he could expect to make on a job) lied on the stand about his personal history to the point where Buckner, when the Dwyer trial was over, convicted his own witness for perjury and sent him to jail.[55]

---

[53] *New York Times,* 7/9/26, p. 7.

[54] Stichman to author, 1965.

[55] This was not the only occasion on which Bielaski got Buckner into trouble. Six months later Fiorello LaGuardia learned that to trap some wholesale bootleggers Bielaski had set up both a fake perfume factory and a speakeasy, which were selling liquor made from denatured alcohol which had been inadequately renatured; he demanded that Buckner indict Bielaski and his colleagues, and Buckner had to take a trip to Washington to convince the Congressman that Bielaski was making an honest attempt to get honest evidence—and that it wouldn't happen again.

Three highly dramatic moments in the trial bore signs of Buckner's theatrical flair. The first of them came on the day of the opening statements, when one of the defendants changed his plea to guilty. A few days into the trial, Stichman suddenly produced as a witness a Coast Guardsman, Paul Crim, who was among the defendants and supposedly a fugitive from justice. Then, defense counsel Benjamin Spellman having made much of the mysterious Bielaski, Buckner swore the investigator as his witness, asked him no questions, and offered Spellman the chance to examine.

Whatever Carroll may have been, Dwyer really was a gentleman. While the jury was out, he came over to Buckner and congratulated him on his summation. "You know," Dwyer said, "while you were speaking, I thought to myself, I really *should* be convicted."[56] When the jury came in with a verdict of guilty against Dwyer and one of his assistants, Dwyer shook hands with the prosecutor, who asked him "if he had not received a square deal." He "replied, with a smile, 'Positively.' "[57]

Most of the defendants, however, were acquitted, from which Buckner drew a lesson for his staff:

In the Dwyer case, Paul Crim testified that he was second in command of a Coast Guard boat which brought in liquor for Dwyer, the commander of the boat being Edward Gallagher who was on trial. Crim's testimony was not disputed. It was corroborated by another member of the crew. I cannot believe the jury had any doubt as to its truth because it was detailed and convincing and yet the jury acquitted Commander Gallagher.

It appeared from Crim's testimony that he suggested both to Dwyer and to his Commander that they bring in some liquor in order that the crew might make some Christmas money. Gallagher told him to sound out the crew and report. Crim did so and the plan was carried out. I can account for Gallagher's acquittal only on the theory that Crim was the moving spirit of the matter. . . .

The law concerning entrapment has been discussed in a previous edition of Scraps where cases were collected and the comparatively simple legal principle stated. What is sometimes overlooked is the fact that there are two separate defenses based on entrapment. One is a legal defense and is addressed to the court either on a motion to dismiss

[56] C. Dickerman Williams to author, 1966.
[57] *New York Times* 7/27/26, p. 1.

or, if the facts are disputed, on a request to give the jury an appropriate instruction. The other defense of entrapment is addressed to the jury. It is based upon the national prejudice against bad sportsmanship. . . . Juries will acquit on the entrapment defense where judges may hold no entrapment is made out within the decided cases. Where the District Attorney's office has anything to do with the situation, most positive instructions should be given the Government official to handle the matter in such a way as to be the least offensive to the jury. The agent should not make the slightest advance. Agents are often so eager to make a case that what is essentially the offering of a bribe becomes imperceptibly the soliciting of a bribe and juries are very quick to pronounce the transition. . . .

Of course, there was no entrapment of Gallagher because Crim was not a Government official and had no idea that the rum running of the Coast Guard would ever become known. And yet the same principle was involved. Here was a man who worked up the deal, who urged his Commander to go into it, and who persuaded the crew to join in the enterprise. This entrepreneur of betrayal of the Government became a witness, received immunity under the law and the jury apparently balked at convicting the man who, although his superior, yielded to the temptation which was organized by the witness. This is indeed a new kind of entrapment defense. But the defense of bad sportsmanship is the same as where the Government agent organizes himself into a bribe.[58]

5

"Buckner went up to do that job as a *professional* job—not as 'public service,'" Justice Harlan said recently of Buckner's twenty-five months as U.S. Attorney. He considered himself the government's lawyer, and the government his client—"in my poor way of thinking," he told the Georgia Bar Association, "one of the most sacred relationships that can possibly exist between two individuals in this world." From this relationship there flowed a code of conduct, which Buckner illustrated for the Georgia lawyers through the case of a mythical Johnson who had his life's savings tied up in a corporation which went bankrupt:

"I say, 'Johnson, you are in pretty bad. I think I can get you thirty cents on the dollar. That will keep the boys in college anyway. You have to give up building the house. I think I can get you thirty cents on the dollar.' I worry about Johnson; I take his troubles home with

[58] *Scraps,* 7/31/26.

me on the subway; I sleep with them and smoke with them; and I think about Johnson while shaving; I throw my morning paper away, and I worry about Johnson the way lawyers do about their clients. I keep on and keep on. Do I go around to my friends, and say, 'By the way, you know I represent Johnson; what do they think of him around here? I think I can get thirty cents for him; do you think I would be a little stronger with the boys if I got him only twenty?' They reply, 'The boys don't think much of Johnson, you know.' 'Well, you don't want me to throw him overboard?' 'Oh, no, no, but I would sort of ease him out.' 'You mean at about twenty?' 'Oh, about fifteen cents.' I go around to others of my friends and I tell them that I represent Johnson and that I think I can get him thirty cents on the dollar, and they tell me that there are others that might be interested in this matter and I had better sell Johnson out a little bit, and pretend to read him the law and make a lot of noise. Now, a lawyer hardly can sink so low, even at the New York City Bar, who could even find the tongue to talk language of that kind.

"Well, will you tell me what is the difference? Will you tell me what is the difference between a lawyer who has a private client and a lawyer who has the Government for a client, who may be in bad? You think you can get the Government ten cents or you may be able to get it fifteen cents. Is there any essential difference between the two cases? When I get through with Johnson, I want to go down and say, 'Johnson, I got you thirty cents.' I want to shake hands with Mrs. Johnson and say, 'I got you thirty cents. A smarter lawyer might have done better for you. A more brilliant man might have done better, but I want to say that no man, who is not any smarter than I am, could have done any more than I have done because I have given you all that is in me. I have given you all the intelligence that I have. I have given you all the brains that I have, and I have given you all the legal judgment and loyal service that I have, and I am very happy to have done this.'

"When I get through with this job, I want to be able to take Uncle Sam by the hand, and say, 'Client, you didn't pay me much; doggone your old hide, you are a skinflint when it comes to pay, but I have got you thirty cents on the dollar. . . .' I can throw back my shoulders and walk out a free man as a lawyer who has done the best for his client, and I can say to anybody that does not like it, 'I have something inside of me that is better than your praise. I have something inside me that is better than asking my wife to dinner; I have got something inside of me, and that is a consciousness, that every lawyer should have, that he had done his level best for his client.' "[59]

[59] Annual Address to Georgia Bar Association, 1925, pp. 20-23.

CHAPTER NINE

U.S. v. Thomas W. Miller

and Harry M. Daugherty

Among the federal matters pending in New York when Buckner took command in the Southern District was a criminal investigation growing out of the payment in 1921 of some $7 million by the United States Government to the Société Suisse pour Valeurs de Metaux. This sum was the sales price plus accrued dividends and interest for 36,344 shares of stock representing 49 percent of the ownership of the American Metals Company. The stock had been seized in 1918 by the Alien Property Custodian, who had been informed by the company, that, although the names on the certificates were those of American citizens, in fact these shares were owned by Metall-gesellschaft and Metallbank of Germany and were therefore subject to seizure under the terms of the Trading-with-the-Enemy Act. On April 7, 1919, the stock was sold to American citizens at auction, and the then Alien Property Custodian, A. Mitchell Palmer, made an announcement: "The German metal octopus spread his tentacles across the ocean and over the United States into Mexico and South America, but for the present, surely, and for all time, he has been driven back, and a wall of Americanism erected which, it is hoped, he will never again be able to scale."[1]

On September 20, 1921, a former captain in the German Army, Richard Merton, who was president of Metallgesellschaft and chair-

[1] *New York Times,* 4/8/19, p. 9.

man of Metallbank, filed claim papers purporting to prove that during the war the stock in American Metals had been owned not by German nationals but by an affiliated Swiss holding company. The United States Government, of course, was not in the business of seizing Swiss-owned assets. Three days after the claim papers were filed, they were approved by Alien Property Custodian Thomas W. Miller, a Harding appointee, and by Assistant Attorney General Guy D. Goff, and Mr. Merton had his $7 million. This was the largest such claim ever approved, and the fastest approval ever granted in a large matter. A similar and less complicated claim involving Standard Oil of New Jersey stock had required 584 days for processing.

Questions about this transaction were raised in the New York *World* as early as the spring of 1922, and President Harding began to worry. He asked Attorney General Harry M. Daugherty to look into the matter, and Daugherty procured a letter from Goff, saying, "The proof in this case was the best prepared proof submitted to the Department in any of the thousands of claims presented as yet."[2] The matter came up again, however, in the Senate investigations of the Justice Department; and when Stone succeeded Daugherty the question of the payment to Merton was pressing business. Special Assistant Attorney General Hiram C. Todd had run into some information on the case while handling other prosecutions, and Stone assigned it to him.

In September, 1925, Todd presented to the grand jury in New York evidence which led to the indictment of Thomas W. Miller (who had since resigned as Alien Property Custodian), and of Richard Merton and his European associates, for conspiracy to defraud the Government of the United States. Frankfurter had known Miller, who was a war hero and one of the founders of the American Legion, from time they spent together at Versailles during the Peace Conference; and he wrote Buckner to find out what was going on. "The Miller case," Buckner replied, "was handled exclusively by Hiram C. Todd. . . . When I came in, I made clear my views about Special Assistants to Colonel [William, or 'Wild Bill'] Donovan, but Colonel Donovan asked me to permit Todd to go on with this matter because he had worked on it several months before I took office. I therefore know nothing about the case except what Todd tells me

[2] *U. S.* v. *Thomas W. Miller,* Record on Appeal, p. 1098.

and I have not had time to talk more than ten minutes about it. . . .
Todd is very much of a prosecutor and I do not think I would take
his judgment, but in this particular case he has stated the facts, which
look bad, and Miller's unwillingness to vindicate himself is to my
mind a very suspicious circumstance."[3]

On December 1 Todd resigned, and Buckner asked Kenneth M.
Simpson (a future Congressman and Republican county leader in
Manhattan) to take a look at the evidence. What Simpson reported
back about the case made Buckner's hair stand on end, and presently
four of the assistants (eventually ten of them) were digging into the
history of Merton's $7 million.

The story which emerged was as follows: In November of 1919,
hard-pressed in the horrors of the postwar German economy and
looking for assets, the Merton family had transferred to its Swiss
holding company its claims to the American Metals stock which
the U.S. Government had seized. About a year later, the Swiss company had entered into correspondence with John Foster Dulles of
Sullivan & Cromwell about the possibility of its recovering this stock
as a company incorporated in a nation which had been neutral during
the war. Dulles replied that no transfer effected in 1919 could possibly alter the legal situation of the period in 1918, when the stock
was seized. Nevertheless, Merton came to America in March, 1921,
to press his claim. Dulles took the question down to the office of
the Alien Property Custodian in Washington, where he spoke with
George N. Williams, Miller's first assistant; and Williams told him
that on the hypothetical case he posed his client would not stand a
chance.

Merton thereupon went looking for somebody who might help
him more than Dulles could, and he was introduced to John T. King,
Republican National Committeeman from Connecticut and Harry
Daugherty's ally in the push which put Harding over in the Republican Convention of 1920. King told Merton to get rid of his lawyers,
that this was the sort of matter best handled by practical men. And
he then introduced Merton to Jesse W. Smith, an easygoing business-
man who had sold his country store in Ohio to go to Washington
with the Harding administration. Smith held no government office, but
he had an office in the Justice Department and lived and traveled

[3] Buckner to Frankfurter, 11/4/25.

with Harry Daugherty—he was Daugherty's best friend, confidant, adviser and bagman. He was, Daugherty wrote later in his book about the Harding administration, "a genial, lovable youngster."[4]

In April, 1921, King and Smith introduced Merton to Miller at the Waldorf Hotel in New York, and then took him down to Washington for conferences with Miller and Williams, who may or may not have recognized Merton's claim as the hypothetical case posed only a month before by Dulles. In any event, Williams gave Merton some advice about how the claim should be prepared. Merton went back to Europe in May, and returned in July with a slightly different claim. Now the November, 1919, agreement which transferred the American Metals claims to the Swiss company was not a deal at all; it was merely confirmation of an oral transfer which had occurred a few days before the United States entered the war against Germany in April, 1917. Under these circumstances the Swiss company would indeed be entitled to the money.

Again Merton saw King, and now an arrangement was made between them. Merton gave King (who was not a lawyer) a $50,000 retainer to work in his interests in this matter, and promised him 5 percent of whatever the Swiss company might recover on its claim. The papers, however, were not yet in order, and Merton again returned to Europe. He came back to New York on September 18 with all the documents; and King and Smith (not Merton) took them down to the Alien Property Custodian on September 20. Three days later the documents had cleared Assistant Attorney General Guy D. Goff, and the money, in Treasury checks and Liberty Bonds, was on its way. Gaily, Miller decided to deliver the checks personally. He came down to New York, where Merton threw a champagne dinner in a private room at the Ritz (King, as a prohibitionist in good standing, delivered the champagne) and gave each of his collaborators a gold cigarette case as a souvenir. The next day Merton handed over to King some $391,000 in negotiable numbered Liberty Bonds which the United States Government had just issued to him. Why King's commission ran to more than 5 percent nobody was ever able to discover.

Fifty thousand dollars of these Liberty Bonds had been sold, through intermediaries, for the account of Thomas W. Miller; that

4 Daugherty and Dixon, *The Inside Story of the Harding Tragedy,* p. 245.

was the basis of the indictment. But Todd had not, apparently, traced the rest. The investigator who did this job for Buckner was Eddie Toland, whom he later described in a letter to Frankfurter as "an F.B.I. man who was sent to me by Donovan. . . . I viewed him for many months with strong suspicion as a 'plant.' I changed my mind completely upon his revelation of extreme loyalty to me personally and to the case generally. He discovered some very vital documents which in that particular case, in view of the general attitude of the powers that be in Washington, could easily have been suppressed."[5]

Toland traced the bonds by their coupons, and found that one large batch had been cashed at a Washington Court House, Ohio, bank of which Harry Daugherty's brother Mal was president. Toland also found that the Department of Justice had issued Transportation Requests to Harry Daugherty and Jess Smith for a trip from Washington to Columbus, Ohio, on the day before the coupons were cashed. Buckner sent David Peck to Washington Court House to study the situation further.

"I found that although there had been a deposit made in the bank of the amount of the coupons," Peck wrote recently, "there was no deposit slip to show the deposit or to whose account they were deposited. I then went over the ledger accounts of all the depositors of the bank to try to find the account to which the credit was made, and there was no such ledger sheet available; and it was noted that there was no ledger sheet for Harry Daugherty, Mal Daugherty or Jess Smith, although it was known that all three were depositors in the bank. I asked the Cashier for their sheets, and she said she had turned them over to Mal Daugherty."[6]

Of those who might be asked to explain this incriminating story, Smith was dead, by suicide or murder on May 30, 1923, in the house he had shared with Harry Daugherty in Washington. Todd had never called Harry to testify before his grand jury investigating the American Metals case, and he had let Mal go after only twenty minutes of questioning, without asking him to produce any records.

In the fall of 1926, after the first Daugherty-Miller trial, Herbert Croly of *The New Republic* received a private letter from Justice

[5] Buckner to Frankfurter, 2/7/41.
[6] Peck to Leo Gottlieb, 8/28/67.

Harlan Stone, criticizing him for implications in the magazine that the Justice Department had neglected to investigate Daugherty during Stone's term as Attorney General. "If Herbert has any more trouble," Buckner wrote Frankfurter rather grimly, ". . . you might let him know that Todd was appointed United States District Attorney for the Northern District on July 7, 1921, by President Harding, which means, of course, that he was virtually appointed by Daugherty. I have ascertained that he resigned from this position very soon, namely, August 29, 1922, and on the very next day was appointed a Special Assistant to the Attorney General at $10,000 a year in order to handle some case or other. This enabled him to receive twice the pay for what I presume was much less work, and I assume, although I have not yet had the matter verified, that it was at this time he opened his New York office as a $10,000 retainer would be a nice thing upon which to open an office. He was continually reappointed Special Assistant as he took up new cases and always by Daugherty because these are not presidential appointments. Therefore, although of course Stone must not have known what was going on, the fact remains that the person chosen to have charge of a case which necessarily involved at least an investigation of Daugherty was a man who was under obligations to him and had served under him." This recital was not a criticism of "Stone's intentions, which must have been of the best," but it did "expose a detail of administration."[7]

Buckner now proceeded to remedy this detail of administration, and in the process became, briefly, a national figure. The prosecution of Daugherty and Miller was, in fact, the most important single activity of Buckner's career, entitling him to a footnote in even a brief text of American history. The significance of the case lies only partly in the rank and station of the defendants. More important, and more gratifying to Buckner, was its demonstration of the government's power to cleanse itself provided significant authority were diffused among administrative branches—and its proof of the superiority of legal to legislative investigation when actual wrongdoing has been alleged. (The Congressional investigations had been mostly a circus.) Against a current of steady disapproval—but not interference—from Washington, Buckner through the first months of 1926 moved to bring the former Attorney General of the United States to trial on criminal charges.

[7] Buckner to Frankfurter, 11/18/26.

His first step was to summon Mal Daugherty back to the grand jury to produce the records of his bank. Mal said he had given the original ledgers for certain key periods and for certain accounts to his brother Harry, who was the dollar-a-year counsel to the bank; and he believed Harry had destroyed them. Buckner called Harry Daugherty, and Harry filed with Judge Thomas Thacher a written statement which Frederick Lewis Allen later immortalized at the head of a chapter in his book *Only Yesterday*:

Having been personal attorney for Warren G. Harding before he was Senator from Ohio and while he was Senator, and thereafter until his death,

—And for Mrs. Harding for a period of several years, and before her husband was elected President and after his death,

—And having been attorney for the Midland National Bank of Washington Court House, O., and for my brother, M. S. Daugherty,

—And having been Attorney-General of the United States during the time that President Harding served as President,

—And also for a time after President Harding's death under President Coolidge,

—And with all of those named, as attorney, personal friend, and Attorney-General, my relations were of the most confidential character as well as professional,

—I refuse to testify and answer questions put to me, because:

The answer I might give or make and the testimony I might give might tend to incriminate me.[8]

Buckner now sent Kenneth Simpson to Europe to talk to the European defendants in the Todd indictment; and the Europeans' lawyer, Martin W. Littleton, went along just in case. "I have hopes of getting something," Buckner wrote Frankfurther, "though I confess I cannot see why they should talk since they can easily remain out of this country the rest of their lives. As I told Simpson they are, at the worst, only 'residents from justice.' "[9] There was no way the United States Government could recover the money from Merton —and, anyway, the nation had grown ashamed of its seizure of private assets during the war; there was a strong movement to return everything to the original owners. Buckner had nothing to lose by offering a deal—especially since the indictment he now wanted was one that would cover Miller and Daugherty, not Miller and Merton.

[8] Allen, *Only Yesterday*, ch. 6.
[9] Buckner to Frankfurter, 2/16/26.

But if the Europeans were eliminated, what crime could the government charge? Bribery was barred by a three-year statute of limitations. "I remembered," Buckner wrote many years later for the benefit of the young lawyers at Root-Clark,

> that Felix Frankfurter had drawn an indictment back in 1906 before I entered the [Stimson] office, in the so-called "cotton leak" cases. On this theory, which was very novel at the time and which involved the giving out of advance information by Government subordinates in the Department of Agriculture concerning a report on cotton crops which was used by New York brokers to their advantage, these cases established a principle that the Government is defrauded if a public official does anything contrary to his official duty regardless of any money lost to the Government. In short, it is embezzlement of loyalty. I told two of the boys to look up Mr. Frankfurter's indictment and any cases upon it. They drew an indictment which withstood the challenge of demurrer.[10]

On May 7, 1926, the grand jury returned an indictment charging Miller, Daugherty and King with conspiracy to deprive the government of the honest services of Miller and Daugherty. King died within a week, leaving only the two former officials as defendants. Under the terms of this indictment, it was not necessary for the government to prove that the Merton claim was bad—just that it hadn't been properly considered. Merton could therefore testify for the prosecution.

On September 7, 1926, the defendants were brought to trial. Buckner was particularly proud of his boys' speed and efficiency in preparing the case: the indictment of former Secretary of the Interior Albert Fall had been presented on June 30, 1924, and was still pending when the Daugherty prosecution began.

Though Buckner had abandoned Todd's indictment, he followed Todd's theory of prosecution. In his day-long opening statement, he set up an easel before the jury, and with crayons of different color drew the pattern of relationships between the German companies and their Swiss affiliate, to demonstrate that Merton's claim was one that an honest man who really read the papers could not possibly have passed. Only after this point had been argued did he come to the relationships of Merton with King, Miller and (through Jess Smith) Daugherty, and to the evidence he would introduce to show who

[10] 21 *Bull,* 4/27/40, p. 174.

got the Liberty Bonds. And the first witness he called for the prosecution was Merton himself.

Particularly after what Buckner had said in the opening statement, he had to handle Merton gently. The government had put Merton up at the Yale Club, and had assigned Kenneth Simpson, a member of the club, to watch his every move. (In fact, Simpson once responded to a paging to a telephone call for Merton, and listened in; Merton found out about it, and the Yale Club expelled Simpson. Buckner felt terrible, but Simpson waved away his concern: "Getting expelled from the Yale Club," he said, "is like getting expelled from Grand Central Station.") Merton went through his paces on his meetings with King, Smith, Miller and Miller's assistant, Williams. (When Miller's attorney, Colonel William S. Rand, objected to the introduction of any evidence about Williams on the grounds that the government could not prove his connection with any alleged conspiracy, Buckner replied, "If the Court please, we do not expect to be able to prove private conversations between Miller and his first lieutenant in his own office with the door locked and the shades drawn."[11]) Though the government could not prove that either Miller or Daugherty had ever laid eyes on the actual claim papers (Williams had handled them in Miller's office and Goff in Daugherty's), Buckner was eager to put them in the record. Judge Julian Mack asked him on what grounds the documents were offered. "Buckner," George Leisure recalled, "with his brilliant mind, said, 'Reasonable availability, Your Honor'—just as though you could look up in a book and find a heading 'Reasonable availability'!" The documents were admitted.

Merton, of course, had every reason to wish to say that the whole deal was perfectly proper—that his claim was a good one, and so far as he was concerned what King did for him was wholly legitimate. He had paid King for good and valuable services, and that was the end of it. Rand, whose client was in deep trouble unless he could explain how the $50,000 in Liberty Bonds had passed through his hands (via brokerage accounts opened for him under other names by friends), decided to use Merton to establish the essential innocence of the transaction. While Daugherty's lawyer, Max Steuer, worried and fussed at the defense table, Rand on "cross-examination" drew

[11] *New York Times,* 9/11/26, p. 2.

from a helpful Merton what amounted to a complete exoneration of Miller. Buckner sat by, not objecting, and the newspapers speculated on what he was up to.

The day after Rand finished, Buckner revealed the strategy. Rand, he claimed, had made Merton his witness; and now the government had the right to cross-examine its own witness. Judge Mack accepted this theory—over the strong objections of Steuer, who truthfully said that he had not made Merton Daugherty's witness at all—and Buckner proceeded to put Merton through hopeless contortions trying to justify the patently invalid claim.

Most of the rest was straightforward, tracing the Liberty Bonds and their coupons through brokerage houses and banks. Buckner's assistant Carl E. Newton drew a chart, copies of which were distributed to the jury, to trace the future history of each of the bonds Merton had given King. The former secretary-treasurer of American Metals, in whose name much of the Merton stock had been registered, testified that until long after the war he had never heard of the Swiss company which supposedly owned it. Buckner showed that on the day the claim was pending for final approval by Goff, telegrams were sent to Miller (who was out of Washington) on its progress— the only example of such urgent communication in the files of the Alien Property Custodian. (To counter Buckner's demonstration that the American Metals matter had moved through Washington faster than any other very large claim, the defense introduced evidence that a $107,000 claim submitted to the A.P.C. by Root-Clark had cleared in 1920 in less than twenty-four hours.) Much of this was not harmful to Daugherty, and Steuer came fully alive only when the government put brother Mal on the stand to say that Harry had destroyed the records which might have proved the deposit of the Liberty Bonds in his, Mal's or Jess' account. On cross-examination, Steuer was the picture of reasonableness, wishing to have all the information before the jury:

"You told [Harry Daugherty]," Steuer inquired, "that you wanted those papers because you had been subpoenaed to produce them before the grand jury in New York?"

"Yes, sir."

"And he told you he had destroyed them?"

"Yes, sir."

"Now, did he tell you at that time—did he say anything at that time of the circumstances under which he destroyed those accounts?"

"He said that he had taken them to the shack and burned them down there."

"That we understand."

"That he couldn't make anything out of them and just simply destroyed them and to forget them."[12]

The defense was straightforward. Williams and Goff, who testified, were the men who had actually passed on the claim. Williams said Miller had barely mentioned it to him, and Goff said Daugherty had never discussed it at all. Under cross-examination, neither was an impressive witness. Williams had to admit that he had not in any other case approved a claim based on an oral transfer, and that Merton's papers now looked weak. Having witnessed what happened to Williams when he tried to argue that the claim was good because the oral transfer was good, Goff (who had since become a Republican Senator from West Virginia and was running for re-election) asserted on the stand that the claim was good because the Swiss holding company long before the war had owned the controlling interest in the German corporations which owned the American Metals stock. This impossible theory of corporation law brought Steuer to his feet to protest, but having said it Goff was stuck with it.

Neither Miller nor Daugherty took the stand in his own defense, though both had been saying to the press for months that at the right time they would explain everything which looked suspicious to the uninformed.

In summation, Colonel Rand relied on the fact that Buckner had not plainly proved actual wrongdoing by Miller. The government's own witness said the claim was perfectly good; indeed, the government had dropped its previous indictment based on the charge that the claim was fraudulent. True, Merton's Liberty Bonds had passed through Miller's hands, but that was not proof that Miller had got them from King—he could have come by them in any number of legitimate ways. Miller had carried the checks and bonds by hand to Merton because the interest on $7 million was costing the government $1,000 a day, and he wished to expedite the matter to save the taxpayers' money.

12 *New York Times*, 9/25/26, p. 3.

Steuer had an easier time, because, while public opinion could scarcely doubt that Daugherty was involved in this dirty business ("A larger jury," the *Times* wrote somewhat sententiously, ". . . was deeply and painfully impressed"[13]), the evidence to connect him with Merton or Miller was scarce. The dangerous fact was the destruction of the bank records, and Steuer met it head on in summation. "It was in some mad, lone moment," he told the jury, "that Harry Daugherty destroyed these sheets. They had been produced before the Todd grand jury in October. The prosecutor had said he didn't want to see them. They went back to Ohio. What happened? Harry Daugherty took them to that little shack of his and his brother's outside Washington Court House. Harry Daugherty, yesterday sought after by all the land, today hounded; a broken man; his life spent; his best friend, the President, dead; his close friend Jess Smith, gone, a suicide; his wife gone; his political career over. He went to the shack—and those whom the gods would destroy they first make mad."[14]

Buckner was having none of this, of course; the case was clear. "If you acquit Harry Daugherty and Tom Miller," he told the jury, "I want no more public office. Acquittal will mean your commendation of the prostituting of public office. . . . Miller took an oath, and with the same hand that swore, he stole. Daugherty took an oath, and through Jess Smith, he stole."[15]

Judge Mack kept the jury out three nights and three days. One of the jurors who was insisting on acquittal in the jury room complained in open court that the delay was putting him under pressure. But Mack was willing to risk it. The fact was that the courtroom was staffed with marshals and guards appointed under the Daugherty regime, and both prosecution and court had reason to fear tampering with the jury. But the dissenters stuck it out, and finally Mack accepted their inescapable disagreement. The final votes were 10-2 for conviction of Miller, 7-5 for conviction of Daugherty. Several jurors later told Buckner's assistants that everybody would have been prepared to find the defendants guilty of taking bribes, but that several were unconvinced that the prosecution had met the standards

[13] *New York Times,* 10/13/25, p. 24.
[14] *New York Times,* 10/8/25, p. 7.
[15] *New York Times,* 10/9/25, p. 1.

of proof of a highly technical indictment as defined in Mack's highly technical charge. "One juryman," Buckner wrote in *Scraps*, "is reported to have rejected documentary evidence on the ground that no man could be convicted of conspiracy on 'inferences.' We have had trouble before with jurymen in considering a charge of conspiracy. Conspiracy sounds like a horrible crime to them and they think of it in terms of a subterranean gunpowder plot."[16]

Daugherty professed himself saddened by the jury's failure to acquit, but Steuer issued a statement explaining it. The jury had been confused, he said, by the "masterly presentation of the case by District Attorney Buckner. He omitted nothing. His opening address was so masterly that we had the comfort of assuming that he would be unable to do anything that would be more injurious to the defense. He presented his evidence in so fair a way that some of the jurors believed it convincing, and, finally, he summed up the case in so persuasive a manner that some of the jurors accepted his arguments in lieu of proof. In short, the one great reason why General Daugherty was not acquitted was Buckner."

Steuer admitted that some suspicion might still hang over Daugherty as a result of his failure to take the stand in his own defense. "It was not," Steuer said, "anything connected with this case that impelled him to refrain from so doing. He would have been glad to have Mr. Buckner ask him anything that had a bearing upon the case. He feared, however—and perhaps absolutely without reason—that Mr. Buckner would cross-examine about matters political that would not involve Mr. Daugherty concerning which he knew and as to which he would never make disclosure. . . .

"The destruction of the ledger sheets did not conceal anything that had the slightest bearing on this case. . . . If the jury knew the real reason for destroying the ledger sheets they would commend rather than condemn Mr. Daugherty, but he insisted on silence."[17]

It is possible to explain Steuer's statement only on the theory that he was sure the case was closed. (He meant the tribute to Buckner's opening, however; Judge Aron Steuer recently remembered that when his father asked him to do some work on the case between trials, "he just threw me Buckner's opening statement and said, 'That's all you

16 *Scraps*, 10/16/25.
17 *New York Times*, 10/11/25, pp. 1-4.

have to know about it.' ") Prominent in Tammany circles, Steuer must have been conscious of the kind of political pressure that a Republican President and Justice Department would bring to bear on a Republican U.S. Attorney to let this particular sleeping dog lie. Buckner had brought Miller and Daugherty to trial; honor was satisfied; why persist?

But Buckner went elsewhere for his advice: specifically, to Frankfurter and Lippmann, and to the partners in Root-Clark. "He laid out the case," Cloyd Laporte recalled, "and asked if he should proceed. If he failed to win it, would it look like a persecution? We all said if he couldn't win it what the public would think was, the law was an ass." Bethuel Webster was returning from his home in Colorado following a brief vacation; Buckner asked him to sound out opinion in the West. By October 20, ten days after the jury reported back its disagreement, Buckner could write Frankfurter: "Just a line at this moment to tell you that I have definitely decided to try the case again, notwithstanding it will, of course, be impossible for me to dramatize with the same surprises as before and notwithstanding the fact that it may come out worse instead of better. . . . All of this is conditioned upon Merton being willing to come back and Littleton is sending him a cable today. He was more of the defendant's witness than mine, and I gave him a pretty rough cross-examination, and he may feel that as a volunteer he thanks me for my applause but respectfully declines the encore, to paraphrase a retort of Ed Warren to me in corporations. This is not yet public."[18]

Arthur Schwartz remembered that at this time Buckner sent him to the library to look up an odd question. "As a general rule, in a second trial," Schwartz said, "if a witness is unavailable you can read his testimony from the first trial. But Buckner could have kept Merton here under subpoena. Had he disabled himself by not holding Merton? I went to look it up, and all the books were out of the library. Someone else was working on the same question. Finally, I came back to Buckner with a memo—you *could* read the testimony. Buckner said, 'I think you're right.' Then I said, 'But, Mr. Buckner, I noticed these other people working on it.' And he said, 'That's all right—I do things that way. It's important enough to be thorough.' "

On November 3, which was election day, Buckner publicly an-

18 Buckner to Frankfurter, 10/20/26.

nounced that he would try Miller and Daugherty again, with a trial date in early December. Although George Leisure and some others on Buckner's staff were convinced that Judge Mack had saved the defendants' hash by delivering a charge beyond the jury's capacity to understand, Miller's lawyers were bitter about some of Mack's rulings (especially his acceptance of Buckner's theory that they had made Merton their own witness), and objected to Mack's taking the second trial. Mack therefore backed away, and the case was assigned to Judge John C. Knox, whom Buckner described to Frankfurter as "an extremely strong character with a great deal of moral fiber. . . . He is nothing like the student of law that Julian [Mack] is, but I am very well satisfied."[19]

But the schedule could not be kept. On November 19 the U.S. Attorney's office made a routine announcement that Buckner had been home for eight days with the grippe, and was not expected in the office for a while; and on December 1 Buckner went to Manhattan Eye & Ear Hospital for a mastoid operation, a very serious thing in those days. His recovery was slow, and after a few days home around Christmas he and Sofy went down to St. Augustine for a ten days' rest that turned out to be a month. During this period, Buckner began backing away from public office. He wrote repeatedly and at length to Gottlieb about the candidates for the Root-Clark office, discussed the men he might want to bring to the firm from the U.S. Attorney's office, the staff he would need on his return to private practice. Meanwhile, in New York, George Leisure, whom Buckner at the start of 1927 appointed chief of the Criminal Division, was supervising a restudy of the Miller-Daugherty case.

The second trial began on February 7, 1927, with both defendants represented by new counsel—the aggressive young Chicago lawyer Aaron Sapiro for Miller, and Harold Corbin of Steuer's office for Daugherty. Sapiro in picking the jury asked each venireman if he was prejudiced against "practical politicians," the sort of men who had to raise the money for political campaigns. One of the prospective jurors was the florist at the Hotel Astor; he said he had known politicians at their best and at their worst. Buckner, after some hesitation, accepted him. Judge Knox said many years later, "I thought that was a mistake—that's when he lost his case."

[19] Buckner to Frankfurter, 11/18/26.

Buckner in his opening statement to the second jury did not make a chart of the relations among the German and Swiss companies. He explained the nature of Merton's claim, the law that gave rise to it and the reasons why both the Alien Property Custodian and the Attorney General were involved: "[I]f the Alien Property Custodian came over to New York, took my hat and overcoat under the mistaken idea that I was a citizen of Germany or Austria, and I wanted to get my hat and overcoat back, I did not go direct to Mr. Daugherty's office . . . and say, 'A great mistake has been made and here is my birth certificate and so forth, I want my hat and overcoat back.' I had to go unto the Alien Property Custodian's office and file my complaint and state the facts and file my proof, and then the Alien Property Custodian sent [me] over to the Attorney General's office, generally with [a] recommendation, though not necessarily so, as to what he thought ought to be done with it. Then the Attorney General, not at all following that recommendation but with his own force of men and taking the great responsibility which was put upon him by the President of the United States . . . conducted an independent investigation and looked over the situation, and if I was right would give me back my hat and overcoat which had been taken away from me under a mistake of fact. But you had to go through the Alien Property Custodian's office before you could tell your story to the Attorney General's people."[20]

The circumstances of the claim itself were given in half an hour, and no special emphasis was laid on Buckner's view of its dishonesty, though he characterized it scornfully (" 'I now recall,' " he had Merton saying to the Alien Property Custodian, " 'that . . . just under the wire before the war, we transferred the whole business . . .' ").[21] He made a considerable point of the fact that neither King nor Jess Smith, representing Merton in the matter, was a lawyer: "John T. King told Merton to get rid of his lawyer and not to get any more. They did not want any lawyers in this situation, [which was] to be handled, as Mr. Sapiro would say, by practical politicians." (Sapiro rose howling to his feet with an objection.[22]) Then Buckner produced for the jury a new and elaborate version of Newton's chart of what

20 *U.S.* v. *Miller,* Record on Appeal, p. 47.
21 *Ibid.,* p. 59.
22 *Ibid.,* p. 69.

had happened to the Liberty Bonds, and began to concentrate his fire upon the $391,000 Merton had paid for a few minutes' service by practical politicians.

"Now, we wondered if by any chance anybody got those bonds who should not. We wondered if they were just absorbed in commerce, as mine are, and yours are, when we sell them, or whether there was something about them that would be interesting. And so we began tracing them. . . . And what do you suppose we have found and will prove to you?

". . . $5,000 of the $391,000 we shall not be able to trace for you. . . . That leaves $386,000. This defendant here, Colonel Thomas W. Miller, the Alien Property Custodian of the United States, got $50,000, traced right either directly or through the proceeds, into his personal brokerage accounts in Wilmington and New York City. That is $50,000. That leaves—you can do it in your heads very easily—that leaves, you see, 386 and 50, 336. . . .

"Divide 336 by three and we get 112—one-third. And $112,000 of these identical Liberty Bonds will be traced for you step by step, by documents, into John T. King's possession. . . . That leaves 224. . . . And [this 224] we will trace for you either by the bonds themselves or by coupons where the bonds cannot be found . . . to the remaining two men of the trio, these two men being Harry Daugherty and the late Jess W. Smith. . . .

"Tom Miller's $50,000 bonds—no dispute about that. John King's $112,000 bonds—we account for the bond itself, sold or still held in hock. A little different with Mr. Harry Daugherty and Jess W. Smith. For example, we will show by documents and records that four of these bonds, or $40,000, turn up in the Daugherty bank . . . put into certificates of deposit to Harry M. Daugherty himself, which are still existent. . . . We found them in the bank in our investigations. . . .

"We will show you that just a few days after Merton and King walked out of that office, just a few days, King sells $24,000 . . . and sends a check to the Daugherty bank. [The records on who got that $24,000 had been destroyed.] . . . That leaves $160,000. We will produce in front of you out of Mal Daugherty's pocket . . . one ten-thousand dollar bond. . . . That leaves 150. We will show by bankers' and brokers' records in Washington, D.C., that Jess Smith, through his account . . . sold over the counter, for raising cash, $40,000. That leaves 110. . . .

"[W]e will show you that the interest on that $110,000 went to Jess Smith. The next coupon date, six months later . . . John T. King again deposited the interest coupons on one hundred thousand, without the ten . . . and . . . he sent a check . . . [and] we find the interest on one hundred thousand dollars' worth of bonds credited to Harry Daugherty's special account. . . . [W]e will show you that on those one hundred thousand dollar bonds . . . no coupons have been presented at all for something like three years . . . since the newspaper publicity, through the Wheeler Committee, concerning this case. . . . [F]or the last three years, those bonds have been in hiding."[23]

The newspapers characterized Buckner's new approach as "inferential"; but it was strong enough to provoke streams of objections, especially from Sapiro. Buckner insisted that there was no need in the case for the prosecution to prove that the government had lost money through the conspiracy, and cited as an example Frankfurter's original case, where a clerk in the Department of Agriculture had sent advance reports to brokers, and had gone to jail for it. Nevertheless, he wanted the claim papers submitted, so the jury could make up its own mind whether any weaknesses in them should be considered; and Knox, like Mack, approved their introduction. Finally, Buckner said, to avoid troubles about the meaning of conspiracy, "Of course we do not prove that officials such as Miller and Daugherty, that they personally handled this matter themselves. The pickpocket has to pick the pocket himself. When you get higher up you have an organization."[24]

Instead of starting with Merton and tracing the claim, then, Buckner started with the Liberty Bonds and traced them. Among his new witnesses were the clerk at Goldman & Sachs who witnessed the transfer of bonds from Merton to King, and the teller at Daugherty's bank in Washington Court House to get the testimony about the destroyed ledgers from someone other than Mal Daugherty. Buckner's assistants and investigators had also been through certain Department of Justice records to spot telephone calls between Harry Daugherty and John T. King, and to tie tighter the knots between

[23] *Ibid.*, pp. 73-80.
[24] *Ibid.*, p. 93.

Daugherty and Jess Smith. Merton, who had agreed to appear again, came on in the middle of the prosecution's case, was handled gingerly, and—Sapiro remembering what had happened to Colonel Rand —was allowed to retire without any cross-examination at all.

On the day Buckner concluded putting in his case ("I always hate to rest, Your Honor," he said, "for fear I have forgotten something"[25]) Buckner wrote to Frankfurter and Lippmann:

"I think myself that I have presented the case better than before because my squad has had time . . . to get the case in better shape, although there is nothing new which is spectacular and direct. I have eliminated all documentary evidence of small probative value and have, therefore, maintained momentum. Nevertheless, the situation is radically different from the other trial. The reason is the jury. The jury appears to be unintelligent, uninterested and wholly uninformed by the evidence. Even the burning of the records appeared to arouse no interest on their part. I believe if the defendants should rest without putting in any witnesses, that an acquittal would result. The only thing in my judgment that could save the case is a defense, and apparently we are going to have a substantial defense lasting four or five days with a probability of Miller himself taking the stand. . . . It is just possible that cross-examination of all the defense witnesses will clear up many details in the case and get the jury interested and informed. . . .

"I am informed that if Miller takes the stand he will say the bonds were turned over to him to make up a political deficit which he and his associates had suffered. Whether he can get away with this, I cannot say. [William Travers] Jerome and [Colonel William] Rand, who knew his defense, were afraid to put him on before. I think Sapiro is much more sympathetic with him, and the lack of sympathy on the part of Jerome and Rand I believe to be the chief reason for a change of counsel. Miller wants an admiring friend as well as a lawyer.

"Another handicap I have suffered is that they did not make Merton their own witness to justify the claim and thus enable me to attack Merton for two days as before. The result is that neither the judge nor the jury has any idea what kind of claim it is up to this point. If there is no defense, I have to handle the whole matter in

25 *Ibid.*, p. 946.

my summing up, and a man cannot carry too big a load in a summing up because that means in the minds of the jurymen . . . too much speech and not enough evidence, even though the documents are part of the records."[26]

Sapiro agreed with Buckner's analysis, and announced that he would offer no defense for Miller, on the grounds that none was needed. Daugherty, however, was in greater danger from Buckner's changed approach to the case. Evidence that the claim was no good was quite irrelevant to the Daugherty prosecution, because there was no way to show that Daugherty had ever had any notion of what the claim was. Stress on what happened to the Liberty Bonds left Daugherty much closer to parity with Miller as a villain. The Steuer office decided to defend.

A good part of the defense consisted of eminent character witnesses —among them, Mabel Walker Willebrandt, who was still in the Assistant Attorney General's post to which Daugherty had appointed her. Buckner and the newspapers were amused at the sight of an Assistant Attorney General coming down from Washington voluntarily to help defend somebody the Justice Department, through its Attorney in the Southern District, was now prosecuting. "[Y]ou are really one of my bosses, aren't you?" Buckner asked on cross-examination.

"If you mean," Mrs. Willebrandt said haughtily, "that I pass on all you do, and approve of it, Mr. Buckner—"

Buckner had been prowling the well of the court, and was some distance away from the witness stand. He reddened, and almost ran toward the witness. "Such as this prosecution, for instance," he called out.

Mrs. Willebrandt raised her eyes to heaven. "I have *nothing*," she said, "to do with this."[27]

Daugherty's major witness, however, had to be Goff—and this time, in a cross-examination lasting a full day, Buckner destroyed the Senator from West Virginia and former Assistant Attorney General. He gave the man every chance to back away from his lie that he had personally examined and approved the Merton application. Slowly, Buckner took Goff through all the duties he had had to perform

---

[26] Buckner to Frankfurter and Lippmann, "Dictated but not read," 2/16/27.
[27] Record, p. 972.

as Assistant Attorney General in the first months of the Harding administration, got him to say that he saw 50 to 75 visitors every day, signed 100 to 150 letters a day, supervised the entire work of the department's Civil Division and Anti-Trust Division, and took responsibility for final approval of all Alien Property Claims. "Would you be surprised," Buckner said, "if I told you that from the time you took office, March 15, 1921, until this claim was allowed, September 23, 1921, there were both allowed and disallowed over your signature some eight hundred claims of the Alien Property Custodian?"[28] No, Goff was not surprised: if that was the record, that was the record. But he had looked over the important papers in the American Metals claim.

Finally, doubtless more in sorrow than in anger, Buckner said, "[H]aven't you . . . testified that you never examined the papers in the American Metals case?"

"I have never testified that I did not examine them," Goff said. "I have testified, if you want me to go back over my testimony—"

"No," Buckner said, "you can answer that one yes or no."

"I won't say I examined every one of those papers, but I examined many of them and I have testified I examined the principal ones."

Buckner said, "I am now talking about your testimony before the grand jury, not when you took the witness stand at the last trial."

Goff, with emotions one can only imagine, said, "Will you read the question and answer to me?"

" 'Q. You never examined the papers in the American Metals case, did you? A. No, sir, I did not.' "

"Now," Goff said, "I don't recall that question and answer. The reason I say that is that question and answer was not put to me when I testified in the first trial in this case."

The cross-examination of Goff in the first trial must have placed Buckner in a most uncomfortable position. The man was a Republican Senator in a marginal state, running a difficult re-election campaign; and Buckner, when all was said and done, did have certain minimal obligations to the party. Now Buckner got even. He toyed with Goff, went over the use of the American Metals case by his recent opponent in the re-election campaign, and then returned to the issue:

"[N]ow, were you asked this question and did you give this answer

28 *Ibid.,* pp. 1047-1048.

before the grand jury: 'You never read a single paper? A. No, sir. The facts in the papers were stated to me a day or two before the claim was allowed'—was that question asked and did you give that answer?"

Goff squirmed. Neither Todd nor Simpson, he complained, had done him the courtesy of showing him the claim papers before he testified. Buckner kept him to his grand jury testimony. "If you say that that question was propounded to me and that I so answered," Goff finally replied, "it is no doubt correct, but I want to correct that testimony in view of the investigation that I have made in this matter, and say to you that some of those papers I did read. . . ."

Buckner was by no means finished with the grand jury minutes. "Now I ask you if you were asked this question and gave this answer before the grand jury? 'Q. And it is your best recollection and it is your best testimony now that in finally allowing this seven-million-dollar American Metals Company claim you depended wholly altogether and unequivocally on the letter from the Alien Property Custodian recommending the claim, together with Mr. Johnson's statement to you as a result of his investigation that the claim should be allowed? A. Yes, sir, I made no investigation of that record.' "

Goff said, "I have no recollection that I made that answer."

Again, Buckner relaxed the pressure just a little; lunch was coming. After the recess, he began again: "Senator, was this question asked you before the grand jury, last year, and did you give this answer? I will read slowly:

" 'Q. And when was it your understanding, as brought out in that first conference, that the subject matter of the claim, to wit, the Germans' equity in the American Metals Company stock, was fully and finally transferred to the claimant, the Swiss Society? A. Now as to that I cannot say, whether I was assured at the first or second meeting, as to when that bona fide transfer took place, but before the claim was allowed the assurance was made to me, based upon the opinion said to have been rendered by a Judge of the Supreme Court of Switzerland, about the practice involved. The opinion is lengthy, and I did not read it.

'Q. You did not read any of the papers? A. No.

'Q. No matter how lengthy or how short it was, you would not have read it in any case? A. No, sir.'

"Was that your testimony taken at that time?"

Next came the disposition of Goff's claim that Simpson had discourteously failed to show Goff the papers while he was on the stand before the grand jury: "Didn't Mr. Simpson have these claim files in the grand jury, that you have seen here?"

"Yes, sir, he did."

"He had them right there, didn't he?"

"He had them in his hand, and he did not show them to me, and I had not seen them, of course."

"Oh, he did not show them to you. Did he ask you this question, and did you give this answer:

" 'Q. Now, Colonel, you have never read these papers, have you? A. No.' Do you remember that?"

"No," Goff said, "I don't recall that. There were a great many questions asked me, of course, in the grand jury room, but I have no recollection of that question being asked; and of course if he had asked me the general question, Mr. Buckner, if I sat down and read that record paper by paper, of course my general answer, no, was correct. I did not read every line in that record. . . ."

"When Mr. Simpson had these papers in the grand jury room, why didn't you ask to see them, if you wanted to see them?"

"Do you want me to answer that question?"

"Yes, surely."

"Do you think," Goff said, "I would have tried to delay the grand jury procedure by taking a record like that, saying to the man that you sent there to examine me, 'You must let me delay these proceedings and read all of these papers'? I would not have done that."

"Well," Buckner said, "I think you should do that, Colonel, since you ask me, when you are asked, have you read these papers—unless you knew positively that you had not read them. Of course, since you never read claim papers, I don't know why you should answer that you had not read any of them, if you had read any of them."

"Well, I said that I had not then read all of these papers in, I suppose, their totality," Goff replied. "Now that is unquestionably the impression that that question made on my mind. The question does not say to me at that time did you read any of the papers, or did you read this paper or that paper? It put up to me the question of the record."

"Now wait a moment," Buckner said. "Wait a moment, the question I just read to you."

"I know you did," said Goff.

" 'Q. You did not read any of the papers? A. No.

" 'Q. No matter how lengthy or how short it was, you would not have read it in any case? A. No, sir.' Is that a mistake?"

"That is a mistake, yes, sir," Goff said, "and I desire to correct it, because I did read some of those papers."

"All right," Buckner said. Next came the question of Goff's understanding of the law under which the money had been paid to Merton, the nature of the claim and the theory under which Goff had approved it. Goff dug himself in ever deeper, until Buckner asked, "Are you saying that the president of the Society who was after the money was mistaken, that Mr. Williams who dictated the letter for Colonel Miller to sign was mistaken, that Colonel Rand, Mr. Steuer and I are mistaken; are you saying all that to get away from the fact that this is the one oral transfer ever acknowledged by the department in its history; is that it?"

"No, not in the least," Goff replied, "because there would be no reason for doing that in the face of the decision of the Swiss judge, who was a member of the Court of Appeals there."

And then the other shoe dropped: Did Goff know that this judge, on whose opinion he said he relied, was not a lawyer at all, but a certified public accountant? No, Goff didn't. And did Goff know that this judge as an accountant numbered among his clients none other than the Swiss Society? No, poor Goff didn't know that either.[29]

Actually Buckner had been reasonably kind. By stressing Goff's political worries in the fall election he prepared the way for disposing of the matter in his summation without making serious charges.

"Let's not have any United States Senator coming in here," he told the jury, "and saying, 'Pooh! pooh! I accept full responsibility; I read all the papers.' Senator Goff cannot laugh off, orate off, or by Senatorial prestige make you forget that Tom Miller got $50,000 for approving this claim in two days. Nor can he, with all his pedigree, his 'present' 1927 model recollection and his knowledge that in West Virginia the newspapers are being read, make you forget that Harry Daugherty and Jess W. Smith got more than $200,000.

[29] *Ibid.*, pp. 1047-1086.

"Senator Goff's testimony in the grand jury room was given in secret. There were no newspapermen present. There was no chance of its hurting him in the Senate or of the people in West Virginia hearing about it. It was different in court. He did not want to admit when newspapermen were present and the people of West Virginia might hear about it that he had placed his signature on any paper of which he did not have full personal knowledge."[30]

In fact, of course, Goff's conduct was worse than that. When he was summoned before the grand juries, the indictment the government sought was one alleging fraud in the claim. To the extent that Goff admitted knowledge of the claim, he was in danger of being joined as a conspirator, which seemed quite unnecessary—especially as he really hadn't ever looked at the claim. By the time he came to testify at the trial, he knew he was in the clear: the telegrams to Miller while the claim was pending before him were demonstration enough that he was not part of the game. Now it was safe for him to go all out for his former boss, and he did so. Reading the record, it is hard to avoid the conclusion that his false testimony convicted Miller—and came very close to convicting Daugherty, too. Again, neither Miller nor Daugherty took the stand.

In summation, Sapiro stressed that if there was anything wrong with the claim, it was Miller's subordinate, Williams—not even accused of anything—who was at fault. One could not hold a man responsible for everything wrong done in his office—why, he did not hold Buckner responsible for the fact that some of his "boy scouts" had argued cases for the government in federal court even though they had not yet been admitted to the bar, which was against the law. (Buckner in the halls afterward said to Sapiro that this was not "straight shooting.")[31] Corbin played a more dangerous game. Buckner, he said, had prosecuted Daugherty to serve his own political ambitions: he wanted to be Governor. Indeed, Corbin said, when he ran for Governor he would have Corbin's vote—but he was not going to "make himself Governor over Harry Daugherty's grave."[32]

The opening was too good to miss. Beginning his own summation, Buckner announced his resignation as U.S. Attorney, "within two

[30] 18 *Bull*, 3/11/27, p. 4.
[31] *New York Times*, 2/25/27, p. 23.
[32] *Ibid*.

months. . . . With my three girls to educate and support," he said, "I
cannot live on my savings any longer." He apologized to the jury
for this intrusion of his personal life, but he felt he had to respond
to Corbin's accusation that he had sought "to injure a fellow human
being for myself or my own preferment."[33] Then Buckner began a
summation which lasted nine and one-half hours, running from Friday
afternoon to Tuesday morning. The case went to the jury on March
1, and deliberations occupied seventy hours. Security was good
enough that when the jury reported that it had reached a verdict with
respect to one defendant but not the other, the newspapers speculated
on which defendant, and whether the verdict was Guilty or Not
Guilty.

On Friday, March 4, after three nights at the Hotel McAlpin, the
jurors returned to say their disagreement was hopeless with regard
to the second defendant, and Judge Knox took the one verdict they
had reached. "I have talked with the foreman of the jury and now
know the facts," Buckner wrote three days later to Frankfurter.
"Miller was convicted in one hour on three ballots. The first vote
against Harry was 7 to 5 for conviction which went up to 11 to 1 and
there it stood for forty-eight hours. Just for your private ear, the foreman and I both feel that the juryman was 'organized,' but I have no
whine or complaint to make even to my friends without proof. It was
an unexpected achievement to get the jury up to eleven. I do not
see what comfort Daugherty's personal or political friends can take
from the fact that one juror suspended sentence."[34]

The indictment against Daugherty was thereupon nol-prossed.
"According to the newspaper accounts," Frankfurter wrote Senator
Burton K. Wheeler, "apparently Buckner of his own motion moved
the court to nol-pros the indictment. That isn't true. The motion was
made by him against his wishes and upon the insistence of the court.
. . . Buckner protested, urged that he be allowed to have a few weeks
in which to think over the matter, report to the attorney general,
and take whatever action was to be taken at the end of that time.
Judge Knox told Buckner that if he did not move to nol-pros the indictment he, the judge, of his own motion 'would take the bull by the
horns and nol-pros the indictment.' To avoid an open conflict with

[33] *New York Times,* 2/26/27, p. 17.
[34] Buckner to Frankfurter, 3/7/27.

[the] court, Buckner thought it better to carry out the court's instructions rather than to have a result achieved in a form that would look like a reprimand by the court. Buckner greatly regretted and still deplores the course of events I have just outlined."[35]

This time there were no speculations by counsel as to why Daugherty had not been acquitted. Goff, indeed, reacted, writing a telegram to Buckner:

. . . [Y]ou are a liar and a coward. Your attack is an overt act in a conspiracy composed of deliberately dishonest and vicious character-assassins, as debased as they are un-American. For weeks your Muscovite hirelings sneaked, snooted, rooted, whispered and telephoned in the filthy slimy gossip of the capital city to gather material for your little strut across the stage in your examination of me a week ago. The success of your hypocrisy and treachery was reflected in the derision and the ridicule with which your examination was received in a crowded court room. You then made honor a jest and the dignity of judicial office a thing of scorn, as you now well know and as you then appreciated. . . . Your cowardice in this proceeding is as insolent as it is notorious. The road of desertion, not resignation, should be left open to you in the hope that the jurisprudence of this nation may be fumigated and freed from the shrinking delinquency and the miserable demagogism to which your connection with the Department of Justice has reduced it.[36]

Postal Telegraph refused to carry this missive, and none of the newspapers printed much of it, so Buckner asked that it "should be embalmed in the pages of *The Bull* forever."[37] Amusingly, this "literary gem," as Buckner called it, was later published in full in Daugherty's book about the Harding administration.[38]

One newspaper (the Cincinnati *Enquirer*) saw in the trial a need for "a larger measure of protection from vicious and irresponsible prosecution. . . . The guilty public official should suffer, but that does not require that the innocent should be subjected to such an ordeal as Mr. Daugherty has undergone at the instigation of partisan political malice." Far more common was the verdict of the St. Louis *Post-Dispatch*:

[35] Frankfurter to Burton Wheeler, 3/15/27.
[36] 18 *Bull*, 3/11/27, pp. 5-6.
[37] *Ibid.*, p. 5.
[38] Daugherty & Dixon, *op. cit.*, pp. 258-260.

It was an oddly sounding charge that Buckner made against the two men—that they had deprived the Government of their best services—but he nevertheless prosecuted it with a thoroughness and vigor that must have challenged the admiration of every man and woman in the United States who loves justice and honesty in the public service. Vengeance upon Daugherty is of little importance, but the warning of what he suffered for his evil-doing has been made with an emphasis that nobody can mistake. The country has Mr. Buckner to thank for that.[39]

In later years, sentiment against Daugherty softened incomprehensibly. Mark Sullivan in *Our Times* recalled visits with the clean old man in his Ohio retirement, and refused to believe he had ever been guilty of anything shady, though Daugherty never explained to Sullivan how or why the Merton bonds wound up in his hands. Judge Knox told Miller at the sentencing (eighteen months and a $5,000 fine) that he believed "the verdict was justified."[40] In one of his autobiographical books Knox noted that in Daugherty's time "the Department [of Justice] fell on evil days, and Daugherty was surrounded by a group of politicians and hangers-on."[41] But in the other book Knox reported that he would have voted as the holdout juror did: "Guilty or not, the evidence presented against Daugherty at that trial was *not* conclusive."[42] To the belief at the U.S. Attorney's office that one of the jurors had been fixed, however, a Washington friend of one of the young assistants probably made conclusive reply: "Nonsense! Harry Daugherty would never have trusted any *one* juror."

In 1940 Buckner brought the story up to date for the young lawyers of Root-Clark. "Miller," he wrote, "served his time and at last reports was holding an official position as Commissioner of Highways in a western state. Harry Daugherty is still living in Columbus, Ohio, doubtless hugging his wrongs when he should be hugging juror No. 7."[43]

---

[39] *Literary Digest,* 3/19/27, p. 11.
[40] Record, p. 1247.
[41] Knox, *Order in the Court,* p. 275.
[42] Knox, *A Judge Comes of Age,* p. 257.
[43] 21 *Bull,* 4/27/40, p. 179.

CHAPTER TEN

Flood Tide

1927-1932

On April 7, 1927, Buckner formally relinquished the position of U.S. Attorney and turned over the office to Charles H. Tuttle, who did not come to visit him prior to the day. "He called me up," Tuttle recalled, "and stated that his resignation was effective and the court was ready to swear me in. He graciously pointed out the files and things of that sort, took me downstairs, sat me down on the chair and said, 'You'll want to judge the staff for yourself. Here's my phone number if you want to call me.' "

Buckner took back with him to his private office three of his assistants at the old Post Office Building—Harlan (whom he had brought), the former Rhodes scholar James A. Farmer, and Samuel Isseks, a Frankfurter protégé from Harvard Law School who had finished his fourth year the previous June, whom Buckner had been paying out of his own pocket because he had not been able to get his appointment through Washington. To say the least, he had work for them in his office.

Indeed, the demand from Root-Clark for Buckner's services was so great that, with the consent of the Attorney General, he began handling a private matter as early as March 8, only four days after the verdict on the Daugherty-Miller trial. This case pitted the investment bankers Dillon, Read & Company, one of Root-Clark's best clients in its financial and corporate departments, against Frank

Seiberling and other stockholders in the Goodyear Tire & Rubber Company, who were alleging various kinds of past hanky-panky in the market and future schemes for the control of Goodyear stock. Former Attorney General George W. Wickersham had been handling the case (though Charles E. Hughes was formally listed as Dillon's senior counsel), but it was the sort of thing that required organization. Pre-trial examinations had begun March 7 in the meeting room of the New York County Lawyers Association, and the firm felt a need for its leading litigator immediately.

Buckner put together a team which by mid-April included twelve lawyers, five of them from his office and three from the staff he had just left at the U.S. Attorney's office. (One other, Robert P. Patterson, had been a Root-Clark associate; and yet another, C. D. Williams, had been until a few months before part of the U.S. Attorney staff, so ten in all were products of the Buckner atelier.) Leo Gottlieb was put in charge of the operation, and filing cabinets began to fill up in the team's special offices at 120 Broadway.

This would have been a difficult case to try, partly because of the complexity of the issues, partly because both sides had a lot to explain; and after a brief look at the situation Buckner put machinery in motion to work out a settlement. He was much aided in this effort by the personalities of both principals, who quite apart from their official legal counsel had staffs of investigators at work to dig up unpleasantnesses in each other's private lives. By the middle of May the case was out of the way, via a complicated settlement which involved a large underwriting of Goodyear bonds to be handled by Dillon, Read, without commission. Buckner's team did not work on the negotiations, which were handled for Clarence Dillon by his associate Ferdinand Eberstadt. "His [Eberstadt's] idea," Buckner wrote Frankfurter, "was that it was wiser on the merits and also created a much better impression for me to plow ahead with my army up to the last moment. I think he was right. The settlement is a highly dignified one and a very honorable one for Dillon, Read, and is also a splendid thing for the company."[1]

There was a great deal of trial business pending at Root-Clark. The firm's Florida clients, acquired in the land boom, needed even more service in the land bust. One of the nation's largest real-estate

[1] Buckner to Frankfurter, 5/18/27.

financing operations, the G. L. Miller Company of Atlanta and New
York, had gone under the previous fall, and Root-Clark, representing
a bondholders' committee organized by George E. Roosevelt, was engaged in actions all over the South. The firm had its own Alien Property Custodian case (involving an attack by the government on the
authenticity of an auction sale of the assets of American Bosch Magneto, a client of long standing; the indictment, interestingly, had been
procured by the same Hiram Todd who had handled the first phase
of the Daugherty-Miller case). A criminal prosecution in this matter
was about to start in Boston. Shortly after the Dillon-Goodyear
dispute was closed out, Buckner arranged to send Gottlieb to help
local counsel. "The client," he wrote Frankfurter, "would like me to
go also. . . . So far as I am concerned I am willing to junior anybody
if the service is really needed and can be paid for, though it would
seem over-organization to have both of us."[2]

Among the cases drawn to Root-Clark by Buckner's fame as U.S.
Attorney were several padlocking matters, in which Buckner cheerfully argued on behalf of the padlocked (especially the owners of the
underlying real estate, who could claim they did not know what their
property had been used for). On appeal in one of these cases, Harlan
wrote a brief 150 pages long. When it came to the argument, Judge
Learned Hand glowered at Buckner and said, "Is this your brief?"

"Yes, Your Honor," Buckner said.

"Well, I'm not going to read it. It's too long."

Buckner said, "Well, it will be your loss, Your Honor. It's a very
good brief. My assistant wrote it and I put my name on it."

In response, the future Justice remembered, Hand threw the document over the bench and onto counsel table with a loud thud of protest. "You can imagine," Harlan recalled, "how I felt. Then, after
the case had been decided, Hand called me in and said, 'Just wanted
to say it was a very good brief.' "

Buckner's publicity even produced a straight criminal client of a
kind very rare in a Wall Street office. This was a struggling importer
named Socrates Moscahlades, who had bought a bonded warehouse
and used his ownership of it to substitute damaged cheese, tapestries,
furs, olive oil and wine for the legitimate contents. Then when arson-
ists burned down the warehouse (which stood in a partly residential

[2] *Ibid.*

area), Moscahlades claimed full insurance on its original undamaged contents. The initial charges brought by Tuttle as U.S. Attorney alleged customs fraud—that Moscahlades had burned down the warehouse to conceal his failure to pay duty on the furs—and it was with this indictment hanging over his head that Moscahlades walked into the Root-Clark offices in the summer of 1927. Buckner was on vacation in Nantucket, and Gottlieb saw the visitor. He called Buckner, uncertain as to whether the firm should take the case; and Buckner, after learning that Moscahledes said he was innocent, told Gottlieb that he didn't believe in turning down business simply because the prospective client looked shabby; the best way to get rid of him was to tell him that the firm would need a $10,000 fee in advance to handle his case. Gottlieb passed along this information, and Moscahlades promptly took a checkbook out of his pants pocket, wrote a check and put it on the desk.

Back in the office, Buckner had an interview with Moscahlades and told him he was taking the case on the understanding that his claim of innocence would stand up, and he would have his own boys investigate it. Then he appeared in court for Moscahlades and successfully argued for an adjournment to prepare the defense. Several junior associates, among them Farmer and the newly arrived Livingston Hall (later to be vice dean of the Harvard Law School), were tolled off to examine Moscahledes, his friends and his books. Meanwhile, Ben Herzberg, a holdover from the Buckner administration in the U.S. Attorney's office, had filed a new indictment, concentrating the government's fire on charges of mail fraud on the insurance companies. Buckner's young men had found that Moscahlades could beat the original indictment, but not the new one.

Buckner called in his client, said that the office was now convinced he was guilty and would not defend him. Much of the $10,000 fee was still unspent; Moscahlades could have it back, and Buckner would recommend him to a good lawyer who wouldn't care whether he was guilty or not. Moscahlades declined with thanks—Buckner was his lawyer, and though he still maintained his innocence he would accept Buckner's advice and plead guilty. Buckner made a deal with Tuttle whereby the U.S. Attorney's office would recommend a light sentence; but Judge Goddard was having none of it, and to the horror of the office Moscahlades got eight years in Atlanta. "The Court," Farmer wrote in *The Bull,* "was somewhat more severe than we had anticipated, but took occasion to commend the way in which our client's case had been handled by Mr. Buckner, stating that but for the plea of guilty, saving the time of the Court and great expense to the Government, the sentence would have been much heavier."[3] It was pretty cold comfort.

The great majoritiy of the cases, of course, were commercial litigations growing out of contracts one of the parties now had reason to wish to break; and the clients wanted Buckner himself to try their cases. Buckner was more or less involved in literally dozens of cases at once. "He was," Justice Harlan recalled, "a great fellow for what he called spinning plates. He would be very busy getting the client happy with the organization, and then he would disappear from the case. If the client got restless because he wasn't seeing enough of Buckner, he would do the necessary, but he was always aiming to work the young men in. He'd turn up again when it was time to try or settle, take off his coat and closet himself with the men who'd worked on it."

Though he would try cases prepared by other offices and handed over to him a week before their appearance on the calendar, Buckner incessantly preached the virtues of preparation by a special staff. Toward the end of his life, he wrote about a judge who after a trial "criticized the chief defense counsel because his case was overprepared. . . . I told the judge there was no such animal—that it was easy to overtry a case but impossible to overprepare a case."[4] Describing a trial to the members of the Chicago Bar Association, Buckner said:

I had, as usual, counsel in the case; namely, six young lawyers who do the work. I always travel with my lawyer. I never take a case unless I can arrange to have a lawyer in the case. These six young bird dogs had been working on this case for ten months. There was not anything at all about the literature of the case that the six of them could learn in ten months that they had not learned, although that involved the examination of somewhere between fifteen and twenty thousand documents. We had, I think, nine stands of file cases in the court. I did not know exactly what they were, except the ones I wanted, but they would come out like pet animals when called.[5]

---

[3] 8 *Bull*, 10/29/27, p. 15.
[4] Buckner, "The Lawyer in Court," 27 *American Bar Association Journal* 5, p. 6.
[5] 13 *Chicago Bar Association Record*, 1/30, p. 101.

In this respect Buckner was the direct opposite of his great antagonist, Max Steuer. Where Buckner would have filing cabinets and a great staff of assistants in the courtroom, Steuer (also short, less well dressed than Buckner) would sit alone at his table without so much as a piece of paper in his hands. His position, he seemed to be saying, was just like that of the members of the jury. Steuer had a prodigious memory, and could keep pages of trial record and exhibits in his head without apparent effort. Except in moments of dramatic emphasis, he would speak softly, and rise apologetically to interrupt with an objection. (Judge Henry Friendly remembered a moment from the first Daugherty-Miller trial when Judge Mack had to make Steuer's inaudible objection for him, calling, "Mr. Buckner—oh, Mr. Buckner! Mr. Steuer seems to wish to say something.") Steuer spoke to the jury both in opening and in summation without a note in his hand, and apparently in a vein of spontaneous conversation. Actually, of course, much of what he did was rehearsed. Leo Gottlieb remembered several visits to Steuer's office, when Steuer, having completed the business at hand, would try out on Gottlieb some of what he intended to say to the jury in the case he was currently trying.

Everyone who worked for Buckner had the rather scary experience of preparing a case for him to try without any guidance whatever. "You quickly learned," Justice Harlan commented, "that if you couldn't swim with the tide, you couldn't work for Buckner." Francis T. P. Plimpton, later to be Adlai Stevenson's aide-de-camp at the United Nations with the rank of Ambassador, remembered that "I nearly had a nervous breakdown over Buckner. When I came to the firm I'd been lassoed into corporate financial. In the fall of '29 I was asked to run the Paris office, and over I went with my wife and two sons. I came back, and Buckner called for me. I'd never been in a courtroom. He asked me to take over the National Cash Register purchase of Remington Cash Register. NCR was under a consent decree from 1917, had to get court approval to go to the bathroom. He said, 'Here it is—coming up for trial in three weeks. I'll give you a couple of good men.'

"He sent me two assistants, and one of them had never been in a courtroom either. We treated it like a closing. Buckner wouldn't see me, wouldn't talk about the case until we got on the train for

Dayton, Ohio. Then he took out the bottle and said, 'Tell me about the case. . . .'

"I remember," Plimpton continued, "in the trial, Jim Rand was on the stand. Buckner turned to me and said, 'Shall I cross-examine?' It exploded in me like a star shell. I said, 'No'—and he excused the witness. He had an extraordinary ability to rely on younger men, and to seize what somebody else had done. The judge decided the case from the bench in our favor.

"There was another moment in that case. A court reporter came up to me and said, 'What was that funny word Mr. Buckner used?' I said, 'It was hegemony—he mispronounced it.' A few days after we got back to New York, Buckner called me into his office. There on the empty desk was a great big office dictionary. 'Will you,' he said to me, 'please look up the word H-E-G-E-M-O-N-Y.' "

Mostly, Buckner picked up the necessary information from his assistants orally. When he had an outside group of "minutemen" working on a case, he would keep up with them not by a flow of memoranda but by Saturday lunches and occasional dinners. "I learned quickly," Leo Gottlieb recalled, "*never* to tell him anything wrong—then if you tried to correct it later, he remembered." The obligation was on the assistant to know the whole case; as Cloyd Laporte put it, "Buckner couldn't stand to be surprised."

For larger matters, once Gottlieb had departed from litigation, Buckner came to rely increasingly on Harlan and Samuel Isseks as his senior staff: "Harlan was the executive officer," said Charles Hilles, son of the Republican National Chairman in the 1920s, who was in the Root-Clark office from 1928 to 1941. "And Isseks was the detail man. He never forgot a detail." He was an enthusiast— "an exceedingly bright fellow," Judge Henry J. Friendly said, "exceedingly nervous and tense. Always had a profound conviction that his own side was entirely right, and not only that the other side was wrong but that their lawyers were crooked. He sometimes got overpersuaded. When he went into the Anti-Trust Division of the Justice Department, he was the most obnoxious trust-buster there. Then he went into private practice, and I don't think anybody was ever so vicious about the Anti-Trust Division."

For Buckner, these excesses were mostly a way of expressing loyalty—though every once in a while even Buckner would find

Isseks' commitment to the cause a trifle overdone. A story around the office told of a case tried in Chicago, when Isseks at the table kept punctuating Buckner's cross-examination with stage whispers of, "He's lying! He's lying!" Finally Buckner turned around and said to Isseks, "What do you want me to do? Kill him?" Isseks' thoroughness and energy were coupled with a great ability to outline a case in full detail without losing the main line of the argument. A few days before a trial, Buckner and Isseks would go down to Atlantic City together and walk the Boardwalk day and night. "Possessing none of the poise and really precocious maturity of a man like John [Harlan]," Buckner wrote Frankfurter in 1941, "he still remains just about the most able and effective assistant I have ever had in a major operation. . . . He sees me every time he is in New York, as he tries to see you very often in Washington. If either of us should tell him to jump out of the window, I think he would do so and wonder about the reasons afterwards."[6]

The staff and Buckner kept each other busy—perhaps too busy. Buckner's contributions to *The Bull* virtually ceased, and he grew increasingly dependent on channels for his information on the life of the office. Though he took endless hours, particularly between November and February, interviewing the new law school graduates and helping them make their start in New York, he was less likely to see his new employees at his home on East Sixty-seventh Street than he had been on University Heights. He was now fifty; the newcomers sensed and appreciated his kindness, and enjoyed the summer parties at Siasconset (especially the annual Saturday night costume parties, when lawyers and their wives dressed as literary characters), but he was inevitably more remote. "He was viewed," says one of the men who joined around 1930, "with a certain amount of amusement by the younger associates. He talked a lot and he was not unrepetitive in his themes." Moreover, he was repeatedly unwell. When not keyed up for trial, he often found it necessary to go home after half a day or come in only for the afternoon. "I prefer to be around part of every day," he wrote Frankfurter, "than to be away altogether."[7]

Though Buckner could not spend energy so lavishly as he had in the early 1920s, during that first spring after his return from the U.S.

[6] Buckner to Frankfurter, 2/7/41.
[7] Buckner to Frankfurter, 6/7/27.

Attorney's office he did invest both scarce time and money in Frankfurter's crusade to save Sacco and Vanzetti. He was one of a committee of about a dozen who paid for the printing of the trial record and for the circulation of the correspondence between Frankfurter and Professor John H. Wigmore, author of the standard treatise on Evidence, who had with ill temper defended the Sacco-Vanzetti trial and Judge Thayer's conduct of it. He gave to friends copies of Frankfurter's book on the case, and reviewed it in *The New Republic* as "a concise, lawyer-like and extremely readable critical analysis. . . . Professor Frankfurter's book is absorbing, but it is uncomfortable. It will leave some with the conviction, others with the feeling and many others with the fear, that Sacco and Vanzetti may be judicially and officially burned to death, not for murder, but for being draft dodgers and communists."[8]

He was pleased at the responsible fuss Frankfurter's book kicked up. "I told Si [Howland] this morning," he wrote, "that it seemed to me that it was your *Atlantic* [*Monthly*] article and your book which brought for the first time portions of the 'conservative' element into the controversy on the side of the defendants. . . . Will you not tell me objectively and without regard to modesty if this is true?"[9] Frankfurter's reply does not survive, which is a pity.

2

Buckner in the late 1920s and early 1930s was, with the possible exception of Max Steuer, the highest-priced trial lawyer in New York. Clients were sometimes shocked by the bills they received. A lawyer on the other side of the negotiations remembered that Root-Clark's client Forster-Wheeler once settled a claim for considerably less than expected in the backwash of receiving a $200,000 bill from counsel. What they were paying for, primarily, was the organization Buckner put behind every matter he accepted.

Buckner's main quality at trial was what Justice Harlan called his "tremendous earthiness in the practice of law." Short and always a little flabby, he was not an impressive figure in the courtroom. His brown hair took on a gray cast, but it remained plentiful, combed high in front with a part just to the left of center, and the youthfulness

[8] 50 *The New Republic*, 4/27/27, pp. 278-279.
[9] Buckner to Frankfurter, 5/16/27.

of his speech and manner was not contradicted by his appearance. His voice was flat and choppy, and his flourishes were dramatic rather than oratorical. He believed in giving a case a rather slow rhythm, leaving time for the least perceptive of the jurors to acquire all the information. He invariably preferred to let witnesses put in their own evidence, even sloppily, and he criticized the lawyer who "thinks that, after all, this witness has not had the benefit of a legal education. . . . [I]t is much more interesting, it is much more professional, if you please, it is much better technique, it is the thing the jury will like better, it is the thing the judge will like better, if you are simply only the friend of the witness; you want to help him; you want to tell him to talk a little louder and tell him not to be excited."[10]

Observing the result of this technique, many lawyers felt that Buckner's introduction of his own case on direct examination was weak. Nobody denied the quality of his cross-examination and of his opening and closing statements—which invariably carried the sense of a plain, blunt, transparently honest man helping the jury uncover the truth. "His was a mind," said the antitrust trial lawyer Hugh Cox, who began his career at Root-Clark, "that did not create complexities—it straightened and simplified. He had an intuitive power of analysis, grasping crucial points so far as his clients' interests were concerned." Perhaps his strongest asset on trial or in negotiations was his exact idea of what he wanted. "The first thing you have to do in any litigation," he liked to say, "is to define victory."

In speaking to lawyers inside and outside his office, Buckner always placed first emphasis on "facts." He wrote for his assistants at the U.S. Attorney's office:

There is a tendency to run off at top speed at the beginning of a new case to "look up the law." What is the law? The law is made up of reported decisions. What are these decisions? They are decisions of the courts concerning certain facts. . . .

[A] man too often is satisfied with a "general" idea of facts. He knows that in a bankruptcy case there is a check signed by the defendant of about $2,000 drawn on about a certain date and drawn, as he recalls, either to the wife or sister-in-law of the defendant. If he knew the precise amount of the check, he might recognize that amount on some book of account which would give him a new lead. If he knew the precise date of

[10] 13 *Chicago Bar Association Record*, 1/30, p. 105.

the check, it might suddenly be revealed to him that the date had significance and articulated with an important date in the case. If he knew
precisely the person to whom the check was drawn, he would suddenly
find himself with material for cross-examination if the person unexpectedly
took the stand without leaving him time for special preparation. I cannot
think of anything so important to a young lawyer (except militant honesty)
as the development of a consuming passion for the facts—all the facts—
detailed facts.[11]

Comments like these created in some quarters the impression that
Buckner regarded law *qua* law as essentially unimportant, but the impression was wildly untrue. Both in his private office and as U.S. Attorney, he subscribed to the Advance Sheets of appellate opinions
for all the younger men, and had the subscriptions sent to their homes.
There were, he told the recipients, two major reasons for reading
Advance Sheets: "One object is to groove the mind with channels of
legal thinking. . . . When one finds a case with the right sort of setting
up excercises he should go through it carefully in order that he may
assemble the premises and proceed to conclusions. Another object is
to secure information. . . . If the decision checks with our instincts
and recollections we may pass it by speedily. If we are surprised at
the decision we would better pause and plough around the lot a
little."[12]

Several of Buckner's contributions both to *The Bull* and to *Scraps*
deal with points of law quite divorced from the immediate factual
situation. Election of remedies, choice of forum, interpretation of
the statute of frauds all appear as relatively abstract questions. Most
frequently, inevitably, the questions of law Buckner explored dealt
with what happens at trials—what sort of questions can be asked on
cross-examination to destroy the credibility of a witness, what makes
a fact acceptable as evidence. ("There is scarcely anything more
difficult to prove in a court room than the delivery of a few parcels
of merchandise or the mailing of a letter."[13]) Occasionally, especially
as a prosecutor, he complained about the state of the law:

The constitutional right against self-incrimination seems to be an archaic
absurdity. It comes down from the date when torture was inflicted as a

[11] *Scraps*, 11/6/26.
[12] 3 *Bull*, 8/12/22, p. 2.
[13] 2 *Bull*, 8/13/21.

means of making people give evidence against themselves. If a man is driving a stolen automobile, I cannot imagine anyone who is a better candidate for a few questions than the driver and yet he has a right to refuse to answer any and all questions on the grounds that the answers may tend to incriminate him. Imagine an office where the stenographer and the bookeeper had a quarrel. The employer calls in his stenographer and asks her to tell him her side of the story. She replies, 'I refuse to answer on the ground that my answers may incriminate me and you must not even use against me the fact that I have so refused. You must forget all about this and if you don't, I shall tell the Bar Association about you.' The employer would discharge the girl on the spot.[14]

Though he recognized that he did it better than most people, Buckner did not think that the actual courtroom trial of cases was a particularly difficult art; and he denied that there was any such thing as a "trial type." He told the City Bar Association once that:

all we have to do is to think of a dozen highly successful trial lawyers and we see at once that instead of belonging to our preconceived "trial type" their differences in personality and method are so great that we are compelled to make twelve types in order to accommodate the twelve successful men. . . . The late Mr. Stanchfield was a very successful and justly celebrated trial lawyer, both at nisi prius and in the appellate courts. He possessed a natural dignity and address which were most effective, but he was not essentially different at the luncheon table. His very presence seemed to inspire respect and attention from court and jury. I am thinking now of an equally famous and successful lawyer[15] whose forte is to climb into the jury box. He possesses very unusual gifts of personal charm and good fellowship. He is not essentially different out of the courtroom. If he were to imitate Mr. Stanchfield the result would be affectation and failure. I think of another successful trial lawyer[16] whose forte is infectious indignation. If he has a case which does not lend itself to indignation he is not much good. I have known this man, who has been very successful at the bar, ever since I came to New York. He is nearly always indignant about something or somebody. Given the kind of a case where he can be indignant without being artificial he is almost unbeatable. A lawyer who is called upon to try his own or other lawyers' cases is sure to fail if he attempts to imitate anyone.[17]

[14] *Scraps,* 10/30/26.
[15] Probably Martin W. Littleton.
[16] Certainly Lloyd Paul Stryker.
[17] Buckner, "The Trial of Cases," 41 *American Bar Association Journal* 271, in Gerhart, ed., *The Lawyers' Treasury,* p. 397.

Buckner himself "was a great plaintiff's lawyer, which includes prosecutor," said Carl E. Newton, who drew the charts which helped to convict Miller. "He was never keyed to the defense—he had to be aggressive. He loved to have the burden of proof, he loved to have the case." His art was to keep the situation simple, and to tie the facts together to make them individually more plausible. With reference to a jury and its attitude toward facts, he liked to tell the story about the barking dog that doesn't bite: "I know it and you know it, but does the dog know it?"

Judge Friendly says that Buckner would have replied to the charge that he was a better plaintiff's than defendant's lawyer with the comment, "That's because the plaintiff is usually right." An interesting aspect of his bias toward plaintiffs' cases is his constant warning to young lawyers against getting into witty colloquies with opposing counsel that will distract the jury from the evidence—which is precisely what the defendant's lawyer would often like to do. "I remember," he wrote in the last year of his life,

when offering a bill of lading in a prosecution during the second month that I ever tried any cases, that it was objected to because I described the paper as a bill of lading, whereas the paper spoke for itself. I, impatient and not waiting as I should have for a ruling, promptly broke in with, "Why, Your Honor, I have a perfect right to describe generically the paper I am introducing; otherwise the jury might think it is a barn door." My opponent [Martin Littleton] immediately replied, "I beg to disagree with the learned District Attorney, as I am sure the jury will consider the paper a darn bore." This caused a laugh at my expense and diverted the minds of the jury from the main facts, which was altogether a mistake.[18]

It was not, however, a mistake from Littleton's point of view.

In presenting facts to a jury, Buckner wherever possible—from his very earliest days in the Stimson office, when he had a replica of the scale built to help convict the sugar trust defrauders—liked concrete evidence. "Go into any of our courtrooms," he told his pupils at the U.S. Attorney's office,

and see how interested the jury are whenever counterfeit money or an interesting check or obliterated ledger is passed around among them. . . . The problem of any advocate is to get the picture that is in the lawyer's mind into the jury's mind or into the court's mind. When this picture is a

18 Buckner, "The Lawyer in Court," *op. cit.,* p. 7.

physical one rather than a metaphysical one, there is no better auxiliary than physical exhibits. When I was Assistant District Attorney I tried perhaps a dozen murder cases although that was not my regular work. I always insisted on a gun, if there was a gun, clothing, if there was clothing, on anything and everything which I could use so long as it was competent and convincing. A brown-rimmed hole in an undershirt is more eloquent than any summing up. So few lawyers seem to realize this except in obvious cases. The principle runs through all trial work, civil and criminal, and almost any kind of case lends itself to some kind of a simple chart or tabulation. Make the eye the ear and you will help your case.[19]

An appearance of total (if pained) objectivity was the target. Buckner was an extremist about objecting to the introduction of testimony by the other side—he did it very rarely. Leslie Arps, who came to Root-Clark shortly before the end of Buckner's trial career, remembered a case where a question by opposing counsel provoked a question to Buckner by the judge: "Mr. Buckner, don't you wish to object to that?" And Buckner replied sweetly, "Why should I? We have nothing to conceal."

Under the heading "Candor," he suggested to his young assistants at the U.S. Atttorney's office that

A highly useful expression for any lawyer is "I don't know." Many lawyers seem to think that such an answer is unfortunate and damaging. Precisely the opposite is true. . . . An equally useful statement is "I admit." If you are arguing in the Circuit Court of Appeals and the decision of another circuit is squarely against you, you should start the legal side of your argument by admitting that another circuit has decided the point at issue adversely to your contention. . . . One does much better with trial courts and appellate courts and juries to admit everything there is against him, both in fact and law, and concentrate upon what is left of the case. This inspires confidence and takes away from your opponent most of his ammunition. It is also clean and honest. . . . One should never apologize for a weakness in his case. He should assert it in order to get the court and jury operating in the precise territory where the battle is to be won, if at all.[20]

Candor came easily to Buckner because he tried few cases where he was not quite confident that he was on the right side. As a pros-

[19] *Scraps,* 4/24/26.
[20] *Scraps,* 5/1/26.

ecutor, he demanded and received nearly complete discretion in deciding which charges his office would press; and even as a private lawyer, as the Moscahlades case indicated, he would usually plead or settle rather than go to court for a client whose story he did not believe. "My own personal rule," he told the Root-Clark assistants toward the end of his life, "is never to argue a case unless I believe the Court should decide in my favor or, at least, that my argument is entitled to a dissenting opinion. I realize that this leaves an extremely small margin between the field of advocacy and the field of judicial decision. . . . At any rate, one way to win cases is to get on the right side. This is also the secret of effective advocacy."[21]

Writing to Frankfurter in 1938, he said, "[P]racticing law on the basis of being on the bench in the same case is lots of fun and in my case proved vastly profitable. I only know one client who quit our office because 'Buckner seems to think he is the other fellow's lawyer.' He was Malcolm Whitman, a non-practicing Harvard Law man and tennis champion. He afterwards committed suicide, but candor compels me to reveal that the motivating remorse may have come from domestic trouble and not from changing from Root-Clark."[22]

Interestingly, it was this case, tried in the late 1910s, which produced the best story of Buckner's stagecraft in the courtroom. This was, as the letter to Frankfurter indicates, a case where Buckner thought he might have the wrong side. "A witness for the plaintiff got on the stand and told a straightforward story damning to our client," Reed B. Dawson remembered. "Buckner knew it was so, and knew he couldn't shake it on cross-examination. During the direct examination, Buckner passed me a paper on which he had written, 'Answer anything.' I fumbled, wrote a reply, passed it to him. We kept passing papers back and forth through the testimony; the jury noticed Buckner wasn't paying attention. Plaintiff's lawyer finished and said triumphantly, 'Your witness.' Buckner didn't notice—he was still reading papers. 'Mr. Buckner, *your witness.*' Buckner looked up. 'Oh?' he said. 'Oh, yes. No questions.' It was the finest piece of cross-examination I ever saw."

Cross-examination was Buckner's special talent. He believed in preparing it in advance, to the point of writing out an outline before

[21] 21 *Bull,* 2/3/40, p. 50.
[22] Buckner to Frankfurter, 4/6/38.

approaching a hostile witness. He reserved his strongest contempt for the lawyer who simply took the witness through his direct testimony step by step, hoping to trip the man up—and more likely reinforcing in the jury's mind the effects of what had already been said. "Suicides are more frequent than homicides during cross-examination," he wrote in the *Harvard Law Review* in a review of Francis L. Wellman's book *The Art of Cross-Examination* (which he did not much like, except as entertainment).[23] The most likely use of cross-examination, Buckner noted, was for purposes of impeaching a witness, for which purposes, Buckner wrote, the trial lawyer should have at his fingertips every available letter the witness ever wrote on the subject under consideration, every piece of sworn testimony from him in previous hearings, every sworn statement and, where useful, all books of account. ("When the witness began lying," Elihu Root, Jr. remembered, "you always felt Emory was rather grieved.") But "the best kind of cross-examination is a cross-examination which is a curtain raiser for the summing up. It is a little difficult to explain what I mean. It is usually possible to bring into sharp relief the theory of the case by a cross-examination, which can eliminate . . . a collateral issue. The essence of such cross-examination is 'what of it?' "[24]

3

The men who worked as Buckner's assistants felt that the case which showed him off to most spectacular advantage was *People* v. *Connolly,* tried during the election campaign of 1928. Maurice E. Connolly had been elected Borough President of Queens in 1911 as a young "reform" Democratic candidate, and had held the position longer than any man had ever before held a single elective office in New York City. In the fall of 1927, an alderman from the borough filed with Governor Alfred E. Smith a petition for Connolly's removal on the grounds of graft in the construction of storm sewers for the borough (a low-lying area much subject to flooding after rainstorms, and requiring as its housing spread an annual expenditure of millions of dollars for sewer systems). Governor Alfred E. Smith appointed Appellate Division Justice Townsend Scudder[25] to be his impartial investigator of the charge and hold the hearings required by law.

[23] 37 *Harvard Law Review,* 402, 403, Jan. 1924.
[24] *Scraps,* 11/14/25.
[25] See Chapter 2, note 25, *supra.*

"Smith," Judge Joseph Proskauer recalled, "wanted to supersede the local DA, and was looking for the right special assistant. Emory was a close friend of Belle Moskowitz, Smith's confidential secretary, and she called to ask me what I thought of him. I said I had complete confidence in Buckner—I knew he would do a thorough, lawyer-like job and not make politics." What Smith needed if the graft in Queens was not to ruin his chance at the Presidency was a Republican lawyer of high reputation who would get rid of Connolly without stressing all the times Smith had worked with him on party affairs. Smith sent Proskauer to ask Buckner to take the appointment as counsel to Scudder in the investigation. Though *The Bull* described the situation as one in which "E.R.B. has again been drafted for public service,"[26] this assignment was a piece of business. In the end, Buckner's personal fee for the job—on top of all expenses, with his staff separately paid by the state—would be $30,000.

To put the case together, Buckner in December, 1927, assigned Harlan to Connolly matters and rented a special office at 2 Lafayette Street for Harlan and five young men who had worked at the U.S. Attorney's office. No more distinguished staff of six has ever been gathered for a single case—a future Justice of the Supreme Court of the United States (Harlan), a future Chief Judge of the Court of Appeals for the Second Circuit (J. Edward Lumbard), the future president of the Chesapeake & Ohio Railroad (Carl E. Newton), the future president of Oberlin College and Ambassador to the Philippines (William E. Stevenson), the future director of investigations for the State of New York (Herman T. Stichman), and a lawyer who would achieve prominence at the New York Bar (Horace G. Hitchcock). Max Steuer, who was a friend of Connolly's, undertook to represent him at the hearings (announcing that he would retire from the case if his investigations revealed any hint that Connolly might be guilty of misdeeds), and immediately launched collateral attacks on Smith's procedures.

While these attacks were pending, in a development which gave Buckner a rather eerie feeling of having been here before, the Mayor, Jimmy Walker, held up the payments to the counsel and his staff. (It was state money, but it had to be paid through the office of the City Comptroller, which was under Walker's supervision.) "The scandal smelled to heaven," Buckner said a year and a half later in

26 8 *Bull*, 12/24/27, p. 1.

the keynote speech of the Republican nominating convention for the mayoralty, "it smelled to Albany, but it did not smell across the river to City Hall."[27] But now Buckner had no need to borrow from wealthier friends, and he paid most of his young men out of his own pocket until, much later, after direct intervention by Governor Franklin D. Roosevelt, the appropriations came through.

What Connolly had been doing is simple to describe but was immensely difficult to prove. There were two fundamentally different ways of making large sewer pipe, either by forming it in the trench or by laying precast sections. One maker of precast sections had a patented "lock-joint" way of connecting the pieces. The city charter required competitive bidding on construction projects and prohibited the specification of patented features by any city engineering department. The bids for the Queens storm sewer got around these laws by setting specifications "copied word for word," as Buckner put it in his opening statement at the Connolly trial, "—word for word, except for the patented features—from the Lock Joint Pipe Company."[28]

Exclusive agent for the Lock Joint Pipe Company in Queens was John M. Phillips, a prominent contributor to and leader of Democratic Party causes. Prior to his acquisition of this franchise in 1917, all Queens storm sewers had been of "monolithic" (laid-in-the-trench) construction; after 1917, 90 percent of Queens storm sewers were laid with precast pipe—and every contract for precast large sewer pipe went to Phillips' company. He raked off in both directions—from the borough by overcharging for the pipe, and from the contractors in pay-offs, because the man who would win the bid was inevitably the man to whom Phillips had quoted the lowest price for pipe. Though there was no mention of the fact at the time, Phillips was an ex-con, so notorious in the 1910s that Whitman when running for Governor in 1914 had featured in his speeches the scandal that Phillips was director of purchasing for state institutions in the then incumbent Democratic administration. Phillips died while under indictment in the Queens sewer case, but he had shrewdly banked his proceeds in Canada; and echoes of the scandal were still being heard as late as 1939 and as far away as London, where the Privy Council in that year decided that Canadian banks did not have to return to the State of

27 *New York Times*, 8/2/29, p. 9.
28 *People* v. *Connolly*, Record on Appeal, p. 88.

New York some $3,405,000 Phillips had socked away in Quebec during his agency for the Lock Joint Pipe Company.

Steuer won his first challenge to the investigation in February, 1928, when the Court of Appeals ruled that Justice Scudder could not as a sitting judge act as Smith's Commissioner in the Connolly removal proceedings. Smith, whose commitment to cleaning up the Queens scandal went much deeper than Democrats Connolly and Steuer had realized, instantly substituted Clarence Shearn, a former judge (who had taken over the Youssoupoff-Widener case for Root-Clark when Buckner left to be U.S. Attorney, and had lost it). "I think," Buckner wrote Frankfurter, "that the Shearn appointment is all right. Of course his methods of practicing for thirty-five years have been diametrically opposite to my own and he does not understand organization, delegation, articulation, group action, and 'profit sharing.' However, we could be much worse off. Judge Scudder was ideal for us because he acted solely as a magistrate and left everything to us, and I in turn left everything to the staff at this particular stage of a most difficult and not altogether encouraging investigation. There have been four or five investigations of this same matter during the past four or five years, all of which have resulted in failure. I now understand the cause of the failure, because the job is a very hard one. At least 90% of the people that we are most anxious to examine have run away from the jurisdiction, taking their books with them. However, I think that in the end we will have done a fair sort of constructive job, even if not at all a sensational one."[29]

Buckner had been continually busy on other matters. He would lunch with the Connolly staff on Saturdays, and take them one evening a week to dinner at the Waldorf Grill. Shearn had set the hearings for April 9. As the date neared, Buckner became more closely involved with the work; and then, a week before the public hearings were to begin, Connolly put Shearn's Commission out of business by resigning as Borough President.

Connolly's excuse was that he could not afford the costs of the defense. Shearn and Buckner had an appropriation of $100,000; Buckner, Connolly later testified at his trial, "surrounded himself with seven or eight lawyers, many of them here today; he employed no less than twenty-five detectives, one of which followed me around. He

[29] Buckner to Frankfurter, 3/5/28.

employed engineers, and I am led to believe that his staff consisted of more than sixty people. They proceeded to operate through the Borough, and subpoenaed everybody, my wife, my wife's people, my brothers. . . ."[30] Mayor Walker fought to get Connolly a parallel appropriation, but even a Democratic Board of Estimate could not buy that one (what, after all, did Connolly have to investigate?); and the failure of the appropriation gave Connolly an excuse to quit. Again, he had underestimated Smith, who promptly appointed Buckner and his staff Special Assistant and Deputy Special Assistant Attorneys General, and empaneled a special grand jury to look into the situation in the Queens sewers. Meanwhile, the state legislature amended the law to make flight and removal of account books under subpoena an extraditable offense, and the witnesses ceased disappearing. This was, however, a rougher business than that; and three weeks before the trial was to begin that fall one of Buckner's most important witnesses "committed suicide" on a lonely road near a cemetery far from his home in the Maspeth section of Queens.

Because much of the spadework had already been done, Buckner's team was able to pilot an indictment through the grand jury by late June. To their great disappointment, they found they could not build an indictment for a substantive crime. Whatever fees had been paid to Phillips by contractors and whatever prices he had charged them for pipe, their testimony that their payments to him had been by voluntary agreement removed the transactions themselves from the domain of criminal law. And Buckner's staff, however large it might be, could not dig up anything that proved bribery. The best they could present was a three-count indictment (which Steuer later forced Buckner to reduce to one count on the ground that he had merely said the same thing three ways), alleging that Phillips, Connolly and Connolly's chief engineer Frederick Seely "did unlawfully, willfully, knowingly and corruptly conspire, combine, confederate and agree together and with each other . . . to cheat and defraud the City of New York out of property . . . obstruct due administration of the law . . . [and] neglect the duties enjoined upon them by law." Phillips was a sick man with a crippled kidney, and on July 3 he died; Connolly and Seely came to trial on September 25, 1928.

Buckner's relatively brief opening statement concentrated on sewers

[30] *People* v. *Connolly,* Record, p. 1669.

and sewer pipe, the Phillips monopoly and the fact that the Borough President had exclusive authority to award contracts. He warned the jury that most of his witnesses would perforce be the contractors, nearly all of whom were hostile witnesses, who "have been kept under subpoena for six or eight months in one way or another."[31] And, inevitably, "a great deal of this case will be what we call circumstantial evidence, detail for detail, and piece by piece."[32] Moreover, "We will not call a single witness who has even seen Connolly and Phillips together since 1921. . . . [T]he indictment charges not lunching together or dining together but working together, and *we will ask you to attach significance to the lack of evidence that they were together,* because we believe that all this evidence will show you that they must have been working together."[33]

There was no doubt that Queens had consistently paid more for pipe than any of the other counties in or near New York, but proving it would not be easy. "The problem was," Carl Newton recalled, "you had all sizes of pipe, and a different price for each size. Hard for jurors to keep all the sizes and all the prices separate in their minds. You don't want a juror saying, 'Hell, I remember they paid only $1.80 in Queens and up in the Bronx it was $2.15; that $1.80 was *cheap.*' " The $1.80 (per running foot) could have been for 24-inch pipe, while the $2.15 was for 72-inch pipe.

To help the jurors keep the prices straight, Newton and carpenters erected in the courtroom, over the weekend of September 30, an enormous chart, four feet by thirty feet, on which the prosecution could chalk comparative prices for each size of pipe as the witnesses testified to their contracts. Steuer opened court on October 1: "May it please Your Honor, I observe in the courtroom a structure that I assume is in some way to be connected or associated with the trial of this case. The defendant Connolly has had nothing to do with its erection. . . . I move its immediate removal from the courtroom. It is placed in the most conspicuous position, adjacent to the jurors; as a matter of fact, they could not have gotten to their seats without circumventing it—and I don't believe that it will be disputed that, being an object of that character, it very naturally would and that it actually

[31] *Ibid.,* p. 91.
[32] *Ibid.*
[33] *Ibid.,* p. 92. Italics added.

did attract attenion."[34] Justice Arthur S. Tompkins allowed it to remain, however, inescapably in the forefront of the jurors' attention; and even permitted the distribution of pictures of the completed chart to the jury when they retired for their deliberations. Steuer in later years would say, "My client was convicted by a chart."

None of this proved, though, that Connolly had profited in any way by the sewer fraud. His bank accounts, carefully examined, were consistent with his official salary—which had been $5,000 a year from 1911 to 1920, $10,000 a year from 1920 to 1923, and $15,000 a year thereafter. He had recently, however, built a rather fancy home, and there was no mortgage on it. Only a few relatively minor checks had passed through his accounts on their way to the building contractor: obviously, he had paid most of his bills for the house in cash. The builder, too, was a hostile witness:

"Q. What is the total amount, approximately, if you can give it to me that Mr. Connolly has provided you with to build this house? A. Approximately $55,000 to $56,000."

"Q. How has that been paid, by checks or paper money? A. Both."

But this was merely holding off the inevitable: "Q. Give us the proportions. Or, let me ask you this: About how much has been paid in paper money? A. About $50,000."[35]

Not the least of the activities of Buckner's bird dogs had been the sniffing out of places where Connolly could have invested or loaned cash. (This was why his people and his wife's people had been subpoenaed.) The investigators found some mortgages he had bought for cash, and some friends and relatives who had been borrowing. "I took the shot at that," Judge Lumbard recalled. "I knew somebody was a good friend of Connolly's, called him before the grand jury and just asked him how much Connolly had loaned him. He said, 'Twelve thousand dollars.' Harlan said to me, 'How in the hell did you know?' But I didn't know—that was just the kind of thinking Buckner stimulated in you."

In all, Buckner pulled from witnesses evidence of purchases, investments and loans by Connolly totaling $145,550 in cash, most of it in thousand-dollar bills. And that was the case.

Steuer defended by offering arguments that the precast pipe was

[34] *Ibid.*, p. 526.
[35] *Ibid.*, p. 1395.

really cheaper than the monolithic, by pointing out that not *all* the prices elsewhere were lower than *all* the prices in Queens, by summoning a string of eager and rather impressive character witnesses—and by calling Connolly himself. His most important technical witness was William H. Burr, dean of the nation's civil engineers, retired head of the engineering department at Columbia, who had been a consultant to the borough. Burr testified that for wet areas precast was cheaper than monolithic because of the extra expense of adding a waterproof membrane to the monolithic and the need to leave monolithic forms in place for twenty-one days after pouring the concrete. As it happened, one of the few major contracts for monolithic construction had been built in one of the wettest areas in Queens.

"Would you be surprised to learn," Buckner said, "that Patrick McGovern bid $200,000 less for monolithic than for precast on the Rockaway sewer?"

"Well," Burr said, "that depends on conditions. I do not know what the conditions are there."

"That depends on conditions," Buckner echoed scornfully. "That depends on how much he has to pay for precast pipe, does it not?"[36]

But Burr, as it turned out, did know about conditions at that sewer. Indeed, he had been the consultant on it, and his signature appeared at the bottom of the blueprint—for a sewer in the wettest part of Queens, monolithic construction, specifying neither the waterproof membrane he had just tesified was necessary nor the twenty-one-day period with the forms in place. Buckner encouraged Burr to take the blueprint with him to look for the expensive requirements during a recess, but Steuer waved away the offer. "To save time," he said rather bitterly, "we'll agree that it isn't there."[37]

Testifying fluently and at length in his own defense, Connolly went through a recital of his political career and statements of the impossibility of his knowing any details about the constructon contracts that came to him for initialing. Phillips he barely knew and disapproved of; and they had been on different sides in some political wars (Phillips had supported Mayor Walker and Connolly had supported ex-Mayor Hylan in a primary contest between the two). Among the questions Steuer did not ask Connolly was the source of

36 *Ibid.,* p. 1567.
37 *Ibid.,* p. 1568.

the $145,550 in cash Buckner's witnesses had seen him spend or lend.

"In the state of the record," Justice Aron Steuer of New York's Appellate Division (who had helped his father in the trial) said a generation later, "Connolly did have a good explanation. He was the executor of an estate, and took fees. He had always been a flashy person who liked to have cash and show cash. But it would have been a plausible rather than a bookkeeping explanation." The best way to give the explanation strength, Max Steuer decided, was to let it come out on cross-examination.

Buckner saw the trap: he did not wish to be the means by which Connolly snuck away from the damning thousand-dollar bills. To Steuer's fury, he did not ask Connolly about the money either. Connolly left the stand without offering any explanations; and Buckner still had the point, unchallenged, for his summing up.

The cross-examination of Connolly was, Buckner wrote later, "kindly and sympathetic," softening up the defendant for what Buckner considered the one important point to be gained. There had been several other investigations of the sewer situation, one of them public; but Connolly had never given any sign he knew there was a problem. Now, "he was shown the book of testimony of such previous investigation and asked if he had read it, to which he replied affirmatively. Up until this time the case had really been devoid of proof as to [Connolly's] knowledge of commonplace rumor concerning corruption in the department involved."[38]

Steuer in his summation covered courageously the question of the cash payments: "All that they ask you to do is to guess that the money came from Phillips. That is all. Nothing else. Just that. If it did not [come from Phillips] it has not anything to do with the case. That is conceded. . . .

"Do you know that under the law the only way you can pay a debt is with currency? Do you know that under the law unless you expressly stipulate to the contrary, if A owes B $500 and A wants to give B a check, plain or certified, for that $500, B does not have to take it? That is not legal tender. . . . [A] man in public office who does not want the transactions which he has had to be public knowledge, uses currency. What of it?"[39]

[38] Buckner, "The Lawyer in Court," *op. cit.*, p. 8.
[39] *People* v. *Connolly*, p. 1826.

Later, Steuer and Judge Tompkins engaged in the following colloquy over the list of legal guidelines Steuer asked the judge to include in his charge to the jury:

MR. STEUER: There is nothing in the law to require him to make payments by checks.

THE COURT: That I charge.

MR. STEUER: The only way a person may legally and with absolute right make a payment is by currency or cash, unless there is an agreement to the contrary.

THE COURT: I charge that, with this addition: That in this case the jurors may consider or may apply their own knowledge of how such transactions are conducted generally by people who have a checking bank account.

MR. STEUER: I except to the modification.[40]

Buckner himself ignored Steuer's comments on cash versus check. On the question of his failure to ask Connolly how he came by the money, Buckner said, "[I]f Mr. Steuer is satisfied to have a Borough President . . . during the very time that Phillips, the Assistant Borough President, you might call him, in charge of sewers in Queens, was grafting three million dollars—if he is satisfied to give lectures on the growth of the Borough instead of telling you where he got $145,550 in thousand dollar bills, or whatever they are, then certainly I am satisfied."[41]

On his failure to connect Connolly and Phillips, Buckner told the jury, "I knew the great plea would be that there is no proof of connection; that when a pickpocket is arrested in the subway, the cop has him by the wrist and he is brought in and there is proof; that when a burglar is caught running away from a house, he is arrested and people see him, and they say he is the man that just came down the fire escape, and there is proof—but that you must not prosecute anybody, you must not prosecute anybody if in 1925 or 1926, the shocking conditions existed here which are revealed by that chart, and you must not prosecute anybody unless some witness is called who overheard some conversation between Connolly and Phillips on the subject.

[40] *Ibid.*, pp. 1923-1924.
[41] *Ibid.*, p. 1899.

"That is the last thing, as I told you in my opening, that anybody would overhear."[42]

The character witnesses were to be expected. "How could Mr. Connolly have been re-elected," Buckner said, "how could he have been re-elected in 1917 and 1921 and 1925 if his reputation was not that of an honest and upright public official?"[43] Finally, as was increasingly common in his later years, Buckner injected a personal note. He disposed of the character witnesses with the statement that "[I]f they were jurors, if they took oath as jurors and heard all the evidence that you have heard in three weeks, every single one of those men would vote for the conviction of Connolly, and I will stake my professional reputation on it."

Steuer went through the ceiling. But one personal comment even Steuer could grant Buckner as a reason for pride. In the middle of an election campaign when Al Smith was running for President, when Buckner's party was eager for the kind of dirt that lay just below the surface everywhere one looked at the Connolly case, Buckner could say to the jury (and to Proskauer and Smith), "I cannot do anything unless I do it and look at it as a lawyer's job. Hasn't it been one, gentlemen, I ask you? Hasn't this been a fair, square, honest nonpolitical effort on my part? Not a politician has been called except men ages out of politics who were called on minor matters like tracing checks and so forth."[44]

The jury was eleven to one for conviction from the first ballot, and on the second day the holdout capitulated. Justice Harlan, as always, wrote the brief by which Buckner blocked Connolly's appeals; he recalled that these were the only briefs he wrote which Buckner went over in close detail. "A great trial," Justice Harlan recalled in 1965. "That chart—and the absence of evidence . . ."

4

Clients poured into the firm—estate work and appellate work for Elihu Root, Jr., corporate work for Howland, tax and financial work for Ballantine, commercial lost causes for Clark (who most enjoyed getting 15 percent for a client where everyone else saw noth-

[42] *Ibid.*, p. 1851.
[43] *Ibid.*, p. 1903.
[44] *Ibid.*, p. 1897.

ing), trials for Buckner. The four young partners elevated in 1925 had all worked in with clients and were all business-holders, though none was yet significant as a business-getter. A tenth partner, Willkie Bushby, was created in 1928 (the next would be John Harlan and Ethan Alyea in 1931). Buckner expanded the office's recruiting efforts from the Eastern law schools to the Big Ten, offering to the deans of the law schools at Wisconsin, Northwestern, Michigan and Minnesota a free trip to a New York interview for any candidate they were prepared to recommend. The office took over yet a third, then a fourth, floor at 31 Nassau Street; by 1932 there were seventy-four lawyers in Root-Clark.

Buckner's own work was a kaleidoscope of the troubles that come to law—will contests, contract cases, stockholders suits, libel suits, antitrust actions. (On one of these, Buckner representing the German potash interests and "Wild Bill" Donovan representing the government negotiated a settlement in their underwear on a train riding through the hot midlands from New Mexico to Chicago.) Buckner's income rose above $100,000 a year, virtually all of which he and his wife managed to spend. All the cases were interesting at the time and soon forgotten in the last-minute drive to master the facts and the law of the next case.

One that was more publicized and more memorable than most was a contract case that happened to be between heavyweight champion Gene Tunney and sports operator Tim Mara. Buckner was called in only a week before the trial by Tunney's counsel, Chadbourne, Stanchfield & Levy, because Mara had suddenly escalated his own trial lawyer to the level of Martin W. Littleton. The complaint against Tunney was that he had welshed on an oral promise to pay Mara 10 percent of the purse (and 25 percent of all subsequent earnings if the title changed hands) in return for Mara's arranging Tunney's fight with Dempsey. Tunney's contention was that he had indeed made such an agreement, but it was to come into effect only if Mara arranged a fight in New York, which he had been unable to do. When first brought, in January, 1927, four months after Tunney's victory, the suit had asked $20,000 plus $25,000. By the time it came to trial, in October, 1930, the ante was up to $20,000 plus $385,000.

The evidence on both sides was almost pure Ring Lardner, and Buckner enjoyed himself. At one point, when Littleton introduced a telegram from Tunney to Mara signed "Golfer," Buckner entered a personal request: "It would be agreeable to me if you stipulate, Mr. Littleton, that this 'Golfer' is Gene Tunney, because both Tunney and I play over 100, but Mr. Littleton plays 85, and whether or not he thinks it fair that a man should call himself a golfer with that score—" But the judge was the slow-moving Peter Hatting, and he said, puzzled, "Is there any dispute that was sent by Tunney, Mr. Buckner?" Buckner said, "No. He called himself a Golfer."[45] From the letters and telegrams introduced in evidence it was clear that Tunney badly wanted a fight with Dempsey, and that he particularly wanted it in New York rather than at Boyle's Thirty Acres in New Jersey (where state law would prevent a decision on points) or in some other city (where the gate would be smaller). Among the complications about booking the fight for New York were that neither Dempsey nor Tunney held a license to fight in the state and that the State Boxing Commission had firmly declared that Dempsey's next defense of his title had to be against the colored heavyweight Harry Wills. Mara knew a lot of people in New York politics, up to and including the Boxing Commissioners and (he claimed) Governor Smith; but Tex Rickard had finally staged the fight in Philadelphia.

Tunney's best witness was James P. Eagleton, proprietor of a speakeasy in the Bronx, who had brought Mara and Tunney together and had listened in on their negotiations. "I spent days drinking beer with him," Justice Harlan recalled, "before he agreed to testify." Then, a few days before the trial, Eagleton called up frantic: "I'm a family man, I've got children to support. Tim Mara says if I testify for Tunney he'll have me closed down." Harlan recalled, "This was something for the boss. I took him down to see Buckner, and Buckner said, 'Don't worry. If Mr. Littleton asks you about your business, you'll have in your pocket a piece of paper from Mr. Harlan you can read in reply.' I wrote out for him the statement, 'I refuse to answer on the grounds that it might incriminate me,' and he took the piece of paper with him."

The trial seemed to be going so well that Buckner and Harlan discussed whether they should call Eagleton at all, but they decided they needed the clincher. Sure enough, Littleton's first question on cross-examination was: "Mr. Eagleton, what is your business?"

45 *Mara* v. *Tunney,* Record on Appeal, p. 134.

Eagleton replied, "Mr. Mara knows my business. He has been in my place of business."

Littleton said, "I do not know what Mr. Mara knows. I know some of the things he knows. I do not know all that he knows. Perhaps I never aspired to that, but I have asked you a question, which I expect you to answer, unless you are unwilling to answer it. Are you willing?"

"I refuse to answer."

"You do? On what grounds?"

"Well," Eagleton said, fumbling in his pocket, "of incriminating myself."[46]

Harlan recalled, "The jury was on the edge of its chairs. We hadn't realized how bad it would look, and now we saw the case going out the window. I couldn't imagine what Buckner would do."

As soon as Littleton had finished his brief cross-examination of the witness, Buckner rose for redirect and asked, "Before the Prohibition Law was passed, what was your business?"

Eagleton gulped out, "Liquor dealer"; and the jury relaxed.[47] Its verdict was for the defendant, but Mara took an appeal; and the Appellate Division paid Buckner the kind of compliment no lawyer wishes to receive: it reversed, in part on the ground that the verdict was contrary to the weight of the evidence. Rather than try it again with that opinion hanging over their heads, Buckner and Tunney decided to settle; and Tunney paid Mara $30,000.

5

Throughout this period, Buckner was closely involved with Republican politics. He made the keynote speech at the 1929 convention that nominated Fiorello LaGuardia (who had to wait another four years to win), and in 1930 he headed a "lawyers' committee" for the election of Charles H. Tuttle. The latter was a considerable sacrifice for Buckner, because the two men did not get along. As Buckner's successor at the U.S. Attorney's office, Tuttle felt his staff had been depleted by his predecessor's siren call first to the Goodyear and then to the Connolly team. On the other side, Buckner claimed, "Tuttle ran [the office] downhill with a speed which can only be achieved by a man who wants the nomination for governor, and wants it along regular

46 *Ibid.*, p. 618.
47 *Ibid.*, p. 626.

organization lines. [Albert O.] Ottinger [Republican candidate in 1928] beat him to it the first time, and he redoubled his efforts to put the staff on the bum."[48] Supporting Tuttle was made even more difficult for him by the fact that Tuttle was a prohibitionist, and Buckner had come to the point where he was demanding "a courageous rebellion against this monstrous and crime-breeding thing foisted upon us by our national government. . . . I am ashamed to say that for eleven years the Republican Party in this state has carried a cocktail glass on one shoulder and a glass of water on the other."[49]

Buckner found, however, the issue he could live with—the fact that the Republicans in the state legislature were committed to continue, and the Democrats seemed committed to stop, the Seabury Investigation of the city government. That, he said, was "the great issue in this campaign . . . a more important issue than any we have had in a generation."[50]

As late as March, 1932, *The New Yorker* was touting Buckner himself, not yet fifty-five years old, as a plausible Republican candidate in that fall's state elections. "An iron realism has so far saved him from such escapades," Alva Johnston wrote, "but count no man happy until he is dead."[51] But while this issue of the magazine was on press, with that macabre relevance that dogs periodical publication, Buckner suffered his first stroke, which would end his public career in both law and politics.

Others in the RCB & H of the 1920s were already gone. Howland had left the firm to become a partner in Guggenheim Brothers at the beginning of 1930. Since then, he wrote in the Sixth Alumni Report of his Harvard Law School class, "I have been worrying not about other people's troubles, as the lawyer does, but about our own troubles in connection with copper, nitrate, tin, and other non-ferrous metals and about the problems involved in reducing our staff in localities as far apart as Chile on the one hand and the Federated Malay States on the other."[52] Ballantine was temporarily out at the time of Buckner's first illness, serving the Hoover administration first as Assistant Secretary and then as Under Secretary of the Treasury. Even Clark had

48 Buckner to Frankfurter, 2/1/32.
49 Speech to Seventh Assembly District Republican Club, 10/28/30, p. 3.
50 *Ibid.*, p. 1
51 Johnston, "Courtroom Warrior—II," *The New Yorker*, 3/19/32, p. 27.
52 Harvard Law School Class of 1907, Sixth Report, 1932, p. 27.

considered public office, and had let Buckner know that he would accept an appointment to succeed Tuttle in the U.S. Attorney's office. But Clark's candidacy, which Buckner vigorously supported, got lost on a political battlefield, and the post went to George Z. Medalie—about whom, incidentally, Buckner was enthusiastic. "Up to the present writing, Medalie is a corking D.A.," he told Frankfurter. "Independent, common sense, modest, shrewd, able. I have asked two or three of our judicial friends. They say so too."[53]

Buckner was not badly hit by the depression—mostly, one of his friends said, because he hadn't saved enough money to have any investments. His wife continued to expand the house at Siasconset, and he undertook duties as president of Nantucket's Sankaty Head Golf Club (where he would make up the deficit, his daughter Ruth recalled, by telling her to give champagne parties at the club for her friends). For Root-Clark, as for many other firms, the first three years of economic collapse were a time of vastly expanding legal income. Bankruptcies and reorganizations flooded the office. But nobody could live through the cataclysm of 1929-32 without re-examining even fundamental beliefs. It is possible that Buckner voted for Roosevelt rather than Hoover in 1932, and certain that for a few months in 1933 he referred to himself as a "Roosevelt Republican."[54] On New Year's Day, 1933, recently out of the hospital and about to return there, Buckner offered his staff a mixture of personal and political reflections:

. . . I would not take too seriously anything that may happen. Perhaps a new system will be better; perhaps worse; perhaps better through a stage and then worse; perhaps worse for a time and then better. A system that witnesses ten or twelve million people without work is, after all, not so perfect as to render re-examination exactly treason, however much we may hope for an end to the depression in terms of the *status quo ante* 1914. . . .

My own idea of personal happiness and an adequate personal contribution to society requires an accepted adjustment to environment—almost, if not quite, *any* environment—and a search for enthusiasms within that environment. The sooner a man discovers (as he can so easily discover, both by experience and observation) that environment *per se* can bring neither the durable satisfactions nor the serious disappointments

[53] Buckner to Frankfurter, 2/1/32.
[54] 21 *Bull*, 439, 9/21/40.

of life, the more quickly will he develop a saving philosophy which defies circumstance. . . .

I am against evangelists, prohibitionists, communists, socialists, Big Navy men, men who wish to be multimillionaires, descent of huge fortunes, Manifest Destiny, payments to veterans not injured in the war, high tariffs, demanding payment of foreign debts, the offering of hecatombs of American Marines to the gods of foreign trade, the taxing of only a minority of voters, doctrinaire reformers, excessive governmental functions and costs, and other things, but I can be quite happy with any of these aversions triumphant.

I am an "internationalist" (whatever that means), in favor of the World Court and some sort of League of Nations, but I am against war and, so as to be clearly understood, against preparedness for war.

I favor radical disarmament without waiting for any other nation. Bargaining concerning the length of knife-blades and concerning their synchronized stropping upon national soles, keeping time with an international metronome—strop, strop, strop, strop,—small nations kindly omit the fourth beat—strop, strop, strop—thank you—is not, in my opinion, a path to peace.

I shall assign to anyone wishing it all my right, title and interest as an American citizen in the dollars to be made in Manchuria by our helping maintain its territorial and political integrity. If our interest be purely eleemosynary, then I move to divert our efforts and money to our own unemployed, deficits, and taxes. If we are neither to fight nor boycott, with possible martial consequences, but merely "tell the world" we shall not recognize a new *status*, then the cable and wireless are an adequate and very cheap megaphone. We do not need the fleet as a broadcasting station.

If one cannot be both an internationalist and a pacifist, as I would like to be, then, after voting for my considered preference, I shall go along with the majority, enjoying myself.

If some or all disagree with any or all of the above, I shall not be disconcerted. Many years ago complacence and some degree of humility followed the devastating discovery that I was frequently wrong. A man must believe what he believes but only so long as he believes it. The Rule against Perpetuities should apply to all personal convictions.[55]

A copy of this document went to Frankfurter, who replied enthusiastically: "It is one of the most felicitous expressions of your general philosophy and says new and wise things which you have not

55 14 *Bull*, 1/7/33, pp. 2-5.

heretofore uttered regarding national and international affairs. I was right years ago in wishing you to become President. Who knows? Had I the talent of Harry Daugherty you might be in the White House— and I, a Harry Daugherty!"[56] Within six months, however, Buckner's tolerance for social experiment had been exceeded by Roosevelt's "state socialism" (both Buckner and Clark were especially horrified as the Roosevelt of the 1932 campaign had been horrified by the idea of deficit financing); and when war came to Europe Buckner was an interventionist—indeed, he reprinted much of this 1933 New Year's message in *The Bull* under the heading "I Was Wrong." By then, his political opinions were of interest really to no one but himself, which he knew and accepted. "I am voting for Mr. Willkie," he wrote Frankfurter. "I don't know him personally, and of course he never heard of me."[57]

6

Buckner's last, longest and saddest trial, twelve weeks in the spring of 1931, grew out of the depression, and perhaps to a degree out of politics. It was a criminal case, in which Buckner sought to defend Saul Singer, executive vice president of the Bank of the United States, which had closed its doors in December, 1930—apparently (not really, as it turned out) destroying the bank accounts of one-tenth of the city's families. Founded in 1913, the bank had grown through spectacular mergers to be in assets the twenty-eighth largest among the country's 27,000 national banks, and in number of branches the third largest in New York State. Its collapse was among the worst tragedies of the depression—especially, perhaps, because it was unnecessary: the bank was solvent and, even after the inevitable losses and costs of liquidation, paid out to its depositors more than seventy-five cents on the dollar. But these developments were in the future in early 1931, when the public was demanding retribution on the officers and directors of the bank, and had found an effective spokesman for the demand in the person of Max Steuer, who first offered his services (without fee) to all depositors of the bank, and then accepted an appointment (again, at his insistence, without fee) as Special Assistant District Attorney to bring the Bank of the United States malefactors to justice.

[56] Frankfurter to Buckner, 1/11/33.
[57] Buckner to Frankfurter, 10/2/40.

Steuer's motivations in coming into this situation as a prosecutor have always been rather obscure. He had never accepted such an assignment before. "I know what it means to charge a person with the commission of an offense," he said in a statement replying to an effort to have him disqualified from the prosecution. "I know what it means to his family, his wife and to his children, to his near relatives and his friends. I have defended persons in that situation. I have wept when they wept and have been as sleepless as they have been."[58] In another part of the same document he observed laconically, "My experience at the Bar . . . has taught me that prosecutors, as a rule, are persons who love human blood."[59]

The reason Steuer gave for undertaking the prosecution of the officers of the Bank of the United States was that "the depositors of this bank are people of my kind and I am interested in them." Most people saw something less altruistic in his activities. The counsel to the bank, and one of its directors was Isidor J. Kresel, who many years before had moved Steuer's disbarment on charges of suborning the perjury of a chorus girl who was suing her boss; and Steuer was known to have a long memory. Moreover, Kresel was at the time of the indictment counsel to the Seabury Investigation of racketeering in the New York magistrate's courts, which would lead eventually to Roosevelt's dismissal of Mayor Walker, who was Steuer's friend. Singer and Bernard K. Marcus, the president of the bank, were leaders in the world of New York Jewry, where Steuer was the outstanding lawyer; but except for one minor matter neither had ever employed Steuer, and he had reason to believe that they had kept him out of some clubs.

Steuer secured indictments against Marcus and Singer, Henry W. Pollock (the Bank's treasurer), Kresel and Herbert Singer, Saul Singer's son, who was a young assistant in the Kresel office. Probably because of their strong involvement with the Seabury Investigation, Charles H. Tuttle agreed to appear for Marcus and Buckner for the elder Singer. Pollock was represented by David Podell, and young Herbert Singer by Harold Medina, then a Columbia Law School professor, later a Judge of the Court of Appeals for the Second Circuit. Kresel himself would have been represented by John W. Davis, former

[58] *People* v. *Marcus,* Record on Appeal, p. 147.
[59] *Ibid.,* p. 129.

Democratic candidate for President; but during the six weeks between indictment and trial Kresel became visibly too ill to stand trial. ("I always thought he was faking, making himself sick by taking some kind of dope," Harold Medina said years later), and his case was severed.

The charges against the officers of the bank were based on their operation of affiliated securities corporations and safe-deposit companies. One of these corporations, which had virtually the same management and ownership as the bank, had by 1929 borrowed from the bank considerably more than the State Banking Department considered proper. Much of the borrowing had been to support the market in the new securities which had united the ownership of the bank and the largest of its securities affiliates, looking toward the sale of a large block of stock to one of the city's more conservative investment houses in late summer, 1929. The investment house had wisely backed away at the last minute, and the securities affiliate was in no position to repay the loans.

To make the books look better, two new corporations summoned into existence for the purpose purchased at inflated prices the securities corporation's stock in a foreign company and in its own real-estate ventures. These new corporations got the money to make these purchases by the sale of their own stock to two safe-deposit companies owned by the bank. The safe-deposit companies got the money to buy the stock of the new corporations by borrowing from the Bank of the United States. In other words, the securities corporation paid back its excess loans from the Bank of the United States with money borrowed from the Bank of the United States by the bank's own safe-deposit companies, two previously nonexistent corporations acting as the conduit. It was a pure bookkeeping transaction within a group of corporations all owned by the same people—as one of the witnesses at the trial said, "a wash." But it fell afoul of the banking law, which prohibited safe-deposit companies from buying common stocks. The indictment charged misapplication of the assets of one of the safe-deposit companies.

No effort had been made to deceive the State Banking Department. All the details had been presented to the department by the bank's accountants on January 12, 1930, a day before the transactions were put through. Yet the purpose of this shuffle *was* fundamentally de-

ceptive. Moreover, it could be demonstrated that the securities corporation had been formed with bank stockholders and bank assets on a
design which yielded extraordinarily heavy profits to Marcus and Singer
and a few of their fellow directors at the expense of everybody else.
Bank examiners had castigated the management in a confidential
report as early as mid-1929; placing the operation in bankruptcy in
early 1931, a few weeks after the bank had closed its doors, federal
Judge John M. Woolsey had denounced the officers of the bank in the
strongest terms. It was not only Steuer who was upset. The underlying
situation which had created the crisis was not inaccurately described
by John T. Flynn in *The New Republic* as "a scheme deliberately
cooked to deprive the bank's stockholders of a large part of the profits
accruing from the management of their funds."[60] Finally, in terms of
purely technical banking practice, the whole business, done in one
day, had been seriously bungled. As Tuttle conceded in his summation
for Marcus, "We have a transaction that is involved, that was carried
through carelessly, inadequately, and in a way which would make a
cow laugh. . . . The details that were left unbuttoned are legion."[61]

By temperament, talent and past experience Buckner was unsuited
to the defense of such a case. He always felt his client had been rail-
roaded. ("The only real crime committed here," he told several friends
in private conversation, "was the crime of the other New York banks
which let this one go under.") The specific activities which the indictment alleged as crimes had not cost the bank's depositors or stockholders a penny. Steuer and the courts had to stretch the law pretty
far to make the indictment good. But in fact Marcus and Singer had
run the bank and the subsidiary corporations greedily, as Steuer
charged. Putting the best possible face on the matter, as Judge Frederick C. Crane wrote for the majority in the 6-to-1 decision of the
Court of Appeals which upheld the conviction of Marcus and Singer,
"Good intentions do not justify the misapplication or misuse of corporate assets when the directors know that the use they are making
of them is not for the benefit of the company, but for the benefit of
other enterprises in which they are interested."[62]

Standard operating procedure at the Bank of the United States was

[60] Flynn, "Using Depositors' Money for Insiders' Profit," 45 *The New Republic* 288, p. 289.
[61] *People* v. *Marcus,* Record on Appeal, p. 5082.
[62] *People* v. *Marcus,* 261 NY 268, p. 278.

about to be made illegal by Congress in legislation most of which was supported even by the American Bankers Association. Buckner's partners Root and Clark had only the year before grown so disgusted with the normal management of trust companies by the New York banks that they had formed one of their own to safeguard their clients' assets. The fact that nearly everybody else in the banking world had behaved as disgracefully as these defendants gave Buckner the feeling that morality was on his side, and in a less frantic period the commonplace nature of their offense would doubtless have preserved Marcus and Singer from criminal prosecution. But Buckner was uncomfortable with clients whose actions had been discreditable, whether or not they had been illegal.

The atmosphere of the trial, held before the depositors had been able to recover as much as 30 percent of their money, could not have been more depressing for the defense. "They talk about public prejudice now," Judge Medina said a generation later. "Well, you should have been there then. There was a queue of depositors all around the courthouse, waiting to get in, every day. They would hiss at you as you went by." And for the first time in a decade Buckner found himself in a position where he could not control the tactics of the trial. Though the Root-Clark office was in charge of the preparation, Tuttle was equally in command in the courtroom. The two men did not get along personally, and they had radically different theories of the trial. Tuttle wished to hold Steuer as narrowly as possible to the immediate circumstances of the juggled loans, while Buckner (convinced that his client had committed no crime and that facts did not damage innocent people) was to a degree a prisoner of his oft-expressed belief that a lawyer should not object to the introduction of testimony.

The record shows, for example, an objection by Tuttle to a question asked by Buckner on cross-examination,[63] an objection by Tuttle and Steuer together to evidence Buckner wished to introduce on direct examination,[64] innumerable statements by Buckner that he did not associate himself with Tuttle's objection to one of Steuer's questions— and then, in the befuddling last week of a long trial, an objection by Buckner to testimony Tuttle wished to introduce.[65] After arguing with each other in open court, the defense counsel would plow together

[63] *People* v. *Marcus,* Record, p. 1986.
[64] *Ibid.,* p. 2016.
[65] *Ibid.,* p. 4824.

through the hostile crowds to continue their quarreling over lunch. Steuer, incidentally, thought Tuttle was right. During the Marcus-Singer trial he would return to his office at the end of the day and sneer to one of his assistants, who had once worked for Buckner, "Tell me, has Buckner ever tried a case before?"

In planning tactics, Buckner was trapped by his prosecutor's approach. One of the most important pieces of evidence in Steuer's hands was a memorandum dated the day after the accountants had told the Deputy Banking Superintendent of what Marcus and Singer planned to do to shift the loans on the books. The memorandum said strongly that the plan would not be satisfactory to the department. The original of this memorandum was missing, and it had been retyped from stenographer's notes. Oddly, that notebook was missing, too, for a long time; but finally it was dug up. Buckner, drawing on experience long past, read the stenographer's shorthand himself and found that while the memo in evidence, retyped after the bank had gone bust, merely expressed the department's displeasure with the projected juggling, the stenographer's shorthand contained the key statement that the Superintendent "might not object."

Buckner hammered on this issue, and tried unsuccessfully to subpoena a bunch of stenographers' notebooks from the Banking Department, by which he said he would show that the entire memorandum had been invented a year after the meeting described in it. He doubtless envisioned a summing up in which he would argue that the loan juggling had done no harm; that the defendants' accountants had approved it and their lawyer (Kresel) had approved it; and that the only evidence against it was a memo faked by a deputy after the bank went smash and the deputy was afraid his own reputation would suffer unless he could show he had opposed this dubious piece of window dressing at the time it was first suggested.

What Buckner could not know was that both the accountants and Kresel had in different degrees given Marcus and Singer away under examination by Steuer in the grand jury room. Accountant Joseph J. McArdle remembered that the Deputy Superintendent had indeed disliked the planned transaction, though he had not specifically disapproved it; and Buckner was reduced on redirect to asking his own witness a question which began with the sour comment, "I will just take your recollection now, like Huyler's Candy, fresh every hour. If you have got some new recollection now on that subject, tell it to us."[66] But Kresel was the killer. Four months had now elapsed since the first onslaught of his dangerous illness, and he was well enough to testify for the defendants. He went through direct examination as expected, but on cross-examination he was confronted by Steuer with his testimony at the grand jury:

"I have nothing to do [with] and did not know of the course that this transaction took. I do not understand why it should have been necessary to have this devious way of having these two corporations. . . . [T]he very fact that it was passed through that way indicates that there was something suspiciously wrong about it. It is unfortunate that the man who was in my employ [the defendant Herbert Singer, Saul Singer's son] was the man who had charge of it."[67]

Kresel now denied that he had said any such thing, and again shorthand notes were produced for Buckner to examine. (He told Steuer the transcription from the notes was correct; and Steuer returning to his office sneered to his assistant, "Buckner can't try cases, but he's a hell of a court reporter.") Steuer and the foreman of the grand jury testified to the accuracy of the grand jury minutes, and a few days after the end of the trial Kresel was indicted for perjury. Buckner again was in the position of savagely attacking his own witness, but now he had more evidence to attack with. His assistant Joseph Schreiber had been through the files not only at the Bank of the United States but also in Kresel's office, and found memoranda and calendar entries proving that Kresel had participated step by step in the discussions leading to the supposedly criminal transactions. Kresel was discredited, but Buckner's task on summation was made almost impossible.

Kresel's testimony had been most severely damaging, of course, to Herbert Singer, whom Medina in his rare interventions had tried to picture as little more than an office boy. Nor had young Singer helped his own cause. Dedicated to the notion that his testimony would free his father, Singer portrayed himself as the mastermind of the deal, and defended it at vast length and in enormous legal detail while Medina tried unsuccessfully to shut him up. Buckner also tried, in charity, to counteract the impression Singer had given. He intervened toward the

66 *Ibid.*, p. 3414.
67 *Ibid.*, p. 4765.

end of the direct examination: "One question before lunch. Herbert, how old were you on the 13th of January, 1930?"

Singer replied, "Twenty-three."

"Twenty-three?" Buckner repeated.

"Yes, sir."[68]

Steuer picked up this colloquy and ridiculed it in his summation, and young Singer was convicted with his father and Marcus. Medina, who had taken the case because Singer had been his student at Columbia only two years before, recalled that "the worst moment I ever had was when the judge revoked bail at four-thirty in the morning, and they led my Herbert across the Bridge of Sighs to the Tombs."

Buckner at the trial stayed with his plans for an accusatory summation. His villains were the Deputy Superintendent, whom he accused of a "dirty, infamous piece of work"[69]; Joseph McArdle, who called the plan "the damn thing" in the grand jury room ("Bootlicking!" Buckner said to the jury. "Bootlicking the grand jury and Mr. Steuer!"[70]); and especially Kresel ("These defendants . . . are condemned, deserted, betrayed by the lawyer on whom they relied"[71]). But the atmosphere was wrong: whatever these witnesses had or had not done to Marcus and Singer, it did not look like much beside the failure of a bank which had had 413,000 depositors. Even a summation which occupies three hundred printed pages could not save Buckner's client.

The jury returned with its verdict at 2:15 on a Saturday morning. Pollock, the treasurer of the bank, against whom there was virtually no evidence, escaped with a hung jury. Steuer refused to approve the certificate of reasonable doubt which would have permitted the judge to continue bail, and the three losers were taken off to cells—first to the common pen, which they shared with the night's haul of thieves and pickpockets. Buckner called several of his assistants; everybody would have to work over the weekend to prepare the papers which would force restoration of bail to the convicted clients. But the papers were still being processed the following Tuesday, when the Singers, father and son, were sentenced and returned to the Tombs handcuffed

[68] *Ibid.*, p. 3685.
[69] *Ibid.*, p. 5253 .
[70] *Ibid.*, p. 5251.
[71] *Ibid.*, p. 5152.

to each other, with Marcus behind, handcuffed to a convicted common thief.

The trial had run from late March to mid-June, 1931, and its last two weeks had coincided with a heat wave that made the courtroom unbearable. The jurors at the end were awarded by the court an extra $500 each for their extraordinary services. The price to Buckner was accelerating collapse of his already precarious health.

In a subsequent trial in 1933, Kresel too was convicted, despite character testimony from Seabury, Smith and Senator Robert F. Wagner; but in 1935 the Appellate Division threw out conviction and indictment, mostly on the grounds that Kresel had not been an officer or director of (or, indeed, the lawyer for) the safe-deposit company whose funds had been misapplied.

On appeal, Herbert Singer's conviction was reversed and his indictment dismissed. "I won it on a jury argument in the Court of Appeals," Judge Medina recalled. "I told the judges, 'You know how these boys in law school are—these law clerks of yours—they think they know everything.'" Judge Crane's opinion picked up this argument jovially with the comment, "We are not unfamiliar with the importance frequently assumed by the young practitioner who is apt to magnify his work and worth."[72] Herbert Singer went on to become a highly successful lawyer in New York; and in 1966 he established a committee to endow a Medina Chair at Columbia Law School. He started the ball rolling with a $50,000 contribution from the foundation established in the will of his father, who after serving not quite two years of a three-to-six-year sentence went off to make a fortune in the oil fields of Texas.

[72] *People* v. *Marcus,* 261 NY 268 at 295.

CHAPTER ELEVEN

Ebb Tide

1932-1941

The last major case to come to Root-Clark because the principals' counsel wanted the services of Emory Buckner was the estate of Miss Ella Wendel, sole survivor of a family of real-estate investors none of whom had managed to produce a child. The value of the estate was estimated in the newspapers at $75,000,000, and it was worth a third of that even at depression prices; and virtually all of it was left to charity. The will was submitted for probate while Buckner was trying the Marcus-Singer case, and was widely publicized. Within a few months, 2,300 people had entered claims that they were related to the late Miss Wendel and were entitled to some of her money. Arthur Garfield Hays and Samuel Untermyer undertook to see that these claimants received the just rewards of consanguinity. Led by the Board of Methodist Missions, the charities formed a committee to protect their interests, began tracking down the claimants for the purpose of settling with them, and in the summer of 1931 hired Root-Clark to handle the litigation.

The charities got to one of the legitimate claimants in Mississippi and bought her off for $25,000; but Hays and Untermyer were on their trail, and the settlement produced nothing but a suit against the charities for fraud, brought in federal court in New York. Buckner argued it on a motion to dismiss in the fall of 1931, in Judge Mack's chambers in the Woolworth Building, on a brief written by Henry Friendly. "I didn't think he argued it well," Friendly recalled, "but, then, it wasn't the sort of thing he did argue well." Meanwhile, the will itself was in limbo, because Hays and Untermyer had challenged the jurisdiction of the New York Surrogate's Court on the grounds that the old lady had been a resident of Westchester.

Nevertheless, Root-Clark proceeded to move for a bill of particulars in which each alleged relative would have to state his reasons for claiming as an heir-at-law and next of kin. Buckner was beginning to organize his teams of researchers, headed by Harlan and Friendly, when in early March, 1932, he collapsed at his home with what he later described to Frankfurter as "a verra, verra light stroke."[1] The effects of the stroke were deepened by Buckner's general state of physical debility, for the fact of the matter was that he had not been really well for two years. He was fifty-four. Old stomach troubles had nagged at him with increasing severity, tiring him, costing him sleep, and to some extent impairing his performance. "The main thing with me," he had written a year before to Gottlieb (who was working on Guggenheim matters in Chile), "is to go on the vegetable wagon, and that I have done completely although even as to that the doctor recommended a compromise when dining out. My greatest trouble is with smoking because of my almost continuous smoking for twenty-five years when not asleep. I have succeeded in reducing that by about half or two thirds and the liquor situation about 50%. It is important in these matters not to get too much 'hipped' on one's diet or health."[2]

Buckner had grown used to feeling poorly, and to working fiercely hard through bouts of discomfort. He had broken his vacation in 1930 for a month in Chicago and California to work on matters involving the McCormick family ("Walter Lippmann press agent," he wrote Frankfurter[3]). In 1931 he was prepared, despite the burdens of the Marcus-Singer case, to undertake a course of six Saturday morning lectures at Harvard, on the practice of the law in New York. And every winter he interviewed 150 or more new law school graduates coming down to look for jobs in New York.

The result was to make a major crisis out of a minor stroke. For

---

[1] Buckner to Frankfurter, 4/6/38.
[2] Buckner to Gottlieb, 1/7/31.
[3] Buckner to Frankfurter, undated, 1930.

four weeks Buckner was held in Presbyterian Hospital absolutely incommunicado so far as office matters were concerned, and then he was rationed to one or two brief telephone calls a day. He wrote a short humorous piece for *The Bull* from the hospital, because, he wrote Gottlieb, "I have so often had colds or grippe or flu and practiced law without interruption on the telephone that I was afraid the boys would become mystified by this unprecedented isolation, and would begin to think I had suffered a nervous breakdown, so I thought I would give them concrete evidence to the contrary."[4] Under doctor's orders, he went directly from the hospital to Nantucket, where he remained, improving slowly, until the end of summer. When he returned to the office on October 1, it was on an afternoons-only schedule; but he did resume control of the Wendel case.

Considerable progress had been made in his absence. The motion for bills of particulars had produced eight hundred such documents, one claiming a relationship in the third degree (nephew), three claiming relationship in the fourth degree, and thirty-three claiming relationship in the fifth degree. Harlan, with Root serving as his senior to reassure the worried clients, moved successfully to dismiss the rest of the eight hundred, and the trial of these thirty-seven began in July, 1932.

The self-proclaimed nephew, Thomas Patrick Morris, represented a serious challenge to the charities, because he could conceivably take the whole estate. He was Irish, supposedly the son of a Mary Ellen Devine who had married John G. Wendel in 1876. He offered in proof of his claim a wedding certificate and a letter sent to him in 1897 from the Wendel firm at 175 Broadway. Harlan and A. Goodwin Cooke of the Root-Clark office went to Ireland in search of Mrs. Devine. "[W]e proceeded northward," Cooke wrote, "stopping at every mud hut on every wandering and forgotten road in the north of Ireland, everywhere finding voluble and enthusiastic farmers who were desperately willing to say anything which might bring a little money into the north of Ireland."[5] But the most important evidence was dug up on the American side of the Atlantic, where one of the lawyers recognized the wedding certificate as something that was in his own family's Bible, traced the publisher in Philadelphia, and

[4] Buckner to Gottlieb, 4/27/32.
[5] 14 *Bull*, 1/1/33.

through analysis of the plates which had been used to print that certificate for almost a century established that its correct date was not the year 1876 but somewhere in the period 1916-23. Less elaborate sleuthing also produced proof that in 1897 Wendel did not have offices at 175 Broadway; and Thomas Patrick Morris, instead of enjoying the proceeds of Ella Wendel's will, went to prison for perjury.

The three claimed relationships in the fourth degree also fell apart at trial, and in the end Root-Clark and the executors of the estate accepted nine of the thirty-three claimed fifth-degree relationships as legitimate. The question then arose, What to do?—and it was to this question that Buckner addressed himself in his afternoons at Root-Clark in the winter of 1932-33. *The Bull* noted "the convention which assembled in Mr. Buckner's room on December 27th and 28th," when lawyers for all the charities gathered with the Root-Clark staff to lay plans for the future. Early that January an equally large convention gathered in the living room of Sam Untermyer's apartment, and Buckner set out for consideration what would later be the essence of a compromise—"a wonderful settlement," Henry Friendly called it recently—that gave the nine accepted claimants about $2 million, and the charities the rest. By terms of a distribution agreement they had all signed with Hays and Untermyer, some sixty heirs of Ella Wendel "received something," Hays wrote "—most of them a substantial sum—some of them a small fortune." Hays himself built his summer home at Sands Point from his share of the recovery.[6] Root-Clark's fee for its services was $400,000.

Buckner did not participate, however, in the final negotiations. On February 24, 1933, he entered New York Hospital for major surgery. "Talk about *your* guesswork!" he wrote Learned Hand four months later. "Here am I having had bellyache and headache for twenty years and no one thought to have an exray look at the gall bladder, which had been carrying around 5 rocks for I don't know how long. I felt so rotten that I worked afternoons only from Oct. 1 to Feb. 24, when the thought belatedly occurred to my dr. and the easy discovery was made. It's not a bad operation—3 weeks and back to work to pay the income taxes—but I got pneumonia and then a second and more serious operation (No! not castration, just intestinal), and the 3

[6] Hays, *City Lawyer,* pp. 335, 336.

weeks became 12 and I am now a month here [on Nantucket] and getting well like a house afire, but it means fall before I go back to work. . . .

". . . *now*—pardon the personal reference to 'my operation'—I can eat *any* damned thing, instead of fussing around as heretofore. I dropped 45 pounds (175 to 130) with that damned pneumonia. I am up to 144 now and hope to *stop* around 160."[7]

During Buckner's twelve weeks in the hospital, the firm received a long-awaited fee, the largest in its history, for its work in reorganizing the Chilean nitrate industry for the Guggenheim interests. (This was the matter on which Gottlieb had gone to Chile.) The partners decided to divide it up immediately, and Clark took the question of Buckner's future, and that of his wife and daughters, into his own hands. He drew up a trust agreement by which Buckner put away irrevocably his entire share of his fee, and sent it up to the hospital via messenger boy with instructions that Mr. Buckner should sign it. Buckner had been near death, and was still very weak and groggy. He looked at Clark's note of instructions, glanced at the document, muttered, "If I were well I don't think I would sign this," and then signed. Eight years later, this trust would provide the great bulk of his estate, on which Sofy would live another sixteen years after his death.

As soon as Buckner was settled in Nantucket after leaving the hospital, he reached out to resume by mail his role in the office. "Am anxious to know how you got along hunting for a first, second or third year man (at a very moderate salary)—or men," he wrote in a joint letter to Gottlieb and Harlan. "It is most uneconomical in money and strength for you fellows to be spending so much time in 'reorganizing work.' . . . It may be that no good men are left and that other offices like ourselves only let out the second and third raters. When the office is improperly organized, senior partners always get the impression that we are trying to run too big a shop. The size of the shop depends upon the number of administrative ganglia—junior partners and senior associates.

"My improvement is remarkable and is faster than Miss Bates [his nurse] thought possible. I shall descend on 31 Nassau after Labor Day with a great noise. I have reason to believe that we are

7 Buckner to Hand, 6/16/33.

very short of stenographers and office boys, another great waste. Even if our fees are one half or less as much as before, we must be efficient or the game is up."[8]

A great deal of this, however, was bravura. In July, though still planning to return to the active practice of law in the fall, he admitted to Gottlieb, "So much happened to me from Feb. 24 on that I have forgotten what we did on recruiting. In December I was in office of afternoons, so must have taken the lead in it. I remember talking to Learned Hand's secretary. It was quite clear he should go to Boston, and I do not remember anyone else or final results. Doubtless I shall as soon as you refresh my recollection."[9]

On October 10, 1933, Buckner returned to the office, eager to work but still weak. His managerial talents were needed, for the firm was entering a long period of declining income, and efficiency of operation, once merely a desideratum, had become a necessity. "I have a vivid recollection," said Abraham Tulin, a friend of all the Root-Clark senior partners from law school days, "of a lunch Emory and I had together at the Yale Club in those days. We were discussing the depression, and he told me it had affected them very seriously. They had an overhead of five or six hundred thousand dollars before the partners could draw a single cent. He said it was a terrible burden to meet."

As a contributor to meeting those expenses, however, Buckner would no longer be able to play a significant role. He had aged; his assistants were shocked by his appearance. Though he himself continued for some time to look forward to a return to the courtroom, it seemed obvious to most of his friends that in the future he would have to function as an office lawyer. Fortunately, the matter that was waiting for him did not require courtroom appearances. It was one of the odd cases spawned by the depression: a railroad suing an estate. The estate, that of Mrs. Mary Lily Flagler Bingham, was one of the oldest clients in the office (she had died in 1917); and the will had set up a trust which had as its "primary purpose . . . the keeping together of the enterprises into which my beloved husband, Henry M. Flagler, put so much of his energy, ambition and life."[10] Now the

[8] Buckner to Gottlieb and Harlan, 5/26/33.
[9] Buckner to Gottlieb, 7/8/33.
[10] *New York Times,* 7/16/33, II, p. 4.

Florida East Coast Railway, which Flagler had built, was in bankruptcy to the point where the holders of the equipment trust certificates were about to seize and sell the rolling stock. The receivers in bankruptcy sued to compel the estate to finance the railroad under the terms of the trust. Recommended procedure for the defendants was obviously dilatory tactics, which Buckner and Harlan followed so successfully that the matter did not even come to trial until May, 1935, when the court at Root-Clark's suggestion appointed an examiner to determine whether even the assets of the estate could "keep together" the battered railroad company. The work could be done from the office, and Buckner, who knew the clients well, was active in it. But there were few clients of that kind; Buckner had never wanted long-standing clients of his own whose demands might interfere with trial practice. For the future, he would have to work mostly as part of a team servicing other men's clients.

He retained his talents as a negotiator, and the men who knew him wanted his judgment. Grenville Clark remembered going to Buckner with the problems of one of the firm's largest clients, the Bank of Manhattan Company, parent of the New York Title & Mortgage Company, which was being sued for fraudulently certifying mortgage certificates. "Buckner said," Clark recalled, " 'Don't worry too much about it—they're suing for too much money and the bank is too old.' And he was right—by putting in dilatory pleas and settling a few cases over four years, we got it cleared up." Indeed, the clearing up was done by Buckner himself, with Gottlieb, because Clark beginning in 1935 largely withdrew from the active practice of law. Buckner, Leo Gottlieb wrote in 1945, "handled the settlement of this case, which involved protracted, complicated and difficult negotiations, with all of the tact, skill and judgment which had made him one of the greatest trial lawyers of his day."[11]

Occasionally, Frankfurter would refer to Buckner matters of some delicacy on which people had come to him at Harvard for advice. A memorandum outlining the origin of one such case survives from 1935, because Frankfurter felt a need to have a document in hand for everyone's protection.

"In the forenoon of Saturday, February 2," Frankfurter wrote,

[11] Estate of Emory Buckner, Memorandum of Leo Gottlieb, 4/12/45.

James Roosevelt phoned me from New York saying that there was a matter in connection with the Department of Justice about which he wanted my advice and, if possible, help. He then stated, in substance, that some friends of his from St. Louis, and some lawyers from St. Louis, were threatened with a criminal prosecution for some alleged delinquencies in connection with the income tax laws; that an indictment was pending, and an early trial in the offing, and that the parties had scraped together all the necessary funds to make a money settlement, and that the check in settlement of the Government's claim was now on the desk of the Attorney General. That [Homer] Cummings had indicated that there should be a settlement in this case, and that because of attacks against Cummings in some St. Louis papers, or for other reasons Cummings is holding up the matter, and in the meantime these people are worrying about the threatened early trial, which in the case of the lawyers carries with it consequences of disbarment.

Roosevelt said that of course if the men are guilty of any wrongdoing they should be punished. His whole interest was that the men should receive prompt fair treatment. I told Jim that if I had his responsibility in advising people about such a matter I should advise them to put the whole case in the hands of Emory R. Buckner. He has had considerable experience on both sides of such tax litigations, and has just the right temperament, and has a special talent for settling controversies that ought to be settled. Such a situation, in my opinion, needs precisely the type of lawyer that Buckner is, namely, free from all possible political or personal association with any of the officials who will have to make the ultimate decision. And Buckner seemed to me particularly indicated as the person to recommend, just because he was a Republican and not a Democrat, and is precisely the kind of able high-minded advisor for people in the situation in which Jim's friends found themselves. . . . I offered to tell Buckner, if Jim desired to recommend him as the lawyer, that I had suggested to Jim that if Buckner were free to do so he should take the case.

Jim said that he would be guided entirely by my judgment, and asked me if I could communicate with Buckner, and that he, Jim, would get in touch with Buckner within an hour. I thereupon put in a long-distance call for Buckner and on reaching him promptly told him my talk with Jim as just set forth.

Late in the afternoon of Saturday Buckner phoned me from New York, beginning his talk with this question, "Tell me, Felix, were you asked by the Administration to look into this tax matter about which you phoned me this morning?" And I replied, "Unequivocally and unconditionally, no. I never heard about this tax matter until Jim Roosevelt phoned me this morning. I have had no communication with a soul about it before or since, and I know nothing more than what Jim Roosevelt told me. It is, of course, too ridiculous to suggest that if I had been asked to look into this matter for the Administration that I would recommend you or anybody else as the lawyer for one side." To which Buckner replied, good-humoredly, "I win a bet of one thousand dollars, for I told my people who said you had been asked to look into it that you could not be else you would not have referred Jim Roosevelt's friends to me as clients, and I just wanted to have you confirm what I inevitably knew. But these men are positive that they were told by somebody that about a month ago the President, when this matter was brought to him, indicated that 'some dependable outside lawyer, like Felix Frankfurter, should be asked to investigate and report on the matter.'" To which I repeated to Buckner that I knew nothing about this business, until Jim Roosevelt phoned me this morning and that he did not by any possibility of interpretation call me up for any other purpose except to solicit some advice for his friends. I told Buckner to make it clear to his clients—if clients they will be—beyond peradventure of doubt that I have and had no relation to the matter except that of recommending to Jim Roosevelt, Emory Buckner as the best lawyer I can think of in New York for this kind of case.

Buckner then told me that it is a very complicated and involved story. . . . But he did not go into the details . . . of the merits of the matter.[12]

Most of the men who knew the value of Buckner's judgment, however, were themselves lawyers, in the business of selling their own judgment; in the past they had referred clients to Buckner not for his wisdom but for skills he could no longer practice. He kept busy. As he had once organized the teams so clients would see the younger men and leave his time free, he now organized so he would see the clients while the younger men worked. He interviewed the new-comers from the law schools—one year he may have spoken with as many as three hundred of them—and he oversaw the day-by-day assignment of personnel and flow of work. He liked to keep up with the young men. "I spent quite a bit of time with him," Hugh Cox recalled. "He was alone a lot in that apartment over the river. He seemed in fairly good shape, but I couldn't really tell. He was still a vigorous and alert man. When I decided to come down to Washington, I remember, we spent till one or two in the morning

[12] Memorandum of conversation between James Roosevelt and F. Frankfurter and Emory Buckner and F. Frankfurter, 2/4/35.

in his apartment while he tried to talk me out of it; a night of very vigorous drinking." Buckner remained an enthusiast, and for many of the men his office off the reception room, while no longer the center of their income, remained the focal point of the office.

Whatever future might have been developed along those lines was a casualty of a second and much more severe stroke in September, 1936, which left Buckner at fifty-nine partly paralyzed on his left side. He was out of the office for a year, so ill that in June of 1937 Gottlieb was able to persuade him to claim disability insurance— but Buckner was an easy target for a claims agent, who persuaded him that his disability was temporary rather than permanent. Seriously and permanently crippled, he returned to the office in the fall of 1937 on a 10:45 to 4:30 schedule. He had by no means quit. "Pasteur," he once told James A. Farmer, "did all his major work after his stroke, and I'm not going to let this lick me."

He was again in financial trouble, and had to write the Harvard and Yale Law Schools for scholarships for his nephew, whose bills he could not pay. He was now sixty, and the fates had to a remarkable degree conspired against him; yet his letters to Frankfurter show only very occasional moments of bitterness. One Saturday he wrote, enclosing clippings of large cases won by contemporaries: "Are we jealous? mean? or just a couple of cocky swell heads? Aren't the three enclosed an instance of the breaks of the law 'game'? Where they have drawn much larger gobs of gum from the slot machine than the coins of capacity they have slipped in."[13] As a nonproductive partner, he felt himself under pressure to reduce his share; and at one point he suggested to Frankfurter he should leave Root-Clark, Frankfurter should leave Harvard, and the two of them should go into practice together. To Frankfurter's gentle declination, he replied:

"I have little doubt of the wisdom of your answer to my question propounded months ago. I too shall probably stay put. Indeed, so chimerical was my whim (though extremely attractive) that I might never have been able to put it over with my own capacities so limited and my specialty possibly never to be followed again on account of 'tension.' Bob Patterson found a Van Webb, Conrad a Hopkins, Buck and Si a Sec and Grenny—but whether two men,

13 Buckner to Frankfurter, 2/15/3?

one proposing to work six months only a year and only ⅔ of each day at that—and a man twenty odd years a 'professor'—could find some men willing to put up huge sums for the pleasure and profit of being their partners may be doubted."[14]

In illness, Buckner drew nearer to his family. His brother Arthur had suffered a head injury in a freak accident in a Pullman car in 1927, and had not been able since to fulfill all the duties of the minister of his congregation in Maine. Now the two brothers saw each other several times a year, in New York or in Siasconset. Their father had died in Nebraska in 1934, but their mother survived, living in relative comfort on the depreciated but still valuable investments in farmland they had made with the money their son Emory sent from New York. Buckner would call his mother in Lincoln at regular intervals. They did not have much to talk about, and sometimes they would just hold on, keeping open the soundless connection between them.[15]

Sofy also had a difficult time, periodically tortured by a bursitis the doctors could not alleviate. "Diathermy," Buckner wrote Frankfurter, "will probably prevent an operation, but two cripples in one house is N.G."[16] The two daughters had married, and the Buckners moved to a somewhat smaller but still luxurious apartment at 130 East End Avenue (where John Harlan lived). The apartment and the country house were both furnished lovingly with antiques chosen by Sofy herself. "For years after we sold it," her granddaughter said, "the antique stores of Nantucket were stocked from our house."[17] Sofy did not like to be in New York: she spent six to seven months a year at the house in Nantucket, and not even the World's Fair of 1939 could delay her departure. "Sofy went on her scheduled date, May 1st," Buckner wrote Frankfurter, "saying her duty in raising her own tulip babies against seeing the million Holland tulips at the World's Fair in the course of two or three weeks should be resolved in favor of her own babies and not in favor of a baby show however magnificent. She is having a grand time working out of doors and inside and her half dozen early-bird

[14] Buckner to Frankfurter, 4/6/38.
[15] James N. Buckner to author, 1967.
[16] Buckner to Frankfurter, 2/3/41.
[17] Emory Buckner Stein to author, 1967.

friends have grown quite accustomed to her going to sleep at the table at dinner."[18]

It was always a source of regret to Buckner that the Frankfurters had never visited their home in Nantucket, and he urged them on every year. "It is only four hours by water from Woods Hole," he wrote. "I, like Marian, do not enjoy water myself, but only once in a dozen years has that boat trip made me queasy. On an excursion from Boston to Plymouth in 1905 or '6 Sofy reported that a few women on board and Buck were the only people who were seasick."[19] At the end of the last summer of his life, Buckner wrote, "We were sorry that you and Marian could not make the trip this year. I hope for better luck another summer, as Marian ought to see the place into which Sofy has poured so much of her soul during the last thirteen years, before it is handed over to somebody else."[20]

For two winters the Buckners tried Florida vacations; they "proved anything but successful."[21]

During the three or four months of every year while Sofy was on Nantucket and Buckner was in New York, one of the young men from the office would live in the Buckner apartment, because he needed assistance with many normal physical activities. Behind his desk at the office, however, he did not look as handicapped as he was, and he continued the practice of law. Most of it, inevitably, was what he called "personal"—managing the clients for whom John Harlan would do the work. Some cases were handled in his name— for example, when the minority of the Board of Higher Education retained him (without fee) to take legal action to prevent the majority of the Board from canceling Bertrand Russell's contract to teach at City College (because Lord Russell was an advocate of free love, not, in those days, because of his political views; Harlan argued the motions with Buckner present in the courtroom, but the court ruled that the minority of the Board had no standing to sue). Buckner was also active in and intrigued by a labor matter, which came into the office, he wrote Frankfurter, "through the very

[18] Buckner to Frankfurter, 5/26/39.
[19] *Ibid.*
[20] Buckner to Frankfurter, 10/2/40.
[21] Buckner to Frankfurter, 2/3/41.

able and attractive [Charles] Wyzanski, of Ropes, Gray. Incidentally, I think he is a grand fellow."[22] To the end of his life, he continued to interview the young men, and to help them where he could. When all else failed, there was law to read; Buckner kept up with the courts and made himself a reference source for the litigators. A few minor honors came. In the spring of 1937, while he was still in the hospital, he was elected president of the Harvard Law School Association of New York City; and in 1938 he was chosen vice president of the Association of the Bar of the City of New York.

Buckner kept himself busy to the point of daily exhaustion; a year and a half before his death he wrote Frankfurter: "I still find myself spending about six hours a day at the office and then calling it a day, and when I get home I am generally ready for bed, as I never go out for dinner or sit up for dinner at our own home."[23] But he recognized that, at least for the time being, his functions as a lawyer were marginal. He closed one letter to Frankfurter with the words, "I am interrupted by a caller. *Mirabile dictu.*"[24]

One of the few bright spots in the last years for Buckner was the appointment of his friend Frankfurter to the Supreme Court in January, 1939. He read almost all of Frankfurter's opinions (except on one subject: "What a strange mental aberration for the CJ to make out of you a tax specialist. Those I seldom read and never understand"[25]). He invariably supported what Frankfurter wrote. "Have just read your opinion concerning Anheuser Busch," he wrote, speaking of a decision that had the conservative community up in arms. "I must say I find nothing shocking in it. I felt much more confidence in its reasoning than in Roberts' dissent. In a day or two I shall have your other labor case. Knowing my hurried 6½ hours a day my views may seem quite unimportant. One forms one's views a good deal by the niching of men, and notwithstanding your former high praise of Roberts, I have never put Roberts in the same class as yourself."[26] Nothing in Buckner's life story is more poignantly attractive than his joy that the junior partner in their

22 Buckner to Frankfurter, 2/7/41.
23 Buckner to Frankfurter, 10/2/40.
24 Buckner to Frankfurter, 2/15/40.
25 Buckner to Frankfurter, 2/15/40.
26 *Ibid.*, penciled addition.

long friendship should begin a new and profoundly important career as he himself decayed.

Buckner was in the office until a few days before his death, from another stroke, on March 11, 1941, at the age of sixty-three. The *New York Times* the next day carried an editorial:

EMORY ROY BUCKNER

Sometimes it has seemed as if the lawyer was coming to be more and more a business man or a specialist of some kind; of the office rather than of the court and jury room. Fortunately the great trial lawyer, a type once peculiarly sympathetic to Americans, is worthily continued. Such a lawyer was Emory Buckner. He gave his cases, criminal and civil, the most careful study from all points. He was rich in surprises. He prepared collaterally as well as directly. In his thirties he was taking part in famous trials. He showed his mettle in cases of conspicuous fraud, murder, political corruption, as later he was to do in momentous civil suits.

Secretary Stimson and former Governor Whitman can testify to his effectiveness. United States Attorney in the Twenties, he was remarkably active in enforcing the prohibition law, which he detested. Characteristically he became a total abstainer while holding that office. Even the suspicion of hypocrisy was hateful to him. As a Special Assistant Attorney General he secured convictions in the intricate Queens County sewer frauds. One pig-headed juror saved the bacon of Harry Daugherty when Mr. Buckner prosecuted him. He was a skillful cross-examiner. In his addresses to juries he was clear, simple and easy, as Joseph H. Choate was before him.

Soon after his graduation from the Harvard Law School Mr. Buckner became a member of a law firm whose members have the art of honorable and various distinctions. Mr. Buckner's high talents, character and industry were accompanied with a great gift of nature or fortune. Most people liked him instinctively. His friends loved him. His name was often mentioned in connection with public office. He seems not to have cared for it; and in later years his health was not of the best. But he was always a good citizen, interested in public affairs, active for law reform; and the friends of John Purroy Mitchel have not forgotten Mr. Buckner's efforts in 1917.[27]

Two days later there appeared in the *Times* a letter from Justice Frankfurter:

[27] *New York Times,* 3/12/41.

I should like to add a footnote to your admirable editorial on Emory R. Buckner in *The Times* this morning.

To his friends—and few men could have left truer attachments behind him—the death of so gay and gallant a spirit means an irreplaceable loss. But the central achievement of his professional life has a significance that deserves to be cherished in public memory.

Nature gave Buckner extraordinary professional endowments. The uses to which he put them were his own superb accomplishment. The greatest of these uses was the way in which he put into practice his uncompromising conception of the function and standards of a prosecutor. His was an instinctive ethical nature, but one whose comic spirit precluded the taint of self-righteousness and the dullness of moralizing.

This strong impulse for right and justice was early confirmed and disciplined through his apprenticeship under Henry L. Stimson as United States Attorney for the Southern District of New York. Buckner's genius for the forum at once manifested itself there. He was happiest and most effective when his great gifts of advocacy were in the service of the public.

As an Assistant United States Attorney, as one of the Assistant District Attorneys of New York County, as counsel for the Aldermanic police investigation, as United States Attorney, and as special prosecutor of municipal malefactors, Buckner displayed uncommon energy and skill in the successful prosecution of subtle and complicated crimes, against powerful opposition.

But what is much more important is that in all these prosecutorial offices Buckner realized that he who wields the instruments of justice wields the most terrible instruments of government. In order to assure their just and compassionate use, a prosecutor must have an almost priest-like attitude toward his duties. Buckner practiced this attitude without deviation.

The quality of this public service is all the more shining in a man so zestful of life, so companionable, so tolerant of the foibles and even of the laxities of others as was Buckner. His pure and rigorous standards in the enforcement of law should serve as an example long to be cherished and one by which to judge others who are entrusted with the responsibilities of criminal justice.

Few monuments remain. There is an Emory R. Buckner Room, an enclave for seminars, in the dormitory associated with the Harvard Law School; a portrait hangs in the Federal Court House on Foley Square; and annually the Federal Bar Association gives an Emory R. Buckner Award to an outstanding practitioner or judge in New York, Connecticut or New Jersey.

Buckner's cases did not make law. His interest was in the result of the case as it would affect the human beings who were the participants, not in the impact of the decision on the lives of others. As a prosecutor, he was moralist enough to believe without question in punishment as the appropriate response to crime. Even after years of immersion in the academic, intellectual and cosmopolitan main stream, his thoughts on the social purposes which are the root of law remained in many ways those of the American frontier, which Frederick Jackson Turner announced as closed while Buckner was still in his teens. To the problems of governance and administration that bemused his friend Frankfurter and made him a seminal figure of the century, Emory Buckner was largely blind. Though he was susceptible to information to an extraordinary degree, the facts he sought were perceptual in a statistical age.

Yet surely he was right on the fundamentals: that people are more important than policies, and that actions speak louder than words. Placing his faith in individuals, he saw the individual at his highest when performing a collaborative, even communal act. The large law firm in the hands of a Paul D. Cravath, a James Byrne, a Walter S. Carter had been at bottom a dictatorial organization, where the word of one man was the local law. Buckner created what he liked to call a "militant democracy,"[28] where even the students felt they had access when necessary to the process of decision.

His joy was in his work, and he never doubted the utility, the essential rightness, of either the work or the joy. "He made people feel," Bethuel Webster said, "that the law was a great calling, not just an occupation." To work with him was a pleasure, even at moments of extreme effort. Men who are leaders of bench and bar, in New York and nationally—whose careers are almost surfeited with triumphs—look back on their association with Emory Buckner as among the significant rewards of their lives. He had a superb eye for talent, and his confidence in the young men whose company he sought gave them confidence in themselves. A believer in persons, he left behind for those who knew him a personal example.

[28] Buckner to Frankfurter, 2/3/41.

INDEX